Healing Depression the Mind-Body Way

Creating Happiness through Meditation, Yoga, and Ayurveda

NANCY CULLEN LIEBLER, Ph.D.,
and SANDRA MOSS, M.S.P.H.

WILEY

John Wiley & Sons, Inc.

Published by John Wiley & Sons, Inc., Hoboken, New Jersey
Published simultaneously in Canada

Drawings by Chris Houghton

The information contained in this book is not intended to serve as a replacement for professional medical advice. Any use of the information in this book is at the reader's discretion. The author and the publisher specifically disclaim any and all liability arising directly or indirectly from the use or application of any information contained in this book. A health care professional should be consulted regarding your specific situation.

For general information about our other products and services, please contact our Customer Care Department within the United States at (800) 762-2974, outside the United States at (317) 572-3993 or fax (317) 572-4002.

Wiley also publishes its books in a variety of electronic formats. Some content that appears in print may not be available in electronic books. For more information about Wiley products, visit our web site at www.wiley.com.

Library of Congress Cataloging-in-Publication Data:
Liebler, Nancy Cullen, date.
    Healing depression the mind-body way: creating happiness through meditation, yoga, and, Ayurveda/Nancy Cullen Liebler and Sandra F. Moss.
      p. cm.
    Includes index.
    ISBN 978-0-470-28631-9 (pbk.)
    1. Depression, Mental-Alternative treatment.   2. Medicine, Ayurvedic.
3. Hatha yoga.   4. Meditation.   I. Moss, Sandra F., date.   II. Title.
RC537.L554   2009
616.85'2706—dc22
                                            2008055886

10 9 8 7 6 5 4 3 2

To the wisdom inherent in each and every one of us—may it prevail and bring forth happiness and vitality.

Contents

Foreword

The ancient, timeless wisdom of Ayurveda, the science of life, focuses on the human being. According to Ayurveda, every individual is indivisible—undivided, total, complete—a unique expression of universal consciousness. Within this life, there is a beautiful amalgamation, which is the union between energy and matter, or rather, the union among the body, mind, and conscious principle.

In the human body, every single cell is a center of awareness and is a functional unit that contains its own intelligence called *mahat*. Furthermore, there is a beautiful communication taking place among cells—this is the flow of intelligence, also known as *prana*. *Prana* is a bridge among the body, mind, and consciousness. It is the manifestation of consciousness into the great five elements—space (also known as ether), air, fire, water, and earth. These elements operate at the cellular and physiological level. The structural aspect of the body is governed by ether (or space), air, fire, water, and earth. However, the functional aspect of the body is governed by the three doshas: Vata, Pitta, and Kapha.

Prakruti is an individual's unique constitution, his or her unique genetic code. The model of *prakruti* in Ayurveda speaks a great deal about the interplay of Vata, Pitta, and Kapha and how they govern our psychophysiology and psychopathology. Over time, however, the bodily doshic ratio of Vata, Pitta, and Kapha can change, and that altered state is called *vikruti*. We are constantly exposed to external environmental changes—diet, lifestyle, relationships, jobs, even seasons. These changes are constantly bombarding the body, and the doshas react in the form of doshic aggravation. This is a crucial point where the disease process begins. *Vikruti*, the altered state of the doshas, can happen on either a physical or mental level.

This beautiful book, *Healing Depression the Mind-Body Way*, explains the interplay among the three doshas. Nancy Liebler and Sandra Moss have nicely blended Ayurvedic philosophy into their unique work in the psychological field.

The many faces of depression reflect qualitative and quantitative changes in Vata, Pitta, and Kapha. When Liebler and Moss speak about the broken brain, they are mirroring the Ayurvedic concept that biochemical disorders can create a *khavaigunya*, or defective space, in the *manovaha srotas*, which is the mind-body connection mechanism. *Manovaha srotas* are the psychoneurological channels through which thoughts, feelings, and emotions flow continuously between the body and the mind. When these channels become blocked, a defective space is created that permits the doshas to accumulate and create psychological problems. Depression is one of these problems.

Nancy Liebler and Sandra Moss have taken the wisdom of Ayurveda and elegantly integrated it with yoga and meditation in this book, creating a healing modality that addresses the whole person. Every sentence of this book breathes the truth of spiritual awakening so that the chemistry of happiness can unfold by metabolizing life, processing matter, and digesting the emotions—all of which creates the chemistry of happiness. If we pay complete attention to our thoughts, feelings, and emotions, a transformation takes place—and through that transformation, we can awaken our own physician within.

Ayurveda explains that every person is a good healer; the body knows how to heal itself. *Healing Depression the Mind-Body Way* offers a new dimension to healing oneself. It teaches us a very simple and practical way to live without suffering from depression. It is my wish that great joy, happiness, and healing energy will unfold in your heart as you read this book.

—Vasant Lad, B.A.M.& S., M.A.Sc.

Acknowledgments

The authors would like to acknowledge the many sages, teachers, scholars, and guides who have illuminated the world with the light of Ayurveda.

They would like to express their gratitude to all of the individuals who have contributed to this endeavor. To James Brooks, M.D., Paul Dugliss, M.D., and Suhas Kshiirsagar, M.D. Ayur. for their encouragement and tutelage. To their agent, Doris Michaels, and to Delia Berrigan-Fakis of the Doris Michaels Literary Agency. To the staff at John Wiley & Sons, with a special thanks to Tom Miller, Christel Winkler, and Kimberly Monroe-Hill for their insight, leadership, and commitment. To Judith Antonelli for exquisitely polishing the manuscript. To Chris Houghton for his artistic spark in creating the illustrations for this book.

Nancy acknowledges her good fortune in having her husband, Bud, in her life. He has been consistently supportive and inspiring—and always lots of fun to be with.

Sandra offers thanks to her husband, Frederick, who sees life through spiritual eyes, and her mother, Fabiola, for instilling in her the importance of living a life filled with Spirit.

Introduction

By picking up this book, you are in good company. You are among the 40 percent of Americans who are, according a report in the *Journal of the American Medical Association*, regularly accessing care from outside the Western medical tradition. People are increasingly seeking treatment based on a paradigm that goes beyond the reductionist view of the human body.

This book is about Ayurveda—the original and ultimate form of mind-body medicine that is the traditional system of medicine in India—and its power to eradicate the root of depression. The central theme of Ayurveda is that nature and the mind-body are aspects of a single continuum of intelligence. Vedic knowledge (dating from India's Vedic civilization, thousands of years ago) explains that what exists in the macrocosm of the natural world also exists in the microcosm of human physiology—in other words, the human mind-body and the natural world are reflections of each other.

According to Ayurveda, human physiology is an ecosystem in which a stressor on any one aspect of the being affects every other aspect. Research in Western medicine is currently validating this concept that has come to us from the ancients. For instance, psychoneuroimmunology (PNI) informs us that the systems of the body are interrelated and that they communicate with one another through messenger molecules. PNI is considered to be one of the most exciting fields in modern medicine. Studies in this field have taught us that, in a very basic sense, our health is the direct result of the relationship between the mind and the body.

The knowledge that has come to us from the Vedic sages and from PNI informs us that the body is the outward manifestation of the mind, of awareness or consciousness. PNI proposes that we can no longer consider the mind as one thing and the body as another, or mental health as separate from physical health. This is new information for us Westerners, who are often inclined to believe that if we are depressed or anxious we should just "snap out of it." That isn't the case. We can no more snap out of emotional difficulties than we can snap out of physical challenges. We need practical techniques to eradicate *the root* of depression and anxiety. This is where Ayurveda comes into the picture.

Refined techniques that help to bring balance to the mind-body were developed thousands of years ago. These techniques are available to us today, and they have never been needed more. Depression is growing by leaps and bounds in every industrialized country in the world. It is considered to be the "common cold" of mental illness. Since depression is caused by a nexus of issues, the likelihood is that there will never be a one-size-fits-all "magic bullet" that will be a cure-all. Instead, monitoring one's lifestyle is and always will be the best way to ensure physical, emotional, and mental health. We wrote this book hoping that it will give you what you need to make the changes necessary to enhance your health and ultimately your happiness.

We urge you to remember that Ayurveda *is* compatible with Western medicine. Whatever Ayurvedic interventions you add to your lifestyle will simply enhance your well-being. We hope that you'll take the suggestions we make to heart and implement them, and that they will, indeed, help you to prevent or undo depression in your life. You deserve to live your life to its fullest, happiest, and healthiest every single day. Your life can only be what you make it. Make it yours and make it great!

We wish you the full realization of your birthright: perfect health and happiness.

Finding Another Way

1

Beyond the
Broken Brain

> In the middle of the path through life,
> I suddenly found myself in dark woods.
>
> —DANTE

If you believe that depression is not just in your head, this book is for you. If you have been in therapy and have popped pills and supplements but still feel like you're not quite right, read on.

Do you ever wonder why your entire being hurts when you are depressed? Have you ever asked yourself, "How did depression take hold of my body, mind, and spirit?" Perhaps you can trace back and pinpoint exactly when darkness struck your life like a hurricane. On the other hand, maybe the blues seeped slowly into your physiology like water into the basement of a house. You see the evidence of the damage but can't find the source of the problem.

Depression can become an unwanted companion casting a shadow on every aspect of your life. Do you feel robbed of liveliness and energy? The menacing presence of a heavy heart, waves of anxiety, or crabby irritability may describe your experience of depression. You long to feel happy, yet you experience a gulf of emptiness inside that nothing can fill. Then again, maybe you have recovered from a bout of depression and want to prevent a recurrence. Having been released from the grip of depression, you now want to safeguard your most precious assets: happiness and vitality.

We wrote this book because we believe that a different way of thinking about depression is needed. As long as our culture is stuck thinking that depression is only about a chemical imbalance in the brain, there will be no cure or plan of prevention in sight. We hold that depression is about more than a "broken brain" (a chemical imbalance) or an emotional problem that you should be able to let go of or talk your way through. It is not an unavoidable genetic problem. Although depression can be a reaction to a trying situation in your life, it does not have to be a permanent state of mind.

The Broken Brain Mentality: If It's Not Your Brain, It's Your "Mother"!

So what is this about a "broken brain," you ask? When Western medical science seeks answers to a problem, it focuses its search on the physical body. That is its area of expertise, and it does this well. First it isolates a disorder to a particular system in the body, such as the circulatory, the digestive, the respiratory, or, in the case of depression, the nervous system. The next step is to centralize the problem to a specific organ, such as the heart, the stomach, the intestines, the lungs, or the brain.

Victory is theirs, Western medical scientists believe, if they can find a causative molecule. When low levels of the brain chemical serotonin were linked to low mood and other depressive symptoms, the medical community thought that it had identified what was wrong in the body and how to fix it; that is how Prozac, a drug that increases serotonin levels in the brain, became a household name.

This line of thinking and its success should not be undervalued. There is a wealth of clinical evidence that biological and chemical processes in the brain influence thinking and emotion. Logic therefore dictates that if those processes go awry, abnormalities of thinking and emotions will result. In other words, if the brain breaks, the emotions suffer; but does this line of thinking really tell the *whole* story?

If the brain is "broken," what caused the breakage? Different opinions exist. Medical doctors are inclined to focus on the physical, whereas psychologists focus on the mind. You are the product of your experiences, the psychologist surmises. Since the neurons in your brain are hardwired in early childhood, the experiences and family patterns of interaction at that time are pivotal in making you who you are today. The biological and chemical processes in your brain, the theory goes, reflect your ongoing relationship with your environment.

Depression, according to this line of thinking, is the result of a lifelong collection of experiences, from childhood to the present. Because memories are stored in your brain, the key to living depression-free is to understand the thought patterns in your head. Therefore, psychologists claim, talk therapy and the changes that result from such therapy are the solution. In other words, if it's not your brain, it's your "mother"!

Treating the Organ of Depression, Not the Cause: What's Wrong with This Picture?

Antidepressant medications artificially and externally manipulate the level of chemicals in the brain. Ultimately, the brain reacts to this artificial manipulation by blunting its sensitivity to these chemicals. This is not unlike hearing loss that results from long-term exposure to excessively loud noise. The person who is taking the medication is then forced to incrementally supply the brain with more and more of the substance in order to achieve its purpose. This is generally followed by the need to take another medication to counteract the negative side effects of the antidepressant. It is not uncommon for people who increase their antidepressant during the day to then need a sedative or a sleeping pill at night. (How depressing!)

The three natural brain chemicals that are associated with feeling good—dopamine, norepinephrine, and serotonin—work in concert with one another. Nature did not intend for one of them to work independently of the others. Nature intended for them to work synergistically and in balance with one another. This is what brings long-lasting relief from symptoms. If one aspect of the body is interrupted, it triggers a cascade of reactions that runs through and disrupts the balance of the entire body. Unfortunately, medications generally target only one or two of the brain chemicals. This partial solution can potentially create other problems.

Given how medical doctors and psychologists perceive the problem of depression, it is no wonder that they focus on the biochemicals and the life experiences that influence brain function. The most common treatment modalities used by Western medicine today are drugs and talk therapy. Drugs, whether synthetic or natural, manipulate the chemicals in the brain. Generally speaking, talk therapy aims at figuring out the inner workings of the mind.

Drugs: A Window of Light?

When it comes to the question of depression, we want you to consider the following: What came first, the chemical imbalance or the episode of sadness? It is generally accepted that a chemical imbalance accompanies depression. Depression is associated with a biological derangement in the brain. This derangement may be triggered by a genetic tendency, lifestyle choices, a tragic event, or a combination of the three. In other words, a chemical imbalance *coincides with* the presence of depression. However, this coincidence (known in science as a *correlation*) does not necessarily indicate causality. It also does not indicate the direction of the causal relationship. That is, does the chemical imbalance cause the depressive episode, or does the depressive episode cause the chemical imbalance?

Antidepressant medications manipulate the level of at least one of the three brain chemicals. Serotonin, norepinephrine, and dopamine are called *neurotransmitters*. Considered mood brighteners, they are responsible for feelings of alertness and happiness. According to Western medical theory on depression, effectively increasing the levels of at least one of these biochemicals should resolve depression in a person.

The value of pharmaceutical interventions to treat depression is currently being questioned by the scientific community. In a study done in the United Kingdom in 2008, antidepressants were shown to be only slightly more effective than taking a placebo. This can be interpreted to mean that people who take antidepressants get better because they believe the pills are helpful and they expect to get better. This placebo effect calls into question whether the antidepressants actually have inherent curative properties. In addition, many researchers are concerned about the negative side effects of the pills. For a variety of reasons, approximately 40 percent of people discontinue their use in the first month. That being said, some people who have experienced severe depression report feeling helped by the medications initially.

Episodes of depression recur in 50 to 85 percent of people who have had one episode. This terribly high recurrence rate has led some physicians to advocate that people who have been treated for major depression remain on antidepressant medication for life, as a preventative measure. Yet even then many individuals do not recover their zest for life, their physical and emotional vitality. In fact, it is reported that 70 percent of people who take antidepressant medication continue to experience lingering symptoms of depression. In addition, a lifelong use of medication may mean living with negative side effects such as dry mouth, rapid heart rate, constipation, dizziness, sexual dysfunction, jitteriness, blurred vision, and memory impairment. In short, medications do not always cure what ails, and they can potentially trigger other problems.

Why keep looking to find a cure in a pill? At best, drug interventions simply soothe the depressive symptoms. This is because pills manipulate one's brain chemicals but do not treat the totality of one's being: body, mind, and spirit. Only a limited biochemical aspect of one's physiology is addressed, and only in a segregated area. When underlying causes are neglected, symptoms tend to eventually recur. However, relief from the darkness of depression must be sought, and antidepressants may, in some cases, provide a window of light. There is anecdotal evidence that this pharmaceutical technology has been helpful to many people.

If you have chosen to take medication to relieve the symptoms of depression, you are not precluded from embarking on the holistic program this book prescribes. The two are compatible and additive in their effects. The whole purpose of this book is to show you how to kick-start your own self-healing mechanisms; to do more than simply address the symptoms of depression. We want to introduce you to a holistic way of treating depression that delves deep into the core of your physiology and sends symptoms scurrying away permanently. We want to offer you a fuller, more encompassing view of the problem, with natural solutions.

There are natural ways of balancing brain chemistry that do not require popping a pill (synthetic or natural). Mind-body techniques are available that bring overall balance to one's physiology and, consequently, affect brain chemistry deeply, safely, and holistically. The body is the best pharmacy, and this is where nature intends for you to go when you need medication.

Treating depression with drugs alone is analogous to using aspirin to relieve a fever caused by an infection. Aspirin merely reduces the fever and makes the patient feel more comfortable. It does not address the cause of the infection.

Brain Chemistry Gone Awry?

A recent study stating that antidepressant medications appear to help only severely depressed people and work no better than placebos in many patients has rocked the perception of the public. "Although patients get better when they take antidepressants, they also get better when they take a placebo, and the difference in improvement is not very great. This means that depressed people can improve without chemical treatments," said Irving Kirsh of the University of Hull in England, the author of the study.

Dr. Helen Mayberg, a professor of psychiatry and neurology at the Emory University School of Medicine, responded to the study by saying, "This [depression] is about very sick people; there's something wrong with their *brains*" (italics added). Herein lies the problem, we think. Even dedicated and well-meaning psychiatrists tend to see depressed patients as cases of brain chemistry gone awry, rather than seeing them as a complex system whose body, mind, and spirit have gone awry.

Approximately 118 million antidepressant prescriptions are issued in the United States each year. Do we really believe that millions of U.S. citizens are walking around with something wrong with their brains that a pill can cure?

Not even a decade ago, physicians treated heart disease by focusing on the organ of the heart, rather than focusing on the person experiencing the disease. Nowadays, no cardiologist would think to give a pill for heart disease without simultaneously discussing the impact of lifestyle on heart health. It is our hope that very soon the psychiatric and psychological communities will shift their current paradigm and begin to think of depression in a holistic manner rather than simply as brain chemistry gone awry.

Talk Therapy: Words and Nurturance

Going to therapy can be extremely helpful for a depressed person. The most common recommendation is to attend talk therapy and take pills. How effective is talk therapy? In some studies, therapy has been shown to improve the symptoms of depression as significantly as medication. These studies have focused primarily on cognitive-behavioral therapy, which strives to bring cognitive awareness to the relationship among thoughts, feelings, and behaviors. There is no doubt that awareness can be a powerful tool for positive change. The hope is that by actualizing personal awareness or insights, people will eventually set themselves free of the same old situations and the same old negative feelings.

There is enormous healing power behind the changes in cognition, behavior, and relationships that are brought on by talk therapy. Everything affects brain chemistry and our overall physiology. If we sit and look at a photograph album and remember the past through pictures, our body chemistry is altered. If we get caught in a traffic jam, our physiology is changed. If we are stressed because of a family conflict or concerns at work, our internal environment is thrown out of balance. Likewise, beneficial changes in the way we perceive ourselves, which can be brought on by talk therapy, are a powerful means to alter physiological chemistry. Effective psychotherapy can be an aid for overall health as well as a treatment for depression. Improved relationships that result from an increased awareness of our thoughts, actions, and emotions can induce positive changes in our being.

However, although therapy certainly offers insight into many of life's problems, by itself it is not a cure for depression, especially major depression. Mild depression is more likely to be treated effectively by therapy. This type of depression is usually time-limited, and increasing self-awareness and experiencing a therapeutic relationship can be very helpful in ending the depression sooner rather than later.

The foundation of talk therapy is the belief that insight leads to change. Talking about life issues is indeed good and helpful. We believe, however, that this is putting the cart before the horse. Improvements in the overall health of the individual—body, mind, and spirit—must also take place if changes in perception (insight) and alterations in feelings are to become permanent. The internal world must move into an overall healthier state. After this psychophysiological shift occurs, insight engendered in the context of a positive relationship can be of great assistance in promoting continuing change.

Mental and physical exhaustion also limits the effectiveness of talk therapy. All too often, a depressed person lacks the mental, emotional, and physical energy to turn insight into action. It is entirely possible to have an intellectual understanding of the connections among thoughts, feelings, and behaviors and still not be able to make changes. It is not uncommon to hear people say, "I know what I should do, I just can't do it" or "I know I shouldn't think like I do—it doesn't help me, but I am unable to change the way I am." Perhaps you have said similar words yourself.

Depression depletes our energy. This emotional malaise (lack of ease) affects every aspect of our being. The talking cure is limited because words are abstract building blocks. They are not the practical interventions that are needed to rise from deep sadness. Talk therapy does not give the necessary physical, mental, and emotional strength to put insight into action. For this—the project of restructuring body, mind, and spirit—we need practical techniques that help us to build ourselves up from the inside out. To fix a crumbling house, the builder starts at the foundation, not the roof. We must do the same.

The condition of depression is all-encompassing. Depression is a physical problem that is beyond the reach of pills, it is a mental problem that is beyond the reach of words, and it is a spiritual problem that requires techniques to help us connect with the abstract qualities of life. Talk is good. It can be exceedingly helpful, but it does not reach the deep physical roots of depression. It affects perceptions and viewpoints and helps us to change the way we relate to ourselves and others. This is wonderful, but it is often not enough.

Fortunately, many practical techniques exist that positively affect our whole being. These work on a totally different spectrum than talk therapy does. When our overall health is improved and our inner source of healing is activated, then talk therapy can become increasingly helpful. (And hopefully you never again need say, "Coulda, woulda, shoulda.")

What If There Were Another Way?

Both drugs and talk therapy have a time and a place. Nevertheless, on the overall effectiveness of treatment, studies say that of all Americans who experience a major depressive episode during their lifetime and use conventional methods of treatment, 50 percent will experience some symptoms of lingering depression and 50 percent will have a recurrent episode. Seventy percent of people who experience a second episode are likely to have a third. In addition, approximately half of the people treated with only the conventional treatment methods for depression show no improvement. Are you wondering why? We were, so we researched it and wrote this book.

There is another way. Let's think about it. Your physiology has an inherent self-repair mechanism. There exists an internal healing intelligence that guides the healing of wounds. This intelligence senses the pain brought on by a cut on your finger and immediately mobilizes a series of reactions to stop the bleeding, form a scab, and induce the regeneration of skin. Elegantly and effortlessly, this process has a 100 percent rate of success, assuming it is not interrupted. It must be successful, for your life depends on it. What if there existed a way to unleash your innate healing intelligence to cure depression?

Depression is a condition that intimately involves many facets of you: your physical being as well as your mental, emotional, social, and spiritual self. This is perhaps why, when you are depressed, everything hurts, nothing seems right, and problems may at times seem larger than life. Do we really think that one single chemical or even a whole concert of such substances is capable of creating an emotion on its own? Can we really expect to solve our problems by talking our way through them? If we could, we would. However, a problem can't be solved with the same mind-set that created it in the first place.

We are not denying that an imbalance in brain chemistry is involved in depression. We merely want to highlight the fact that the interplay of molecules in the brain is incredibly complicated. Brain health is affected by much more than the quantity of brain chemicals produced. Hormones, for example, greatly influence the workings of the brain. Food, in turn, influences the production of the hormones, and our emotions often guide our food choices—for better or for worse. All aspects of our physiology are interwoven. Mother Nature is a weaver, and she has woven every thread of our being into one tapestry, which is maintained by our lifestyle. This is the point of holism.

Holism goes deeper than the eye can see. Human beings are more than the mortal packaging they inhabit. We are a creation of our consciousness. In fact, in a deeper reality, an energetic pattern of vibration underlies the totality of our being—body, mind, and spirit. From a holistic perspective, matter is energy and energy is matter, so there is no separation between body (matter) and mind (energy). Where attention goes, matter flows, it's been said. The implication of this philosophy is tremendous: it implies that we can use our consciousness to create our worldview, our mind, and our body—and to heal. We do this by enlisting a consciousness-based health program based on the ancient science of Ayurveda.

Ayurveda: Weaving the Fabric of Health

During the Vedic epoch in India (about five thousand years ago), there lived sages, wise men and women, who developed a system of health called *Ayurveda*. This ancient science has recently been revived, to the delight of millions. Ayurveda provides an instruction manual for unleashing the self-repair mechanisms that are inherent in our physiology.

Ayurveda can help us to do this because it looks at the human being from a deeper reality than Western medicine does. Ayurveda moves beyond studying the systems of the body to studying the underlying energetic patterns, the vibratory essence of the human being. Its concepts readily correspond to modern theories of quantum mechanics physics, which are increasingly deciphering the energetic nature of the human body, mind, and spirit.

Ayurveda is considered by many to be the original holistic science of health, and we think it is the ultimate system of mind-body medicine. The solutions for depression offered in this book are based on this ancient science of healing. Following the Ayurvedic path will help you no matter where you are on the continuum of mental and physical health. Ayurvedic interventions will enhance your well-being whether you are battling a major depressive episode, are trying to beat the blues, or simply need support coping with the problems of daily living.

If you are currently taking medication and choose to continue, this holistic program will help you to achieve radiant good health. On the other hand, it can help you to transition away from medication, if it is judiciously applied in consultation with your physician. Ayurveda can also help people who have never experienced depression but who want to keep any possible genetic tendencies at bay by maintaining a state of optimal wellness. Fundamentally, this knowledge can help anyone who wants to uproot depression from his or her life.

Ancient Science, Modern Wisdom

Ayurveda is the world's oldest system of natural medicine. Whereas fads come and go, Ayurveda has had five thousand years to work out its kinks, toss what doesn't work, and refine what does work. Native to the Vedic civilization of India, it predates Chinese medicine by several hundred years. So are you scratching your head now, wondering why you have never heard of it? Maybe you have.

Ayurveda is the tree of knowledge from which many popularized therapeutic interventions have grown: for example, aromatherapy, sound therapy, vibrational-energy therapy, herbal therapy, massage therapy, polarity therapy, chakra therapy, and yoga postures. As a complete system of health, however, Ayurveda has been introduced to the

Western world only in very recent times. We and a lot of other people who have experienced its benefits think it is here to stay.

Ayurveda has had such longevity because it helps us to maintain ours. *Ayur* and *veda* are two Sanskrit words that mean "knowledge of living." This explains why the focus of Ayurveda is to teach us how to live our lives vibrantly by creating good health every step of the way. As a matter of fact, Ayurveda defines health as a state of complete physical, mental, emotional, social, and spiritual well-being. Health is not merely the absence of disease and infirmity. This ancient science offers the epitome of a holistic approach to living life with zing. Think of Ayurveda as Mother Nature's spokesperson, giving instructions on how to weave threads (our daily actions) into a vibrant tapestry (our physiology).

Ayurveda is, however, more than an instruction manual for how to live our life. It is all about awakening the incredible "physician within" to actualize our potential to heal. More specifically, as will be explained, the physician within can be conceptualized as the natural intelligence inherent in all of us. This natural intelligence can heal a cut on our finger, bring balance to our brain chemistry, and even heal a broken heart. Explaining how natural intelligence works and how it can be unleashed is the job of Ayurveda.

Why, then, does undoing depression seem so hard? Even when you have a road map, the difficulty often lies in following it: getting the correct orientation, reading the signs, staying on course, and making the right choices at crossroads. Yet even for these challenges, Ayurveda proposes a solution: expanding your awareness. This is the key step, the answer to safeguarding happiness, to living life with zing. Before you dismiss the rest of this book because of statements that may seem overly simplistic, unrealistic, and unconvincing, let us offer you a glimpse of the belief system underlying the Ayurvedic worldview.

Ayurveda is ancient yet ultramodern. It is ancient when measured by chronological time, because the gems of wisdom it offers are timeless. The Ayurvedic framework is described by the sages in metaphorical and poetic language rather than with modern terminology. Ayurveda is ultramodern, ahead of its time, because its fundamental concepts are currently being explored and expounded upon by those at the cutting edge of modern science and technology: quantum physicists and molecular biologists, among others. We expect that in the future, as modern wisdom catches up with this ancient science, *Ayurveda* will become a household name. As you read about Ayurveda, you will often realize that we are telling you what you already sense, can validate through your experience, and intuitively know to be correct. The beauty of this system of health is this: it works!

Often the brain must be fed before the mind can open. Therefore, throughout this book, we intend to draw parallels between ancient precepts and modern scientific knowledge. From the onset, let us underscore that Ayurveda represents a complete system of health. Although its roots trace back to the ancient Vedic civilization of India, its principles are universal in their applicability.

Seeing Life through the Eyes of the Vedic Sages

The ancient sages and the scientists of modern times have one fundamental thing in common: both strive to understand the nature of the universe and its inner workings. How they go about doing this determines which category they fall into: sage or scientist. Addressing the question of how each group (and everyone in the academic disciplines between the two) arrives at an understanding is beyond the scope of this book. Suffice it to say that this is the issue that fills the corridors of universities and drives the creation of volumes of academic manuscripts.

As far as we know, the Vedic sages did not sit on sterile laboratory benches, make use of scalpels, or experiment on other living beings. They did not use microscopes, employ molecular biology techniques, or have mechanical computers to solve complex mathematical equations. What they did have was the earth around them; this was their laboratory. They made connections based on no other reference than life as they saw it. Traditionally, it is believed that the nature of the universe was revealed to them while they were in a deeply meditative state of mind. (Einstein did this too, you know, and so can you.) Essentially, the Vedic sages realized the following:

As is the microcosm, so is the macrocosm.

As is the atom, so is the universe.

As is the human body, so is the cosmic body.

As is the human mind, so is the cosmic mind.

This verse states that living beings are microcosms of the universe itself. The Vedic sages understood that we are made up of the same elements as the cosmos and are influenced by the same forces. The fire that burns deep within the belly of our planet is the same energy that drives digestion in our stomach and intestines. The element that makes up the earth we walk on creates our physical body. The expansive space that surrounds us is as vital to the universe as it is to the working of our brain. The mineral composition of the water in the sea is similar to the fluid inside our cells. The elegant workings of the universe are mirrored in our cells.

If human beings are, in effect, a reflection of the universe, then they are also subject to all the laws that govern the universe. The same natural intelligence that controls the rhythms of the seasons also regulates the inner workings of our physiology: our digestive, circulatory, endocrine, reproductive, respiratory, and nervous systems. The same force that drove a seed to create an oak tree also drove a single cell to create the wonder that is you.

Before we start to get too heady, let us explain how the concept of natural intelligence and life-energy relates to the task of daily living. Our physiology is a manifestation of the natural world. Life-energy is blocked when our connection with the energy field that underlies the natural world is disrupted. Disease ensues when the flow of natural intelligence transmitted through our mind, our body, or our spirit is impeded.

Every day, through every action we take and every decision we make, we are guiding the flow of this life-energy. Our decision to live in accordance with the laws of nature or against them brings consequences. It determines the health of our physiology and the well-being of our mental and emotional life. Teaching us about these laws and, therefore, restoring the flow of connection to natural intelligence is the goal of Ayurveda.

Ayurveda focuses on the person who is experiencing the symptoms rather than on the symptoms themselves. Therefore, instead of the one-size-fits-all Western medical approach to treating the brain, Ayurveda offers a comprehensive plan that addresses the uniqueness of the individual, starting at the level of spirit, beginning with consciousness.

Rather than focus on the treatment of a symptom, Ayurveda addresses the underlying cause that created the fertile ground for an ill condition to flourish. This is why we have begun with an introduction to this science of living, which offers knowledge on how to live life rather than on how to get rid of a symptom. This is also why we believe that Ayurveda can teach us how to create happiness in our lives.

The following chapter will discuss the Ayurvedic paradigm of depression. The benefit of this worldview is that it opens the gateway for the treatment and prevention of depression. Only a multidimensional analysis of the problem of depression can bring about a holistic solution to the condition. Let's get to the root of the problem. The answer to depression is in the minds of the Vedic sages.

Depression: A Slow Leak in the Basement or a Dramatic Tornado?

Before we proceed, we would like you to consider the evolution of your current predicament in terms of the many aspects of your being:

* What analogy would you use to describe your unique expression of depression? Think back on your experience of depression. How would you describe it? Would you say it came on like a slow leak in the basement of a house? Was it not easily identifiable until it had already caused damage? Or did depression hit you like a dramatic tornado? Can you trace your bout of depression back to a specific triggering event?

* Depression happens—it evolves and changes. What were the first telltale signs of depression in your life? Did the symptoms change over time? Can you correlate any lifestyle habits or events that triggered them to change, for better or for worse?

* Depression is created one act at a time. How did your symptoms of depression affect your physical self (your general health and your physical stability and strength)? Your mental self (your thinking and perception)? Your emotional self (your feelings)? Your social self (the manner in which you relate to others)? Your

spiritual self (your ability to remain mindful of the abstract aspects of life)?

- Depression is undone one act at a time. Describe any interventions that have been successful for you in undoing depression. As you describe them, consider which aspect of your being you are addressing. In other words, how were you able to support your body, mind, and spirit to restore physical, mental, emotional, and spiritual well-being? Be specific.

- Think back to a time in your life when you were not experiencing depression. In fact, think back to the best time of your life. How would you describe your physical, mental, emotional, social, and spiritual self at this point? Please realize that this describes your true nature.

2

Why Depression Happens

> Enlightenment, peace, and joy will not be granted by someone else. The well is within us.
>
> —THICH NHAT HANH

According to Ayurveda, happiness is our birthright. In the quiet of our minds, most of us agree. We intuitively know that we are capable of more positivity than we often experience. We sense an inner vault of happiness and vitality, but we have difficulty accessing this treasure. We wander through life searching for the key that unlocks that vault, often to no avail.

What has happened to our happiness? We have not really lost access to our birthright; we just think we have misplaced the key. What we have actually done is to forget how each choice we make, every step of the way, affects our experience of happiness.

The sunflower has no choice but to turn its head toward the sun. In this way it survives and flourishes. We, on the other hand, possess an intellect that gives us choices. Unlike the sunflower, we often forget that we are an inherent part of the natural world and are subject to its laws. We make mistakes in many of our daily choices about food, sleep, exercise, and how we use our time. The mistakes are often made unwittingly; nevertheless, the body is adversely affected. In this way we block our ability to experience happiness and we create depression. The good news is that what we create, we can undo. By embracing the holistic nature of our body, mind, and spirit, we'll find the key, unlock the vault, and realize our birthright.

The Novelty of the Ayurvedic Approach

Ayurveda goes where therapy cannot reach and offers what medication cannot provide. It tells us how we create and can undo depression. In its toolbox, Ayurveda has many practical techniques to help us regain vitality and happiness. It can help anyone who is stuck anywhere on the continuum of depression. If you suffer from the blues, have gone through the tyranny of recurrent bouts of depression, or simply wish to maintain your emotional wellness, you will find Ayurvedic treatments to suit your unique needs.

The Ayurvedic theory of physiology corresponds more readily to theories held by modern physicists than to traditional medical theories. Both the Vedic sages and contemporary quantum mechanics physicists regard human physiology as a pattern of vibrations that exists in a sea of consciousness (intelligence). Sages and physicists, working thousands of years apart, have used similar words to describe the reality of the human being in the universe.

Understanding the Ayurvedic worldview changes the way we understand our physiology. First, the Vedic sages urge us not to think of ourselves as solid, unchangeable beings. According to them we are in constant flux, living in a sea of consciousness. Second, they instruct us that our physiology is an extension of the environment. This means that we affect and are affected by everything that exists in this sea of consciousness. Third, the sages proclaim that our physiology is a pattern of vibrations orchestrated by natural intelligence.

In order to understand our physiology, it is imperative to understand how nature works. Nature organizes everything. It is constructed in layers, and what we see with our eyes is only the manifest layer.

There is a logical, sequential unfolding of the different layers of nature. As we move through the layers of nature—as we go from the seen to the unseen—energy structured in different patterns is revealed to us. In this manner we find that the essence of our physiology is energy. This does not negate, however, that at the manifest layer we are solid beings. (Of course you look solid, feel solid, and are solid.) At a more fundamental level, however, you—the complete you—are one seamless energetic system, and every aspect of your being affects the totality. When we learn how to address the underlying layers of our physiology, we can effectively promote health and wellness.

How Is Depression Created?

Depression happens. It can seep into an individual's body and mind like a slow leak, like water into the basement of a house, or it can arrive like a windstorm, coming suddenly and with dramatic force. Depression is influenced by genes, life situations, and the state of one's general health. We should not underestimate the impact of the wear and tear of daily living on our physical, mental, and emotional health. Regardless of the origin, Ayurveda gives us hope by offering strategies for keeping depression at bay.

The Vedic sages don't want to talk about your brain (or your mother!). To them it is all about the flow of life-energy throughout your physiology. When life-energy is depleted or blocked, physiological problems ensue, including depression. This is because energy supports all functioning. We are, basically, energetic beings.

When blockages in our physiology impede the smooth flow of energy, we become ill. If we are vulnerable to depression, this is the way in which illness will strike. Life-energy is the power behind our thinking; it provides us with the ability to create and experience joy. It is also the engine that generates good physical health. Our mood, our thoughts, and the state of our general health all reflect the transformation of life-energy from nature into our physiology.

Basically, anything that blocks or depletes our available life-energy is an agent of depression. The culprits are many, but chronic stress tops the list. Physiological aging (which is not necessarily the same as chronological aging) is second on the list. As we age, it becomes increasingly difficult to ward off the negative effects of stress; we more readily build up impediments to the free flow of our energy network. If this buildup is not regularly and effectively addressed, it will eventually weigh down our spirit.

Understanding how our life-energy becomes blocked involves a basic principle: as transformers of energy, we use our five senses to take in the world around us. In fact, human beings digest everything that is taken in through the senses. You literally are what you eat. However, let us define the word *eat* as the process of ingesting and digesting everything we consume through our body, mind, and spirit.

If our physical, mental, or emotional digestive ability becomes less than optimal, we can become overwhelmed with undigested matter, causing a disruption in any given aspect of our being. Oppressed by this condition, we become depressed.

Another basic Ayurvedic tenet is that just like animals, plants, and minerals, human beings are an integral part of the natural world. Our physiology has genetically programmed biorhythms that are intimately attuned to the rhythms of nature. Our evolutionary trajectory has not taken us away from the need to follow the dictates of Mother Nature. However, unlike other creatures in the natural world, we have the ability to wittingly and unwittingly engage in habits that create physiological imbalances. Think about it: no sentient being in the wild works eighteen-hour days, and cows don't eat pizza at midnight. Habitual behaviors that violate the laws of nature bring derangements to our body, mind, and spirit and eventually pop up as depression and other ailments.

In short, we create depression when we deplete our vital energy; when we accumulate gunk in our seamless energetic system, thereby blocking access to the free flow of our life-energy; and when we incur imbalances in our physiology.

How Is Depression Undone?

To undo depression we must create its opposite: vitality. Happiness is the byproduct of a healthy physiology that is filled to the brim with vitality. The ultimate source of vitality is the natural intelligence that underlies the universe. We create vitality by promoting the free face of natural intelligence.

As we go through life, with the passage of time, we often become more entrenched in our ideas about who we are, failing to become who we could be. It is part of human nature that without intervention we will repeatedly return to the same solutions and the same habits. Through the repetition of mental, emotional, and behavioral patterns, we create deep grooves in the nervous system. Each thought, behavior, and feeling triggers a release of neurochemicals, which in turn structure our physiology. With these structural patterns set in place, we are driven to repetition. This has led some scientists to say that we actually become "addicted" to our emotional, mental, and behavioral patterns.

In order to heal depression and create happiness in our life, we need to alter our neural and biochemical patterns. As this psychophysiological shift occurs, our repertoire of emotional, mental, and behavioral responses is expanded. This expansion directs every aspect of our being toward vitality. In order to alter our neural and biochemical patterns, Ayurveda holds that we need something much deeper than thinking or talking about problems or taking pills.

To counter depression, Ayurveda employs strategies that infuse vitality into body, mind, and spirit and thus inherently work to undo depression. These strategies generate a vibrant life force, resolve blockages, and correct imbalances. Highly practical, they are easy to understand and put into practice.

As agents of vitality, Ayurvedic strategies have important factors in common. First, they help us to harmonize with the rhythms of nature. Second, if energetic blockages exist, they activate the physiology to initiate purification, helping the mind and the body to attain clarity. They also help us to optimize our digestive abilities so that we can efficiently transform thoughts, emotions, and food into usable energy. These interventions work at the level of consciousness—the foundation of our being—and thus untangle the roots of depression.

The following list of antidepression strategies is designed to unleash our innate healing potential by creating the opportunity for natural healing to take place:

1. **Understand that consciousness underlies body, mind, and spirit.** In chapter 3, we discuss the fact that consciousness, the intelligence that guides nature, is the basis of everything in the universe. We explain that the human body is not merely a

hunk of matter but rather a pattern of vibration emanating from an underlying field of energy. This notion can serve as a trigger for a shift in paradigm that has the potential to revolutionize medicine and radically change the way we treat depression.

2. **Learn to identify your unique manifestation of depression.** The Ayurvedic perspective on depression allows for fine-tuning the assessment of symptoms. It correlates particular symptoms with elemental imbalances in the different facets of the being. Depending on their unique physiological disturbance, individuals are likely to express one of three archetypes of depression: Airy Depression, Burning Depression, or Earthy Depression.

   In chapter 4 we illustrate a case of Airy Depression, which is marked by anxiety. In chapter 5 we present a case of Burning Depression, which is often characterized by a wall of frustration, anger, and irritability. And in chapter 6 we describe a case of Earthy Depression, which is marked by physical inertia and emotional lethargy.

3. **Optimize the digestion of food and experiences by body, mind, and spirit.** In chapters 7 and 8 we show that depression encompasses the entire body, mind, and spirit—not simply the brain. Depression can result from the inefficient digestion of food by the body or of life experiences by the mind. Either way, we can block the free flow of energy and dampen the expression of happiness. Our digestive fire must be optimized at every level of being for efficient psychophysiological functioning to occur.

4. **Nourish the physiology with powerful rest.** So important are rest and sleep for the undoing of depression that we have dedicated two chapters to these topics. In chapter 9 we discuss how the regular practice of meditation provides deep rest for the physiology and purification for the nervous system. In chapter 13 we illustrate how sleep deprivation makes the mind and the body vulnerable to mental and physical stress. This stress inevitably results in blockages in our energetic network or imbalances in our physiology. Fatigue creates depression; deep rest is curative.

5. **Use tailor-made exercise programs, yoga poses, and breathing techniques to undo depression.** To undo depression we must forgo

the idea that one size fits all. In chapters 10, 11, and 12 we shed light on how to use breathing techniques, exercise, and yoga poses to undo depression. We guide you in designing a program that addresses your particular expression of depression. As agents of vitality, breathing techniques, exercise, and yoga poses serve to invigorate the physiology. They promote the generation and free flow of our life force. The general theme of these chapters is "different strokes for different folks." Pick the curative strategies that are right for you.

6. **Use food as medicine.** Ayurveda encourages us to think of food as packets of information that bring us the natural intelligence of nature. In chapter 14 we discuss the fact that the solution to depression may be found in the morsel at the end of our fork. Of equal importance, we believe, is the point that it is not *what* we eat but *how* we eat that brings vibrancy to body, mind, and spirit.

7. **Use meditation as medicine.** In chapter 9 we highlight that the regular practice of meditation relieves stress and boosts physical, mental, emotional, and spiritual energy and the expansion of awareness. We cite scientific research that has been replicated and validated that demonstrates the efficacy of meditation as an antidepressant strategy.

Of the myriad strategies available, meditation is the main agent of vitality. Meditation kick-starts all of our self-healing mechanisms. It provides the deep rest that is required for natural healing to take place. At a profound yet subtle level, it purifies body, mind, and spirit. It promotes our digestive capacity by igniting our metabolic furnace. Most important, it allows us access to happiness and vitality—our birthright.

Antidepression Strategies

Make a paradigm shift in the way you think about the essence of your being. Here are the seven strategies again, in a more succinct form. Which of the following do you think would help you the most?

1. Opening your mind to the understanding that the human body is not a hunk of material, but rather a pattern of vibration emanating from an underlying field of energy.

2. Identifying your unique manifestation of depression in terms of your energetic self.

3. Optimizing the digestion of food and experience by the body and mind.

4. Nourishing the physiology with powerful rest.

5. Promoting the free flow of your natural intelligence in your body through a tailor-made exercise program, yoga poses, and breathing techniques.

6. Using food as medicine.

7. Using meditation as medicine.

Awakening Your Inner Physician

Think about the last time you were sick with an infection—a cold or a stomach virus, for example. How did you know you were getting sick? What were the first signs? What did you do about it? What worked best for you? What can you learn from this experience about your body's ability to regain physical health and wellness? Are you aware of the body's healing intelligence, which guides the healing of wounds? Where do you want to begin in the process of awakening your inner physician?

3

The Many Faces of Depression

The closer a man gets to knowing himself, the less
likely he is to trip up on his own illusions.

—ARTHUR MILLER

Most books on depression provide a long list of symptoms
to help the reader assess whether he or she is actually suffering from this affliction. Perhaps you have taken such an inventory
and have wondered what to do about the symptoms that did not fit
with your experience of depression. With more contemplation, you may
have noticed that some symptoms seem contradictory. For example, if
depressed, you are likely to oversleep or not be able to sleep at all; eat or
not eat; be anxious and irritable or lethargic and weepy. Does it not make
you wonder why, regardless of your pattern of symptoms, the recommended treatment plan is often one size fits all? What accounts for this?

A one-size-fits-all treatment for depression is the result of thinking
of the body from a mechanistic paradigm. The assumption behind the
Western medical approach to treatment is that all bodies function
the same way. Therefore, regardless of the constellation of symptoms
that a person experiences, the logic of this approach is that a single

treatment plan should suit every case. The truth is that there is no one-size-fits-all treatment for depression.

Reductionist Thinking about Depression

The Western scientific view of the body is reductionist. It sees the body as a machine that is made up of different components, each identified by the function it plays. Medical scientists have studied each of these systems as a separate entity, and modern medical care breaks down the treatment of the body into specialties. For example, a dermatologist treats skin disorders, a neurologist treats brain and nervous system dysfunction, a cardiologist treats heart problems, and an endocrinologist treats our hormones. This perhaps explains why Western scientists have focused the study and treatment of depression on a single body part—the brain.

Reductionist thinking falls short when it comes to treating diseases that cause your entire being to go awry. Depression is a case in point. It wreaks havoc on our endocrine, respiratory, cardiac, and immune systems, to name a few. Our digestion, immunity, sleep function, thinking, sex drive, and motivation are also greatly affected by depression. Scientific studies have repeatedly pointed out that sadness hurts the heart, and there is indeed a strong association between depression and heart disease. It is not uncommon to hear that during a bout of depression, preexisting conditions of any sort worsen. For example, for some people, skin disorders become activated, which can signal a hyper-reactivity of the immune system; for others, their immunity plummets and they fall prey to every germ to which they are exposed.

Not until recently has Western medicine suggested that even though the different systems—digestive, nervous, endocrine, respiratory, immune—are separate, they might (and do) interact closely with one another. Fortunately, mind-body medicine and the emerging field of psychoneuroimmunology are bringing the issue of the unity of the mind and the body to the forefront of modern science. The Vedic sages, on the other hand, understood this concept a very long time ago. They looked for the unity that underlies all of the systems in our physiology rather than focusing on the systems' diverse functions. This is the holistic approach that we need when we study the global affliction of depression. A deeper understanding of the interrelationship of the many aspects of one's physiology allows for a more precise diagnosis and a treatment plan that is based on the unique needs of the individual.

Changing Paradigms of Depression

Let us consider how the paradigm of depression has changed. Our current mechanistic worldview reduces the human being to something akin to a tinker toy wrapped in a bag of skin. Depression was once considered an ailment of the spirit; only in modern times has it been relegated to a chemical imbalance in the brain.

The notion that depression results from a nexus of risk factors is gaining popularity. However, practice has yet to catch up with theory. Moreover, even when the body, the mind, and the spirit are all taken into account, the treatment continues to be focused on brain functioning. At best, interventions are generally geared to supporting brain function through a brain-healthy diet (addressing the body), changing thought patterns (addressing the mind), and realizing that you have a "higher self" (addressing the spirit). To make the psychophysiological shift that is required to end the tyranny of depression, however, our culture must adopt a paradigm that results in interventions that delve deep into our very essence—consciousness. In order for this to happen, a consciousness model of the human being must replace the current mechanistic model.

The Vedic sages viewed the human being as a pattern of vibrations, a seamless energetic system whose point of initiation is cosmic consciousness. The individual is the embodiment of a field of pure potentiality. In other words, the sages believed that the intelligence that underlies the universe resides in us as well. This natural intelligence controls our inner workings with the same care and precision with which it controls the blossoming of a flower in a garden, the development of a fetus, or the healing of a physical, mental, or spiritual wound.

Lest you think that this is some New Age mumbo jumbo, let us tell you that the latest scientific research in a variety of disciplines affirms that there absolutely is unity among body, mind, and spirit. From deep within the mountain of evidence of cutting-edge science, a voice is shouting, "Wake up and smell the holism!" We think that this is the voice of reason.

We have consistently used the terms *mind-body, physiology*, or *body, mind, and spirit* to underscore the underlying unity of the workings of our being. The elemental you—your most basic form—is most accurately described as a seamless energetic system. We might not look like we are always changing, but in fact we are in constant energetic flux. Behind our static outer appearance, all our functioning—the dynamic internal state of biochemical reactions, the internal communication among cells, and the continuous flow of energy throughout the mind-body—is regulated by guiding principles that organize and govern the entire system and keep us constantly adjusting to internal and external change. Ayurveda calls these organizing principles *doshas*.

The doshas are common to all of the systems in our physiology. Ayurveda focuses on this commonality (the doshas) instead of what is separate and distinct. Whether we are dealing with cells, tissues, organs, or the entire mind-body, the doshas, or guiding principles, orchestrate function across the board. With this knowledge, we recognize our mind-body as indivisible and its functions as supremely interconnected.

When you look in the mirror, you see a solid form that is yourself looking back at you. Nevertheless, you are aware that under your skin there are organs, muscles, tissues, and bones that create the structure (the body) that you see before your eyes. Even deeper, at a microscopic level, the total physical system is composed of cells. At the molecular level, the building block of a cell is DNA, the blueprint of all biological matter.

Atomic particles (protons, neutrons, and electrons) exist at the foundation of the cellular level. Protons, neutrons, electrons, and all other subatomic particles are conceptual representations of fluctuations of energy. It is here, at the deepest quantum level of nature's functioning, that we find a field of pure potentiality, of everything that can be. It is at this level that we find the energetic foundation of matter.

Modern Western scientists, through their in-depth studies in bio-chemistry, genetics, and molecular biology, are beginning to understand how matter works. They are also gaining knowledge on how energy affects matter. However, at this point, in order to understand functioning at the quantum level (how energy becomes translated from the field of pure potentiality to our physical reality), we still must look to Vedic knowledge for guidance. What did the Vedic sages know?

The Ayurvedic System of Doshas

From their in-depth study of nature, the Vedic sages observed energy disguised in the form of five elements. From the subtlest to the most perceptible, they are as follows: ether, air, fire, water, and earth. Everything in the natural world contains these five elements. This is the case whether we are talking about minerals, plants, or animals.

According to Vedic knowledge, these five elements combine into three fundamental fields. Air and ether combine to form Vata dosha, fire and water combine to form Pitta dosha; and earth and water combine to form Kapha dosha. But the doshas are *not* "things." They are the guiding principles in nature.

The doshas are among the first manifestations that sprout from the field of pure potentiality into the realm of matter. In turn, Vata, Pitta, and Kapha dosha orchestrate the functioning of the pattern of vibration that creates the elemental you. Let us explain this in the words of modern physicists.

Albeit with different language, modern quantum physicists echo Vedic knowledge. They tell us that five spin types (elements) form the most basic concepts in particle physics: (1) spin 2 (graviton) relates to the element of space, (2) spin $\frac{3}{2}$ (gravitino) relates to the element of air, (3) spin 1 (force fields) relates to the element of fire, (4) spin $\frac{1}{2}$ (matter fields) relates to the element of water, (5) and spin 0 (Higgs field) relates to the element of earth. Physicists assert that everything in creation is derived from the combination of these five fundamental spin types into three superfields: gravity, gauge, and matter. Gravity is produced from the combination of spin 2 (space) and spin $\frac{3}{2}$ (air) and corresponds to the classical definition of Vata dosha. Gauge is produced from the combination of spin 1 (fire) and spin $\frac{1}{2}$ (water) and corresponds to Pitta dosha. Matter is produced from the combination of spin 0 (earth) and spin $\frac{1}{2}$ (water) and corresponds to Kapha dosha.

Here's another way to think about it: The analogy of primary colors has often been used to explain the fundamental nature of the spin types in the creation of all forms of matter. Combinations of blue, yellow, and red form all of the other colors of the rainbow. Purple, for example, is red plus blue. In this way, every possible manifestation of universal intelligence represents a combination of the five spin types.

The three doshas (Vata, Pitta, and Kapha) operate in the macrocosm of the universe as well as in the microcosm of the human being. Every aspect of the natural world, including the human being, is a pattern of intelligence, and it is the doshas that govern the workings of this pattern of intelligence. Knowing how the doshas influence your individual mind and body is the key to functioning in harmony with nature. The necessary tools are awareness and intentionality. Awareness of how the doshas function allows us to become intentional about our daily choices and habits in order to keep our physiology in a state of balance.

Think of the doshas as master homeostatic mechanisms that keep your mind-body on an even keel. The doshas maintain your internal equilibrium in the face of external changes. There is survival value in this. For instance, even on a cold winter day, you maintain a constant internal temperature, which is required for the proper functioning of your physiology.

The doshas impart the intelligence of nature into your physiology. They function as guiding principles to govern the major processes in the mind-body. Your physiology is constantly being affected by its environment, yet for proper functioning it has to maintain homeostasis. If this natural internal balance is not maintained, the proper functioning of the physiology is compromised. It is the doshas that allow the maintenance of homeostasis.

Through the process of daily living, we incur imbalances at the doshic level. If these imbalances go uncorrected, the intelligence of nature will not be properly translated into our physiology, which will then be unable to initiate its self-repair mechanisms. Over time, left uncorrected, imbalances disrupt proper functioning and eventually cause disease.

Depression is no exception. According to Ayurveda, disruptions at the level of the doshas are at the root of all disease processes. Ayurveda gets to the root of the problem of depression because it understands how to diagnose, treat, and prevent the doshic imbalances that create it.

Pulse Diagnosis: Detecting Doshic Imbalances

Ayurvedic practitioners are trained to detect vibratory patterns that emanate from the physiology. They do this primarily through a technique called *pulse diagnosis*. Pulse diagnosis reveals a complete picture of the workings of the physiology. It details what is happening at the gross physical level as well as at the doshic level, where physical functioning is orchestrated. The pulse offers a window into the state of the mind-body because blood is the one substance that circulates through every organ, tissue, and cell in our body; in doing so, it picks up information about the state and functioning of the physiology. This information is revealed in the form of signals, the meanings of which have been thoroughly mapped out by the Vedic sages. Subsequently, reading the pulse leads to highly refined diagnoses.

Many physicians who are trained in both Ayurveda and Western medicine attest to the fact that pulse diagnosis offers a wide window into the physiology. Western diagnostic techniques can detect a problem only when obvious signs and symptoms are revealed in the physiology. Pulse diagnosis, on the other hand, reveals the early stages of imbalances that precede illness. By detecting the state of the doshas, we can identify and treat the root causes of our symptoms before the symptoms even materialize. Symptoms are a last stage in the disease process.

Doshic Diagnosis

Even if there is no Ayurvedic practitioner in your area, you can still gain insight into your doshic imbalances. Understanding how the doshas work will help you gain these powerful insights.

Each of the doshas orchestrates particular functions in the physiology. By learning what is under the purview of Vata, Pitta, and Kapha dosha, you can begin to decipher the patterns that are indicative of imbalances. Once you understand the patterns, the next step is to utilize the wisdom of the Vedic sages, using their deep understanding of how the natural world works in order to bring balance to your physiology.

Vata dosha governs the nervous system and is therefore the guiding intelligence that coordinates all movement. It is involved in the flow of energy and circulation within the physiology and controls the communication among cells and among organs. This is because communication inherently involves the movement of information between objects. By relaying information between our internal and external environment, Vata keeps our internal biorhythms in tune as well as attuned to the cycles of day and night and the changes of the seasons. Vata dosha guides the body's adjustments to change—be it physical, mental, psychological, dietary, or environmental.

Pitta dosha governs all of the transformative processes that occur in our mind-body. At the physical level, Pitta transforms the food we eat into energy, but its role is not limited only to the digestive system. Pitta functions wherever there is a need to transform one substance to another, so the emotional and intellectual processing of experiences is also under its purview. This dosha is the basis of our metabolism because it is responsible for the transformation of physical, mental, and emotional experiences into vital energy.

Kapha dosha holds everything together. Kapha governs the formation of physical structure; it is responsible for the strength and cohesion of cells, tissues, organs, muscles, and bones. Likewise, at the mental and emotional levels, Kapha regulates the stability and stamina of our thinking and emotional processing. The integrity of our physiology is under the purview of Kapha dosha. It governs our immune system and is intimately involved in maintaining our health in the face of external physical threats, such as germs.

In Other Words: Different Ways of Understanding the Notion of a Dosha

The ancient Ayurvedic concept of the dosha has its modern counterpart in biology, molecular biology, genetics, and quantum physics.

The body has thousands of homeostatic mechanisms, which regulate everything from blood oxygen levels to complex kidney functions that maintain fluid balances. Like the doshas, these homeostatic mechanisms have one objective: to preserve as constant the conditions of life in the internal environment.

DNA is like a microchip of pure biological intelligence that is inscribed in a chemical cipher called the genetic code. The doshas function like DNA. They are a dynamic blueprint from which each unique physiology is built.

Modern quantum mechanics physics and Ayurveda use different languages to describe the same phenomenon. The sages speak of five *mahabhutas* that combine to form each dosha, whereas physicists discuss how five spin types combine to form three superfields. Both agree that these form the basis of every aspect of the natural world.

The Three Archetypes of Depression

Using the theory of three doshas allows for specific diagnosis and tailor-made treatment for depression. All disorders, including depression, happen over time. An imbalance in a dosha is a process that begins when a particular dosha is aggravated. Over time, if the imbalance is left uncorrected, a disruption in the healthy functioning of the physiology occurs. Eventually noticeable symptoms appear that relate back to the doshic imbalance. Depending on their specific doshic disturbance, people are likely to express one of three archetypes of depression:

1. **Airy Depression.** Disturbances in Vata dosha yield a depression that manifests with a loss of enthusiasm and with anxiety as the predominant secondary emotion. The individual has difficulty falling asleep. The driving internal perception is the feeling of being overwhelmed or out of control. The root of the problem is likely to be found in a lack of stability in life patterns. Difficulty sustaining a major life change can be a trigger for this archetype of depression. Nourishing the physiology and stabilizing the nervous system are the main therapeutic techniques.

2. **Burning Depression.** When a perturbation of Pitta dosha occurs, the metabolic processes are blocked. Irritability and frustration are so prevalent that they can often mask a gulf of sadness. The individual's sleep is disrupted because the mind wakes up long before the body is fully rested. The driving internal perception is the feeling of having blocked possibilities. Approaching life with extreme intensity and a pattern of overdoing may be at the root of the problem. To resolve this type of depression, the physiology must be cooled off, literally and figuratively. Decreasing intensity is as essential for recovery as getting deep rest.

3. **Earthy Depression.** When Kapha dosha is disrupted, solidity and stability morph into feelings of being weighed down. Lethargy, lack of interest, and being overly sentimental keep the individual feeling stuck. Excessive sleep is a key feature of this archetype of depression. Helping individuals with a Kapha imbalance to overcome inertia is a challenging task. Interventions must address the heaviness experienced at every level in the mind-body. Ayurvedic purification treatments greatly assist in resolving this type of depression.

In subsequent chapters, we will discuss three cases that illustrate each of the archetypes of depression:

1. **Arial's Story: Anchorless in the World.** This case illustrates Airy Depression, triggered by a disturbance in Vata dosha and marked by anxiety.

2. **Barbara's Story: Burning to Cry.** This case illustrates Burning Depression, associated with an imbalance in Pitta dosha and marked by a wall of anger and irritability that masks sadness.

The Makings of Depression: Brain Chemicals and Their Elemental Counterparts

It's not just low serotonin that's making you blue. Depression comes about through a nexus of factors, and its tentacles affect your entire being. Once it's seeded in your physiology, it impacts your neurotransmitters. Different types of derangement in these biochemicals lead to different symptoms. In fact, the chemical derangements mirror the categories of elemental imbalances set forth by Ayurveda.

Archetype	Elemental Imbalance	Chemical Derangement
Airy	Vata imbalance	Low serotonin
Burning	Pitta imbalance	High norepinephrine and/or dopamine
Earthy	Kapha imbalance	Low norepinephrine and/or dopamine

3. **Ed's Story: Needing to Liven Up.** This case illustrates Earthy Depression, a problem with the functioning of Kapha dosha that results in the buildup of blockages in many aspects of the physiology.

Depression: It's Elemental!

Questionnaires are limited in their ability to fully assess the depth and breadth of a multidimensional problem like depression, especially given the fact that each of us has a unique physiology. Questionnaires can, however, be helpful in pointing us in a general direction. To this end, we have devised a series of questions (see page 42) in the hope that answering them will get you thinking about depression from an Ayurvedic perspective. The case histories in the upcoming chapters will help you to refine your understanding of how doshic imbalances lead to different manifestations of depression. Don't pigeonhole yourself until you have read through all of the chapters.

Some individuals will readily fit into a distinct pattern of depression; others will find that their manifestation of depression is like a collage, created from bits and pieces from each of the three archetypes of depression. In still other cases, individuals may find that they have experienced distinct symptoms from each of the three categories at different times. For instance, it is not uncommon for an individual to move from one category to another. You might start out with an Airy Depression and, over time, if the root cause is not addressed, develop other imbalances that result in an Earthy Depression.

1. When you experience depression, what are your predominant secondary emotions?

    A. Fear and anxiety

    B. Anger and resentment

    C. Emotional numbness

2. When you experience depression, what is your driving internal perception?

    A. Feelings of being overwhelmed or out of control

    B. Feelings of frustration and the sense that my ability to move forward is being blocked by others

    C. Feeling stuck and powerless to change

3. When you experience depression, how is your sleep pattern affected?

    A. I have difficulty falling asleep.

    B. My sleep is prematurely interrupted.

    C. I sleep too much.

4. When you experience depression, how is your desire for food affected?

    A. I have no desire for food.

    B. My desire for food is not affected.

    C. I desire foods that comfort me.

5. When you experience depression, how do you relate to others?

    A. I feel insecure in relationships.

    B. I tend to want to control my relationships.

    C. I either get clingy or tend to withdraw.

6. In general, what is your first response to feeling emotionally hurt?

    A. I cry.

    B. I respond with sarcasm and biting remarks.

    C. I tend to keep my feelings to myself.

7. How would you describe yourself when you are not depressed?

    A. I tend to be enthusiastic and lively.

    B. I tend to be dynamic and intense.

    C. I tend to be good-natured and easygoing.

8. How do you communicate with others when you are not depressed?

    A. I tend to be a better talker than a listener.

    B. I am easily annoyed by people who talk too much.

    C. I am a good and patient listener.

9. How would you describe your energy level when you are not depressed?

    A. Physical energy comes to me in bursts.

    B. I have a lot of energy and stamina.

    C. I use my energy slowly and steadily.

10. When you think back on how you became depressed, which of the following would you say was a significant contributing factor?

    A. Lack of stability in life patterns

    B. Approaching life with extreme intensity and a pattern of over-doing

    C. Difficulty overcoming inertia

If you have answered mostly As, then you are likely to be experiencing an Airy Depression; if Bs, a Burning Depression; if Cs, an Earthy Depression. If your answers were fairly balanced among all three choices, you most likely have a mixed pattern of depression.

Reading the next three chapters will help you home in on the physiological imbalance that is steering your depression.

4

Airy Depression

> We must become the change we
> want to see in the world.
>
> —MAHATMA GANDHI

Airy Depression is triggered by disturbances in Vata dosha. This archetype of depression is characterized by a loss of enthusiasm and by loneliness, anxiety, fear, and worry. The individual reports feeling overwhelmed by a life that seems out of his or her control. There is a pervading sense that one's mind is being pulled in many directions. Feeling mentally overworked, the person experiences diminished creativity, mental focus, and clarity. An unstable memory and scattered thinking add an underlying sense of anxiety and not feeling grounded. Aches and pains, malaise, and unrelenting fatigue are physical symptoms often associated with Airy Depression.

Faced with the option to fight, flee, or freeze, an individual with an Airy Depression will opt to flee under stress. Fleeing can, for example, take the form of keeping oneself occupied in an effort to avoid dealing with mental, emotional, or physical issues. In other instances, a person may tenaciously hold on to false ideas and beliefs even when faced with evidence to the contrary in an effort to escape dealing with a deeper reality.

One of the main factors in the onset and perpetuation of Airy Depression is a lack of stability in life patterns. Often, episodes of Airy Depression occur after an individual has sustained a major life change that has disturbed the structure in his or her life. Long-standing sleep debt and mental or emotional fatigue can often be found at the root of the problem. Unfortunately, one of the first telltale signs of this archetype of depression is the presence of a sleep disturbance—namely, insomnia. The inability to get a good night's rest adds momentum to a depressive episode.

Without correction, an imbalance in Vata dosha can potentially trigger an imbalance in Pitta dosha and morph into a Burning Depression. Likewise, a prolonged episode of Airy Depression can easily turn into an Earthy Depression. Nourishing the physiology and stabilizing the nervous system are the main therapeutic techniques to undo an Airy Depression.

Arial's Story: Anchorless in the World

As Arial began to talk, she folded her arms across her chest. Her body seemed to collapse into itself with every word she said. Her delicate frame appeared overly thin, and her face had a mask of tension and worry. With a quiver in her voice, she explained, "My life is drifting away from me, and I feel empty and hollow inside. I don't have a clue about what's going on with me lately. I have a beautiful family and a great job, but many days it all just feels like too much. My husband is annoyed at me because I have lost enthusiasm for the things we used to do together. I don't know what he expects of me. I feel so overwhelmed—like a rubber band that has been stretched so far it has lost its zip."

For Arial, life had become a game of catch-up. She woke up every morning feeling overwhelmed: "My days have gotten wild. I've lost all sense of a routine. Every day is different, and I just feel completely out of control."

Six months earlier, Arial received the promotion she had been wanting for years. "I was flying high for weeks," she said. The job meant a transfer to another state, a move she enthusiastically looked forward to making. Her face was tear-streaked as she explained that recently the job has seemed empty, the pursuit of success devoid of meaning. Adjusting to the new location was harder than she thought it would be. She missed her extended family.

Arial was also having difficulty adjusting to the demands of her new position. She explained, "When you have an upper managerial position, you never know what crisis will come next." As she wiped a tear away, she explained that she has yet to confront a major crisis, yet she perceives a necessity to be on her toes constantly. Anticipating the inevitable emergency, she regularly checks her phone messages in case she has not heard the phone ring. "My cell phone has become an appendage to my body," she said.

Wringing her hands, Arial explained that she has been concerned because sometimes her thinking doesn't seem clear: "I'm scared that my thinking is foggy and my replies are scattered." To handle this, she drinks a lot of caffeinated beverages: "Coffee in the morning and diet soda in the afternoon." She grabs lunch on the run, and by four o'clock, she exclaims, "I feel like there is a fan blowing confetti inside me!"

By the end of the workday, Arial is running on fumes; however, this is when her job of active parenting started. With tension in her voice and a look of defeat on her face, she muttered, "I worry if I have enough energy to be emotionally present for my kids—but I do help with homework and drive them to their activities. By eleven o'clock I feel as if I could drop. Instead, I lie awake thinking of all the things I will have on my plate the next day."

To unwind, Arial usually chills out in front of the TV for an hour or so before bed. "It had better be a show filled with action and suspense," she noted. "Anything else would bore me." Her other form of relaxation is exercise: "I also run every day. It gives me energy. I don't know what I would do without it. It's the only time my mind stops racing."

Ayurvedic Diagnosis

From the Ayurvedic perspective, Arial would be diagnosed with an imbalance in Vata dosha that has led to depression. Her symptoms fit the archetype of an Airy Depression. The predominant issue is her loss of enthusiasm for the things that formerly brought her joy. We see that she is also anxious.

Vata dosha, the combination of the elements air and ether, governs the nervous system. This dosha becomes disturbed as a result of too much activity and not enough rest. The excess activity stirs up the air that composes Vata, essentially turning a breeze into a tornado. From a Western medical perspective, this means that the nervous system is in a prolonged state of hyperexcitability, which leads to its inevitable collapse. Our bodies require rest, and when we exert ourselves too much for too long, the physical mechanisms that promote physiological balance become deranged. In its attempt to keep up with itself, the body revs up its production of biochemicals—not just in the brain but throughout the body. At some point, physical fatigue sets in as a depletion of hormones and neurochemicals occurs.

What triggered the tornado? Upon receiving her dream promotion, Arial said she was "flying high for weeks." It is not uncommon to let our feelings guide our lifestyle. Arial responded to this feeling of heightened energy with overactivity. Her nervous system became revved up and eventually went into overdrive. The physiology can't maintain a constant state of arousal without becoming imbalanced. The new job was the trigger for the tornado, but it was her adjustment to its demands that caused the windstorm to continue unabated.

Moving to a new state energized the tornado. Psychologically and emotionally (in addition to the physical strain of packing and unpacking), moving literally displaces us. A move to a new state entails dealing with everything from breathing unfamiliar air to having to locate a new dry cleaner and grocery store. When these places are found, the faces are unfamiliar, leaving one with a sense of loneliness. In addition, Arial had to help her children adjust to a new home, a new neighborhood, a new school, and new friends. Newness signifies change, and the constant adjustment to this change is demanding on one's entire being: physical, emotional, mental, and spiritual. Furthermore, change and the demands of adjustment tax the physiology—the nervous, endocrine, immune, and digestive systems—and, in Ayurvedic terms, can trigger a derangement in Vata dosha.

At the emotional level, the first thing we see is a drop in enthusiasm. Arial reported that her husband is concerned because she has lost her enthusiasm for life and for the things that previously made her happy. She feels sad and worried. The job she so desperately desired is now lacking in meaning and interest. Her primary internal emotion is feeling out of control. As she aptly explained, "I feel so overwhelmed—like a rubber band that has been stretched so far it has lost its zip." In other words, Arial has lost her resiliency.

At the physical level, by her own admission, she is exhausted. Ironically, she is depleting her remaining energy reserves by doing things that will give her temporary quick bursts of energy: jogging and gulping down caffeine-loaded drinks. She reports grabbing lunch on the run. There is no time in her day to do anything to nurture her physical body. Worrying about her relationship with her husband and children is further draining her vitality.

Arial describes feeling as though a fan were blowing confetti inside her. This is a very accurate metaphor for what is happening to her physiology as a result of her Vata derangement. At this point, Arial does not believe that she can stop doing and going. She has fallen into the habit of keeping herself in overdrive, in high gear. She seeks stimulation in everything she does. Internally, worrying (excess mental activity) is a way to keep the mind stimulated, albeit not productively. Externally, watching suspenseful TV shows stirs up the brain much in the same way that jogging revs up the body. It is no wonder that she has one of the main symptoms of a severe Vata imbalance: insomnia.

Psychologically, Arial is ungrounded. Up to now, one of her main sources of stability has been her relationship with her husband, and now he is pulling away. This disturbance is a stress on her heart, rousing her emotional whirlwind and feeding into the vicious cycle of instability. Her Vata imbalance is affecting her ability to think clearly. In fact, a Vata imbalance causes people to lose their problem-solving ability. In Arial's case, she thinks that she is losing her husband, but her ungroundedness gives her no sense of control over this event. Instead, she is holding on to what she can control: the cell phone. A Vata derangement frequently causes a person to become hypervigilant, perceiving that there is a crisis around every corner.

Spiritually, Arial is without an anchor. Unfortunately, she is not unlike many people who are caught in the web of overactivity. Running from one external thing to another, Arial has lost her sense of internal self. At a superficial level, she has lost her awareness of how her lifestyle affects the whole of her being. At a deeper level, she has lost her connection to the unchanging aspect of life that exists within and underlies everything.

Becoming Reanchored

Becoming reanchored and filling Arial's emotional void calls for balancing Vata dosha. Arial learned the source of her imbalance and how her lifestyle choices exacerbated her condition. For those who, like Arial, suffer from this archetype of depression, the sense of self-worth is generally dependent on being active, on constantly doing and going.

We suggested short-term interventions at first. Herbs eased Arial's anxiety and insomnia. She was able to get some much-needed rest, and the clarity of her thinking improved. Once she had more energy, she was ready to implement changes to her lifestyle.

Arial also learned to meditate. The mental technique that she began to practice was profoundly helpful. It became a regular part of her everyday life. The daily practice of meditation helped her to create an internal infrastructure of support and expand her awareness. Her particular meditative practice also gave her nervous system a deep rest, which enabled her to settle down. Her insomnia permanently disappeared.

The next therapeutic task was to help Arial nourish her physiology and rebuild her physical energy. A key point was to have her understand that her physiology is part of the natural world and subject to the dictates of nature. This understanding helped her to realize the importance of stabilizing her daily routines.

Vata imbalances are corrected when people follow natural biorhythms. Consequently, Ayurveda recommends taking our cue from the rising and setting of the sun. If we go to bed close to ten at night and rise at six in the morning, we garner nature's support. In addition, Arial was encouraged to set aside time to eat her main meal at noon in a quiet and comfortable setting. This is when our digestive fire burns as hot as the midday sun, so our physiology can metabolize (cook) our food most efficiently. Proper nutrition is a necessity for the resolution of depression.

We encouraged the regulation of Arial's metabolism by suggesting that she eat at approximately the same time every day, and we recommended good-tasting foods that would resolve her particular doshic imbalance: warm, heavy foods to infuse her physiology with groundedness. In this way, Arial came to understand that food can be medicine.

We all tend to move in the direction of our imbalances, and Arial was no exception. Her revved-up physiology erroneously sought solace through unfocused activity. Daily jogging was only depleting her energy, so we suggested a series of restorative yoga poses and breathing exercises instead. At first she greatly missed running. Eventually she realized that it was being outdoors that she missed, so she began taking walks with her husband in the morning and evening.

If you are wondering who has time for meditation, walks with one's spouse, and leisurely lunches, the answer is you do. Once your physiology becomes balanced, your internal world gains order, and this is reflected in your success in the external world. Everything seems easier. When you have more mental and physical energy, your efficiency increases. Following Ayurvedic guidelines helped Arial to reconnect to her inner source of strength and vitality. In time, her natural enthusiasm resurfaced and her anxiety vanished.

Do You See Yourself in the Mirror?

1. To which aspects of Arial's personal history or story do you relate?

2. Consider how Arial responds to the situations in her life. How do her responses to her life situations resonate with your tendencies? What are the similarities and differences between you and Arial in your responses to life stressors?

3. As a result of your unique tendencies, which aspects of your being are the most adversely affected by depression (that is, your physical, mental, emotional, or spiritual self)?

4. When you are faced with adversity, which aspects of your being offer you strength?

5. How does an imbalance in Vata dosha affect your physiology?

6. What lifestyle choices might be exacerbating a Vata imbalance in your physiology?

7. What lifestyle choices might restore balance to your Vata dosha?

8. Which Ayurvedic interventions described here do you find most interesting? Which interventions do you think could be helpful to you?

5

Burning Depression

> Anything that has real and lasting
> value is always a gift from within.
>
> —FRANZ KAFKA

Burning Depression is triggered by disturbances in Pitta dosha. Individuals with this type of depression report feeling as if their efforts are thwarted by others. This inner perception that their possibilities are blocked leads to pervading feelings of irritability and frustration. Often these strong emotional reactions mask a gulf of sadness. An underlying fear of failure or of losing one's competitive edge also exists. People with a Burning Depression may experience bouts of jealousy, feeling that others have it easier than they do.

Faced with the option to fight, flee, or freeze, individuals with a Burning Depression will opt to fight under stress. In this archetype of depression, a restricted sense of awareness is often at the root of the problem. With diminished powers of discrimination, Pitta-imbalanced individuals are unable to see how their actions affect others and how they play a role in any given situation. Consequently, they blame their predicament on others. Sharp criticism is dished out about how others should behave and what they should do. There is often an increased desire to control how people do things, presumably in an effort to have things done the "right" way, meaning *their* way. Individuals with a Burning Depression often resort to outbursts of anger or sarcasm as a primary means of making their case.

Inflammatory conditions often arise throughout the body, such as skin problems and eruptions (including rashes and acne), digestive disturbances such as ulcers, and irritation of the eyes. An increase in the frequency of migraines is often reported. The person often feels relentless muscle tension. Interruption in the sleep cycle (early-morning awakenings) is often reported.

A life of high intensity and excessive competitiveness may be at the root of the problem. The main therapeutic techniques are cooling off the physiology. Expanding one's awareness and broadening one's horizons are essential.

In a person with a Pitta imbalance causing a Burning Depression, it is common to also find an underlying imbalance of Vata dosha. Like wind fanning a fire, this imbalance directly affects Pitta dosha, leading to a burned-out nervous system. Consequently, attention must be guided toward rejuvenating the physiology by decreasing the inflammatory process at every level. The person needs to calm down (balance Vata dosha) and cool off (balance Pitta dosha).

Barbara's Story: Burning to Cry

Perched on the edge of her chair, Barbara was the picture of tension and frustration. It had been suggested by her boss that she had a problem managing anger. Unflinchingly, Barbara told a different story: "Ironically, I think I have lost my edge. I am fat and flabby—and so is my brain. This is not who I am. My brain used to be razor sharp. I could tune out the world and get my work done. Everyone looked up to me. Now I feel out of sorts. The other day I overheard someone say that I was an overbearing crab."

Barbara felt baffled by her predicament. "I guess I am irritable sometimes, but so what? If people did what they were supposed to do, I wouldn't get so frustrated. I go the extra mile—always! But it's the schmoozers of the world who end up going places." With this statement, she began a tirade against the people at work. Barbara obviously felt terribly misunderstood.

It was particularly difficult for Barbara to discuss her emotions in any depth. All verbal paths of inquiry seemed to hit a wall of anger. With red eyes, tears burning to come out, she related a series of professional and personal experiences that led to frustration and disillusionment. Until recently, Barbara explained, she didn't take the time to think about her emotions—or, as she condescendingly said, "ponder my navel." Instead, it seemed that she managed her emotions through active participation in competitive sports. Tennis was her favorite, but since a knee injury had taken her out of the competitive league, she had lost interest in all sports. Barbara defensively said, "There's nothing as good as tennis."

Sounding both lonely and bitter, she said, "I miss going to the court after work. Now I go home, check e-mails, and return a couple of phone calls. Then I pour myself a glass or two of wine to unwind—it's good for the heart, you know."

Ayurvedic Diagnosis

Although Barbara did not identify herself as being depressed, she does present the clinical picture of a person who is suffering from a depressed mood. She eventually acknowledged being exhausted at work because of difficulty maintaining sleep at night. She has gained weight because of a sharp decrease in activity and an increase in eating. Her self-esteem, according to her report, has plunged. At work she has difficulty concentrating on tasks.

From the Ayurvedic perspective, Barbara's imbalance in Pitta dosha has led to depression. Her symptoms fit the archetype of a Burning Depression. Her prevalent internal perception is one of feeling thwarted, of possibilities being blocked; this is externally expressed as frustration and irritability. However, a deep sadness hides behind this wall of anger and antagonism.

When asked if she had considered the fact that she might be depressed, Barbara seemed surprised by the question. "You think I am depressed? This is just how I am," she snapped. Like many people, Barbara believed that being depressed meant being under a cloud or being immobilized by sadness. On the contrary, for individuals who are experiencing a Burning Depression, irritability often covers up a sad mood and low self-esteem. Barbara had gone undiagnosed for so long because her primary way of functioning in the world was to plow through undeterred, in spite of her internal experience of herself.

Pitta dosha governs the transformation and generation of energy at every level of the physiology. At the physical level, it functions like a stove in our digestive system, helping us to turn food into energy. At the mental level, it's the power that helps us to digest life experiences.

Pitta dosha becomes disturbed as a result of overdoing, pushing too hard, and not taking time to integrate experiences. At risk for this type of depression are individuals who push themselves constantly because they equate achievement with self-worth. In the case of a Burning Depression, the unmeasured intensity causes the individual to eventually burn out or blow up.

Let's take a closer look at Barbara. Metaphorically speaking, she is like a pressure cooker that is unable to let off steam. Her internal perception of having blocked possibilities and of being thwarted represents the lid. The feeling of being blocked is at the root of Barbara's acerbic personality. As the pressure builds, she boils over. As she explained, "I am so frustrated, I feel as if I could explode." The external expression of this imbalance is irritability, hostility, sarcasm, and sharp criticism of oneself and others. This is how Barbara relieves the internal pressure, the internal steam that has built up in her physiology.

From a Western medical perspective, a Burning Depression involves an imbalanced production of excitatory neurochemicals, primarily norepinephrine and dopamine. When noreprinephrine and dopamine are in balance, they provide drive, determination, and energy. In excess they create a desire for thrill-seeking behaviors and aggression. Furthermore, the excessive release of these neurochemicals is accompanied by a deluge of stress hormones—with cortisol leading the way—that promotes an inflammatory physiological state. What exists in the microcosm of the physical body also exists in the macrocosm of the mind. It is therefore not uncommon to find inflammation running wild in the body, with symptoms ranging from skin disorders to ulcers and heartburn to, deeper still, heart disease. As we see in Barbara's case, her emotions and mental predisposition have become inflammatory as well.

What causes the burnout or the blowup? Metabolizing food or experiences involves four key steps: ingestion (taking in), digestion (breaking down), assimilation (absorbing), and elimination (excreting waste). When Pitta dosha is in balance, there is a great capacity for efficient metabolism. In other words, there is a great ability to withstand tremendous amounts of stress before succumbing to its negative effects. A balanced Pitta dosha enables individuals to be hard-driving and often very successful at whatever they do. However, one thing can lead to another, and doing too many things with a great deal of intensity can often cause an imbalance. The brightly burning fire of Pitta generates a lot of energy. Unfortunately, this splendid energy can be misused, to the detriment of one's body, mind, and spirit. In essence, the fire begins to burn itself out.

The issue for individuals with a Pitta imbalance is that they can ingest and digest efficiently, but assimilation is amiss because they don't take time to integrate. They are metabolizing so quickly that they don't reflect on how their lifestyle is impacting their physical health. Nor do they find value in analyzing emotions. As Barbara so aptly put it, "I don't have time to ponder my navel." Eventually, awareness becomes restricted. Like a horse with blinders, Barbara has been running a race and losing sight of how lifestyle choices affect her mind-body, how she feels emotionally, how her behavior affects her relationships; last, but certainly not least, she has completely fallen out of sync with the spiritual aspects of life and living. This is a prescription for a Burning Depression.

The wonder of Burning Depression is that those who have it can continue functioning and be unaware that they are depressed. At the emotional level, individuals like Barbara are quick to register frustration. More gentle emotions, such as sadness, are left unattended until they demand recognition. In addition, a Pitta imbalance triggers a tendency to be hypercritical of oneself and others. Individuals become preoccupied thinking about perceived hurts. Their ability to recognize anything past frustration, hurt, or anger is impaired.

In Barbara's case, her emotions affected her behavior and adversely impacted her performance and relationships at work. She reported being recommended for an anger management class, yet she had no awareness of how her behavior had triggered this recommendation. Her intense flame had become a wildfire burning everything in its path. Like most people with a Pitta imbalance, Barbara had a great deal of energy for external achievement and could, as she said, go the extra mile. If an individual continues to run, taking no time for reflection, intensity builds on itself and eventually burns itself out.

Barbara had developed negative coping mechanisms to deal with her physiological imbalance. At the physical level, for example, she had been overeating in an effort to "quench the burning sensation" she experienced in her stomach. Unbeknownst to her, an ulcer was the source of the uncomfortable sensation. Lost in her intensity, Barbara was unaware of the cues her body was giving her.

It had also become habitual for her to drink one or two glasses of wine a night. In the short run, this provided a respite from her intensity, but in the long run, downing alcohol intensified the Pitta imbalance in her physiology even further. Drinking one or two glasses of wine a night was, for Barbara, like pouring gasoline (a type of alcohol) on a flame. Alcohol inflames the physiology, including the heart.

Drinking alcohol on a regular basis also caused a disruption in her sleep patterns. Although she did not have difficulty falling asleep, she did have trouble maintaining sleep. Barbara reported crashing at night only to wake up a few hours later feeling hot, irritated, and restless. She would often be awake for a few hours, then fall asleep again in the early hours of dawn—shortly before the alarm would announce the arrival of a new day.

Alcohol on My Mind: The Effect of Spirits on Your Mind-Body

To drink or not to drink—that is the question. Research studies have suggested that imbibing alcoholic beverages is good for the heart. Giddy with delight, many of us have taken to toasting our health with a glass of wine in hand. How is that good for the heart? By helping you to relax, even for a short while, alcohol lowers blood pressure, and this in turn is good for the cardiovascular system. Furthermore, it's been reported that chemical compounds in the skin of grapes help to reduce plaques and even prevent stroke.

Unfortunately, although a moderate amount of alcohol is arguably good for the physical heart, this same amount can be detrimental for the emotional heart. Because it triggers feelings of sadness, alcohol serves as a depressant. Sadness may eventually evolve into feelings of nervousness and anxiety, as well as mental lethargy and physical fatigue during the subsequent hangover. With increased regularity and quantity of consumption, it is more likely that the symptoms will intensify, eventually rendering the drinker anxious and depressed. A person's mood is exaggerated by the use of alcohol. If someone is depressed then while drinking, they will probably become even more depressed.

Alcohol *can* act as a tranquilizer, reducing stress for moderate drinkers. Some studies define moderate drinking as a total of two to three glasses of wine per week. Anything more than this only increases stress on the body, especially when the drinker stops for a time or as tolerance for the substance increases.

Because alcohol slows down and relaxes ("depresses") the central nervous system, it also slows down brain function, breathing, and pulse rate. With increased alcohol consumption, the body's cells and organs become less able to perform efficiently. Eventually, sedation and drowsiness occur.

For people who have been alcohol-dependent a long time, the substance can have a toxic effect on their neurotransmitters. Alcohol triggers an increase in the amount of circulating cortisol, which in turn reduces serotonin, norepinephrine, and dopamine.

One would logically expect, therefore, that alcohol consumption would be a causative agent of depression. Nevertheless, studies have shown that drinking alcohol does not necessarily *cause* depression or anxiety. In other words, not all heavy or longtime drinkers will become depressed. However, if you are already experiencing depression, alcohol can trigger an exaggerated expression of associated symptoms.

Alcohol can also indirectly contribute to the development of a depressive mood. It does this in several ways. First, although alcohol depresses bodily functions, it often stimulates the expression of emotions. It inhibits function in the part of the brain that enables us to control our behavior, which releases us to express all manner of emotion——the good, the bad, and the ugly. Taking other drugs can increase the effect of both the alcohol and the other drug, especially if the other drug is also a central nervous system depressant, such as a tranquilizer or an antihistamine (allergy medication). Second, alcohol stresses blood sugar control and can cause episodes of hypoglycemia (low blood sugar), which in turn can lead to a depressed mood. Third, by disrupting sleep, alcohol makes it difficult for a person to get the restorative rest that one needs to function properly.

Cooling the Fire

In a return appointment, no sooner did Barbara settle in than she pointedly exclaimed, "I've thought about what you said. Maybe I am depressed. It doesn't matter what's wrong. I just want to fix it and get my edge back. Tell me what to do—I'll do it." The task at hand was to offer practical solutions to lessen the internal pressure that Barbara was experiencing. In terms of the metaphor of a pressure cooker, the first step was to open the release valve ever so slightly.

The main therapeutic task was to cool off Barbara's physiology. A reduction in Pitta dosha would dramatically relieve the physical, mental, and emotional pressure that she was experiencing. We therefore introduced herbs that infuse the body with calming, cooling energy. As her internal intensity lessened, it became easier for Barbara to make lifestyle changes. Not only did she reduce her intake of alcohol, she also began eating light and cooling foods that would reverse her imbalance (see chapter 14).

Being unable to maintain sleep was causing an additional imbalance for Barbara—a derangement in her Vata dosha, the controller of the nervous system. This derangement was having the effect of fanning the fire, making Pitta further out of balance. Our first recommendation was that she limit her intake of alcohol to two to three glasses of wine per week. Herbs were recommended to balance both Vata and Pitta doshas. Additionally, doing a self-massage with herbalized oils helped to cool the physiology and calm her nervous system.

We also recommended yoga postures and breathing exercises to help her release muscular tension (dissipate the "heat" in her muscles). Barbara explained that while she was doing the cooling breathing exercises, she felt as if she were releasing waves of heat through her nose.

Since we all tend to move in the direction of our imbalances, Barbara had been drawn to hot, spicy foods. An important Ayurvedic principle was introduced to her: like increases like, and opposites balance. Consequently, in order to reduce the heat in her physiology, she would profit from the ingestion of soothing, cooling energies. Through her mouth, she would benefit from foods that would not inflame her intestines. Through her senses, she would benefit from taking in the refreshing sights and sounds of nature. Logical and keenly astute, Barbara initially scoffed at this suggestion—it sounded, she said, "too New Age-y." Here was the opportunity to help her make a paradigm shift.

Groundbreaking scientific findings tell us that the essence of the physical, concrete, material world is energy. In essence, everything is a pattern of vibration in a sea of intelligence. The implication of this is powerful: our physiology is an extension of the natural world. Barbara understood that she was in constant interaction with the natural world and could use her participation in nature to heal.

A walk in the moonlight is one of the prescriptions for balancing Pitta. Whereas the sun has a heating effect, the moon offers the opposite: it soothes and cools. By walking in the moonlight, Barbara would infuse her physiology with a balancing vibration. In fact, this became a favorite activity and illustrated to Barbara another important Ayurvedic principle: the world is our pharmacy, and its healing effects are validated through personal experience.

We also recommended aromatherapy. The Vedic sages understood, and modern science confirms, that the nose is the gateway to the brain. Aromas effectively stimulate the olfactory nerve, thereby causing a release of neurochemicals in the brain. Each aroma carries a particular vibration, an energetic message to the physiology. For Barbara we recommended using rose essential oils. Roses carry the energy of compassion, allowing for acceptance of oneself and others. In Barbara's case, compassion served as an antidote for the desperate feeling of competitiveness that was fueling her drive and making her ragged.

Ultimately, it was through expanding her awareness that harmony and balance were sustained. Meditation offered a way to take the lid off the pressure cooker. As her awareness expanded, she was able to keep "the big picture" in mind and to remain focused without such a blinding intensity. Keenly brilliant and more energetic than ever, Barbara was astounded that she could experience calmness and a sharp edge at the same time. At work, success became the norm again—this time with less pushing and more joy. Laughter began to come easier to her, and so did exercising for pleasure rather than for competition.

Do You See Yourself in the Mirror?

1. To which aspects of Barbara's personal history or story do you relate?

2. Consider how Barbara responds to the situations in her life. How do her responses to her life situations resonate with your tendencies? What are the similarities and differences between you and Barbara in your responses to life stressors?

3. As a result of your unique tendencies, which aspects of your being are the most adversely impacted by depression (that is, your physical, mental, emotional, or spiritual self)?

4. When you are faced with adversity, which aspects of your being offer you strength?

5. How does an imbalance in Pitta dosha affect your physiology?

6. What lifestyle choices might be exacerbating a Pitta imbalance in your physiology?

7. What lifestyle choices might restore balance to your Pitta dosha?

8. Which Ayurvedic interventions described here do you find most interesting? Which interventions do you think could be helpful to you?

6

Earthy Depression

Life is movement. The more life there is,
the more flexibility there is, the more fluid
you are, the more you are alive.

—ARNAUD DESJARDINS

Earthy Depression is generally caused by an imbalance in Kapha dosha. In this archetype of depression, symbolically speaking, the characteristic solidity and stability of the earth element congeals, causing an individual to feel "stuck" at the physical, mental, and emotional level. The Kapha-imbalanced person often reports feeling weighed down by life and unable to move forward. Earthy Depression is characterized by physical and mental lethargy, dullness, and a lack of interest and motivation.

Deep sadness is often rooted in excessive sentimentality. The individual usually has a strong attachment for the way things were. The ability to metabolize past experiences is often diminished, so he or she carries around undigested remnants of the past. This condition can often keep a person from moving forward in life.

Faced with the option to fight, flee, or freeze, individuals with an Earthy Depression will freeze under stress. The stress of meeting deadlines causes them to procrastinate and creates obstacles to performance. Subsequently, they have difficulty completing projects.

This lack of progress and achievement further cements their feelings of sadness. They often have a diminished sense of self-esteem and an increased longing for the days when they felt better about themselves. Unfortunately, they feel paralyzed to make any changes toward a more positive state of being.

Physical manifestations of this archetype of depression include eating and sleeping in excess, which often leads to weight gain and increased lethargy. The main therapeutic goals are helping the individual to overcome inertia and addressing the heaviness experienced at every level in the mind-body. The therapeutic task is to ignite the digestive fire (*agni* in Sanskrit) in every aspect of their physiology: physical, mental, and emotional. Additionally, by undertaking the purification of the physiology, the individual begins to feel invigorated and uplifted. Earthy Depression is often experienced following a prolonged bout of either Airy Depression or Burning Depression.

Ed's Story: Needing to Liven Up

Ed walked into the office looking as if he were carrying the weight of the world on his shoulders. Apathetic, with eyes turned downward, he sank into a chair. Heavyset and sturdy, Ed brought to mind the picture of an immovable mountain. His voice sounded as heavy as molasses, and at times he struggled to piece sentences together. "The last time I felt this bad was about ten years ago," he said. "I didn't want to come here today, but my wife says that I've fallen in the muck again." Sounding defeated, he added: "She's probably right; she usually is."

Engaging Ed in conversation was like pulling teeth. Tediously, he described his first bout with depression. It occurred when he was twenty-three years old, after his fiancée called off their wedding. The second episode happened shortly after his youngest daughter left home for college. Now, at age fifty-eight, Ed said that the heaviness struck shortly after he retired from a job he had had since he was thirty years old.

Hopelessness about the future seemed to be the main theme in Ed's description. He denied having suicidal thoughts but hesitantly acknowledged, "I often wonder, what's the use?" He had fallen into an unhealthy rut. His days had turned into nights, and his nights into days. Frequently, he would go to bed at four or five in the morning and sleep until one or two in the afternoon. Ed's primary diversion was watching TV. He did chuckle ever so slightly when he guiltily confessed, "I can watch infomercials for hours." He admitted that he snacked all the time, especially during the night. He had gained fifty pounds in the past year—"mostly from pastries and milk shakes," he explained.

Ed was amazed that he could feel exhausted after ten hours of sleep. He was not deriving energy from sleep, nor was he getting energy from food. He described getting a quick pick-me-up from his high-fat, high-sugar snacks but then falling into a deep mental stupor for hours afterward. "My wife worries, and I feel bad about that," he concluded.

It was obvious that Ed's wife, Janice, was worried about her husband. She explained, "I've been down this road before. This time, I am really scared that I am going to spend the rest of my life with a couch potato." According to Janice, Ed's current bout of depression was more severe than the previous bouts. "During the last episode, Ed was working. Now he has nothing to force him to get up and get going. Now he seems lost—to himself and to me. He forgets things—he can't seem to carry a thought from one day to the next. If I get frustrated and remind him of a chore or a responsibility, he sinks his feet into the ground like a stubborn child." With a quivering voice, Janice said, "I don't think he wants to help me at all. What's more, I don't think he loves me anymore. I miss our physical life together." Shyly she added, "Nothing interests him, not even sex."

Ayurvedic Diagnosis

Ed's wife is correct to be concerned about him. The statistics on the recurrence of depression are staggering. The number of prior episodes predicts the likelihood of developing a subsequent episode. Approximately 50 to 60 percent of individuals who have had one episode will have a second. Individuals who have had two episodes have a 70 percent chance of having a third; and individuals who have had three episodes have a 90 percent chance of having a fourth.

Ed's what's-the-use attitude is understandable. For years, he took antidepressant medications and went to psychotherapy. Fifteen years ago he was hospitalized and received electroshock treatments. None of these interventions was successful in the long run. All of them failed to reach the root of the problem. According to Ayurveda, in order to eradicate his depression, Ed needs to understand that his lifestyle triggers his physiological vulnerabilities. Having this knowledge will open the door to a plethora of practical techniques to help him achieve balance and prevent relapses.

Ed has a tendency to develop an Earthy Depression. Deep sadness, lack of interest, and a sense of being stuck are the primary manifestations of this type of depression. Ed's what's-the-use attitude indicates his internal perception: a lack of motivation leading to hopelessness. Excessive sleeping (hypersomnalence) and eating are often used as comfort techniques. Mentally and emotionally, excessive sentimentality and attachment to the past are at the root of his problem.

Kapha dosha governs the structure and cohesion of the overall physiology. It is associated with strength, stability, and structure. A preponderance of this dosha in a person brings to mind the image of a mountain. As if emerging from the earth, Ed has a solid physical structure and a stable presence. When he is in balance, a sense of contentment and dignity accompany his every act.

At the physical level, this dosha regulates biological strength, natural resistance (immunity), and proper body structure. At the psychological level, it affords stability of mind, emotional endurance, and mental stamina. However, when this dosha of benevolence goes out of balance, strength turns into rigidity and stability turns into inflexibility. Individuals with a Kapha imbalance can become immobilized, as if locked within their own structure, be it physical, emotional, or mental.

Worse yet, an imbalance in Kapha dosha triggers a toxic accumulation in the physiology. This gunk, known as *ama* (Sanskrit for "undigested"), then clogs the flow of energy throughout body, mind, and spirit. We all digest food and experiences differently. When there is a Kapha imbalance, digestion slows down and *ama* begins to accumulate. This is what has happened to Ed. The source of his sadness is depressing gunk.

Ed's toxic accumulation of depressing gunk is a result of the fact that his metabolic furnace has shut down—physically in his belly and metaphorically in his mind. His ability to digest experience has been compromised. Digestion and assimilation—two of the four components of metabolism (see chapter 5)—are not working in his favor. What he ingests through his mouth or his senses is not being broken down, nor is it being assimilated. Consequently, he is not receiving nourishment at any level. The reason for this breakdown is that the "digestive fire" (*agni*) in the essence of his being—that which transforms one thing into another—has been snuffed out. Without this fire, Ed has no spark for life.

Ed has had three episodes of depression. Each episode has been associated with a major life change: his fiancée breaking up with him, his daughter leaving home, and retirement. The emotions triggered by these events were difficult for Ed to metabolize, to integrate. In a manner of speaking, Ed's pain comes from emotional indigestion.

The flip side of our greatest strength is our greatest weakness. What attracted Janice to Ed was his stability, dependability, and reliability. Because he is out of balance, however, his emotional stability has turned into rigidity. Faced with retirement, he feels hopeless, unable to imagine creating a new way of living. He is stuck in the past. His mental and emotional structure has become solidified, not unlike earth that has gone through a drought. Reliability has become a compulsive tendency to stick to routine. As his wife explains, dependable Ed has become emotionally clingy. Janice feels suffocated by his frequent whiny phone calls to her at work asking when she is coming home.

Ed has sunk into a lifestyle that enhances the heaviness he feels in his heart. He is weighed down with extra flesh. He eats to comfort himself. Rather than providing him with nourishment, the food is blocking the flow of energy in his body and mind. It is not being digested properly, therefore it is creating a toxic accumulation. The results of this "indigestion" are cloudy thinking, an overwhelming sense of being stuck in his body, and an inability to lift his spirit.

Changes to the structure of Ed's life, such as retirement, brought about a jolt to his Vata dosha, which governs his nervous system. Change is hard for everyone, but this is especially true for those who are already experiencing a Kapha imbalance. When his nervous system receives a jolt, Ed feels different from usual. Almost by reflex, he attempts to settle his physiology in order to maintain his usual way of experiencing himself. To balance the unsettled, ungrounded feeling that the change has triggered, he reaches for that which is grounding: a stable routine, extra rest and sleep, and the comfort of sweet, heavy, and oily foods. Basically, he leans in the direction of his imbalance. In the short run, extra rest, excess sleep, and heavy foods do pacify Ed, but in the long run, they further imbalance his Kapha dosha.

Telling Ed to liven up and let go of his emotional baggage would be futile. He physically cannot do this until the digestive fire of his mind-body is ignited. His physiology needs to be brought back into balance. Once it is in balance, Ed will more readily be able to leave the past and move into the future. He will be helped psychologically and spiritually through physical interventions. In order to enliven his spirit, we first have to lighten his physical load.

Igniting the Fire

We want to ignite Ed's *agni*, his power of digestion at the physical, mental, and emotional level. Physically, we want to break down the existing *ama* and promote its elimination. To this end, Ayurvedic purification techniques are a must. Think of it this way: in order to function properly, we are not unlike our cars; we need to clean out the dirt and grime in our systems. When impurities and toxins accumulate at the cellular level, they impede the flow of natural intelligence throughout. The cells then lose their access to this intelligence. They forget how to function. Removing *ama* from Ed's physiology is therefore the first step in his recovery from depression.

We recommended that Ed undergo Ayurvedic purification techniques, known as *panchakarma*. Panchakarma is an extensive process geared to purify the body of toxins and undigested matter that results from an improper diet and lifestyle. Full-scale panchakarma is a specialized treatment requiring expert supervision as well as labor-intensive methods administered by Ayurvedic technicians. However, some purifying measures can be done at home.

Ed initiated an at-home panchakarma purification process. His diet consisted of light and warm foods that are easy to digest and that infused warmth and liveliness into his physiology (see chapter 14). Soon after changing his diet, he reported feeling lighter physically as well as emotionally. Now he could begin to entertain the idea of moving his body, of taking a walk instead of sleeping when he felt an attack of lethargy midmorning. This was the first step in reigniting his digestive fire. The second was to enlist the power of herbs for additional purification. The purpose of the herbs was to encourage proper elimination and to prevent the future buildup of *ama*.

Gradually, Ed's internal biorhythms once again began to mirror the cycles in nature. This was an important step in his recovery from depression. When we disrupt our internal biorhythms, be it through insufficient or excessive sleep or by sleeping during the day and staying up at night, we lose nature's support for a well-functioning metabolism. Nighttime is when the "garbage crews" come out and clean up the physiology. If we are awake, these midnight riders (immune cells) cannot do their job, and we become clogged with garbage (toxins, or *ama*). There is a time and a place for everything, and excess sleep, especially during the day, is a thief of energy. It further sets our physiology out of balance.

To light a fire, a little bit of oxygen is always necessary. We prescribed Ayurvedic breathing exercises to fuel Ed's body with oxygen—or, in Ayurvedic terms, to ignite his metabolic fire. As he began to practice these exercises regularly, he noted that it was as though a light had turned on in his brain.

In addition, we suggested that Ed learn to meditate. The regular practice of meditation helped Ed to purify the more subtle aspects of his being, the mind and the emotions. Making a connection to the spiritual aspects of life also helped him to see change as a necessary part of the evolutionary process.

Do You See Yourself in the Mirror?

1. To which aspects of Ed's personal history or story do you relate?
2. Consider how Ed responds to the situations in his life. How do his responses resonate with your tendencies? What are the

similarities and differences between you and Ed in your responses to life stressors?

3. As a result of your unique tendencies, which aspects of your being are the most adversely impacted by depression (that is, your physical, mental, emotional, or spiritual self)?

4. When you are faced with adversity, which aspects of your being offer you strength?

5. How does an imbalance in Kapha dosha affect your physiology?

6. What lifestyle choices might be exacerbating a Kapha imbalance in your physiology?

7. What lifestyle choices might restore balance to your Kapha dosha?

8. Which Ayurvedic interventions described here did you find most interesting? Which interventions do you think could be helpful to you?

7

Metabolizing Life

When you are a master of your body, word and
mind, you shall rejoice in perfect serenity.

—SHABKAI

There's nothing wrong with feeling sad. A feeling of sadness can actually be a helpful signpost, telling us that something in our life is wrong and requires attention, or it can be a natural response to painful circumstances (such as death or divorce). If we listen, our emotions serve as guides. They can give direction and inform us about our state of being. Our emotions let us know if we are on the right track in myriad ways: nutritional, relational, physical, spiritual, and occupational. Sad feelings can be a valuable sign that it is time to make lifestyle changes. For instance, it can be your body's way of letting you know that it is time to slow down and get more rest. The blues might be asking you to pay increased attention to your behavior. They can serve as a warning—like a fever at the onset of a cold—that your body is struggling with a disease process. Sadness might be a cry from the spirit telling you that a significant relationship is changing and requires attention.

Emotions are an aspect of our whole being. We can't just isolate one because we don't like it and chop it off. Emotions serve a purpose.

70

They provide depth and breadth to our lives. They assist us in growth if we learn to become aware of the messages they send. A person who is in good emotional health recognizes feelings, calls them by their names, and uses them as guideposts.

Depression often gets a foothold in our psyche when we ignore our inner feelings of sadness. Unattended to, sadness can ultimately cause blockages in the mind, the body, or the spirit. In this way, feelings of sadness can morph from being helpful guides to being menacing jailers, threatening to take away our birthright of happiness and vitality. Depression can incarcerate us in a state of oppression when it takes hold of our physiology. However, where attention goes, energy flows; when we place our attention on our sad feelings, when we use them as guideposts, the blockages clear, freeing us to move on to other experiences. This is what metabolizing life effectively is all about.

Processing Matter, Digesting Life

According to the Vedic sages, one of the main causes of all mental and emotional disease is the inability to process the emotions that are generated by life experiences. Processing an experience is analogous to digesting and metabolizing food. In fact, this is an accurate statement in terms of $E = mc^2$: all matter is energy, and all energy is matter. If an experience were a piece of bread, this would mean taking it into your system, breaking it down, incorporating useful parts into your body, and sending the rest down the digestive chute to be eliminated.

People who live in a state of balance and enjoy health and wholeness can do this. They are able to fully process negative experiences and difficult emotions in a reasonable amount of time. They are able to let go of negativity and move on with their lives. For others, processing takes more time.

Some people are not able to digest experiences very quickly. Their power of transformation is not optimal. Excessively slow mental or emotional digestion causes negative impressions to stick around for a long time. These negative impressions, in turn, affect current thoughts and feelings, which results in emotional imbalances. In other words, even though we may not be having problems in the present, we can be continuously traumatized by past experiences.

Letting Go of Old Baggage

Our physiology can become exhausted from carrying around emotional baggage. Past problems can cause emotional problems in the present. For instance, we may remember a negative situation that happened ten years ago and think, "Why did that happen to me?"

Our mind may become attached to finding an answer. When the stress is still lodged in our mind, the brain will re-create the experience based on its memory of it. The body will reexperience the trauma and lodge the memory even deeper in its tissues. The mind-body will feel the experience as intensely as it did when the injurious event actually happened. Our *perception* of life events affects us even more than the events themselves.

A person with an excellent emotional metabolism can be resilient in the face of normal life stressors. This person springs back and moves on. If our emotional metabolism is weak, we hang on to stress. This sets into motion a process that can create depression. Rerunning old movies in our mind affects our body at the cellular level. We literally become stuck in a rut, because we become accustomed to the release of the brain chemicals that are associated with our habitual neuronal pathways. We tend to return to the same ways of thinking, feeling, and behaving. Nevertheless, changing our way of being and our worldview is not as easy as simply snapping our fingers. Altering how we process experiences requires a psychophysiological shift. How do we accomplish this?

Although we have warned you about the dangers of carrying emotional baggage, we are not simply saying to you, "Just let go of it!" (The infamous *it* refers to whatever is causing you distress: your beliefs, your ideas, past crises, present dilemmas, your spouse, your boss.) In order to get rid of depression, we must certainly let go of depressing stress in our system. It is absolutely necessary to let go of all manner of negativity and stress in order to be healthy, yet we acknowledge how difficult it is to do so. You cannot simply will your brain to do it. This only causes more stress in the system and is counterproductive. If personal will were enough, the likelihood is that we would all use it; after all, misery hurts.

Therefore, telling you to just let go would not recognize the intense fatigue that your physiology has acquired from replaying the old movies of your life. Nor does it take into consideration the energy that is necessary to lessen the accumulated mental and emotional gunk that is weighing you down. Destressing and degunking require energy and internal strength. Unfortunately, when we are depressed, we do not have the internal strength to simply shake off whatever is oppressing us.

In order to begin anew, we need to ignite the digestive fire in our being. Once we do this, we will begin to digest our life experiences efficiently, so that they don't stick around and weigh us down. According to Ayurveda, we do this by expanding our awareness. Awareness serves as a fuel that lights our inner fire, improving our capacity to transform our mind. If awareness becomes one-sided, depression may soon ensue. An expanded awareness relieves stress by helping us to see the big picture. Events and circumstances that formerly caused us to feel bad can be viewed from a different perspective. Yet awareness goes beyond mental processing or our level of intelligence.

The Danger of Object-Referral

To the Vedic sages, the intellect is not something we measure with an IQ test or judge by an individual's academic performance. Rather, it is the mental faculty in charge of discriminating between ourselves and everything else. It is also the aspect of us that mediates between what we see (the material world, the world of the senses) and what is unseen (the energy world, the world of the spirit).

Object-referral occurs when the intellect is exclusively directed outward, toward the objects of experience. In this state of mind, we focus our awareness only on what can be seen, heard, touched, tasted, and smelled. In effect, the intellect deals only with what it absorbs through the five senses, ceasing to believe that anything exists beyond what it perceives. The material world becomes its only reality; the spiritual world is ignored. (By *spiritual* we mean the abstract or nonmaterial aspects of life.)

In a state of extreme object-referral, our intellect is lost to an external world of constant distraction. Disregarding the inner life of the self, we focus only on objects outside ourselves. Moving the mind from one external focus to another eventually brings about fatigue, stress, and anxiety. For example, looking for happiness in adventures not yet experienced or in a newer and better pleasure is bound to create stress. Eventually, mental clutter and emotional fatigue soil the mind and make it fertile ground for depression.

Object-referral means that the reference point of our existence is the ego, our social self. In a state of extreme object-referral, we relate only to what is external to us. Consequently, the ever-changing circumstances, events, people, and things that are inherent to the outside world exert too powerful an influence over us. For example, we may value ourselves only for what we possess, how we look, and what we accomplish. Singularly seeking fulfillment and personal power in objects of experience makes us feel fragile. We forget that we are more than meets the eye.

Fear and vulnerability accompany a state of extreme object-referral because everything that gives our life meaning is changing and impermanent. If our intellect focuses on the external world to an extreme, we lose a true sense of our own worthiness. This leaves us with no idea of the extent of our personal power. We lose touch with the underlying reality of life and living.

Self-Referral: Freedom from Tyranny

If the outward turning of our awareness is object-referral, its polar opposite is self-referral. Self-referral is the turning inward of one's awareness to gain the experience of the unchanging inner world, the unseen world, the world of one's spirit.

When we are in a state of self-referral, our attention turns to deeper levels of the mind. In a subtle but profound way, we experience the unified nature of life. This increases our awareness because it infuses natural intelligence—the intelligence that underlies and governs the universe. Self-referral anchors us to a deeper sense of the self. Inevitably, fear and vulnerability dissolve. When one has the ability to experience self-referral as well as object-referral, there is a deeper enjoyment of all aspects of life—the internal and the external.

Imagine living life with an internal sense of "I am greater than these circumstances." This is the feeling that is evoked by experiencing self-referral. It is a feeling of freedom and expansion that offers relief and renewed hope. As such, experiencing self-referral serves as an anti-depressant, one that doesn't come in a pill. Not only does it give you a sense of perspective, it also empowers you. It might not be possible to change events and others around you, but by changing your inner physiology and psychology, you can change your perceptions and gain a new perspective and deeper insight. Old circumstances can look completely different. This is what happens when we expand our awareness.

Self-referral is not a completely foreign concept. We all have experienced a state of self-referral at some point or another, and many people know how to access it. It usually comes in the form of a spontaneous intuitive experience, but we can also engage in a state of self-referral in a systematic and regular way. Engaging in self-referral is not a purely mental exercise, nor is it a reflective type of introspection. It is a direct inner perception of the consciousness that underlies all thoughts and emotions. This state of awareness can be attained in many ways, but meditation is the path we recommend. Through the proper practice of meditation, one can ensure a systematic attainment of the state of self-referral. Eventually your practice will become an integral aspect of your life; in turn, this will be reflected in your way of being.

Finding Balance, Expanding Awareness

Focusing on the external aspects of life is a good and necessary process. Nevertheless, in today's achievement-oriented world, most of us unfortunately spend all of our waking time engaged in object-referral. The process of self-referral is often neglected. The great irony is that when we live life in this way, we are cheating ourselves from having the balance we need for maximum success in our activities. This is because we are putting blinders on our awareness.

If all we experience is object-referral, we limit our connection with our internal fountain of energy. At the mental level, we lose perspective and clarity of thought. Mental fatigue overwhelms us, inhibiting our ability to glide through the transitions that life imposes. At the emotional level, we run the risk of becoming handicapped, unable to experience a full range of emotions.

Neglecting self-referral can be an invitation for problems; depression is one of them. If we turn our ear to the words of the Vedic sages, it becomes easy to understand why depression has become an epidemic of modern living: entire societies are addicted to external pleasures in an effort to find internal fulfillment.

In order to find true and enduring fulfillment, make engaging in self-referral a regular practice. This is not unlike brushing your teeth in the morning. You wouldn't think of going a day without finding time to clean your physical self. Why, then, would you consider getting on with your day without purifying your awareness?

Through the systematic process of self-referral, we expand our awareness. When we have a panoramic view of our life, past and present problems take on a different proportion. Our mind is able to grasp more layers of reality and thus perceive life with more depth. A fuller vision of life appears in front of our mind's eye when we practice self-referral as well as object-referral.

Along these lines, depression can be thought of as a symptom of one-sided awareness. It frequently occurs when the mind becomes exhausted because it is in a state of extreme object-referral. The extent of object-referral often determines the depth of depression. In a state of extreme object-referral, we fail to grasp that fulfillment comes from an inner bank of vitality, strength, and joy; it comes from a deep energy source, the intelligence that underlies the physical world. A state of extreme object-referral locks the doors to this bank and dooms the person to eternal poverty—that is, if you consider vitality and its by-product, happiness, to be among the riches of life.

It is with expanded awareness that we sense the effect of our lifestyle on our physiology. Awareness functions like a sensor, helping us to tune into our internal and external environments. It is the faculty that allows us to process and respond to information appropriately. In the hurly-burly of life, we forget that we are whole beings. We neglect to take into account the totality of our being when we are deciding on a course of action. We forget that our life force must operate holistically, for the benefit of all facets of our being. We allow our surface desires to dictate our choices, and in doing so we make mistakes. These errors in choices put our system even further out of balance. Like a leaning tower under the force of gravity, we are pulled in the direction of our imbalances by momentum.

Constricted awareness depresses the body. At the physical level, it indirectly disrupts the free flow of our life force. When we can't intuit what our physiology needs or how our lifestyle affects us, we run the risk of getting caught in a cyclone of destruction that leads to many ills, only one of which is depression.

Unfortunately, once depression takes hold in the physiology, it further constricts awareness. In an effort to escape our depression, it is common for us to become unaware of what is in our best interest. We make poor choices; we go on gunk-collecting sprees and dump dead-and-dumb food into our system. We bombard our awareness with mind-dulling entertainment. Neglecting to be kind to ourselves, we push ourselves beyond our limits and then fuel our body with caffeine, nicotine, and other stimulants. When our physiology shouts for help, we refuse to hear. Inevitably, our metabolism comes crashing down, dragging our vitality (and happiness!) with it. The gunk that weighs us down snuffs out the metabolic fire of our being.

Ama: The Gunk of Depression

When our vitality is weak and our metabolic fire is burning low, it is easy to accumulate gunk in our mind-body. According to Ayurveda, gunk is the thing that disease is made of because it blocks the free flow of our innate intelligence at different levels of our being. This gunk, or *ama*, is a product of inefficient metabolism. There are three types of *ama*: physical, mental, and emotional. Physical *ama* obstructs our biological processes and is formed when the food we eat is not digested properly. Emotional *ama* is a residue carried from one experience to another, obstructing the full enjoyment of the here and now. Mental *ama* blocks access to our inner knowledge, our intuition.

Ama cements depression, causing some of its main symptoms: low energy and fatigue, cloudy or slowed thinking, poor memory, appetite disturbances, increased sensitivity to pain, headaches, backaches, sore muscles, constipation, and low immunity to disease. The first thing that people feel when they begin to succumb to depression is often a sense of malaise. It is not uncommon to hear people say, "I just don't feel

Ama . . . in Other Words

Modern medicine recognizes *ama* and the dangers it poses. Physicians speak of excess cholesterol, free radicals, trans-fatty acids, and uric acid as causes of disease. These are all examples of *ama*. When someone has coronary bypass surgery, inflamed plaque (a modern English word for *ama*) is removed from the arteries to prevent heart problems. We are advised to go to the dentist regularly to have our teeth cleaned. What is the dentist removing? *Ama*!

As the eyes are the windows of the soul, the tongue is the window of the digestive system. In fact, it is the only part of the digestive tract that is visible to us. Sometimes you can see *ama* on your tongue.

If you'd like to see some *ama*, eat a big dish of ice cream shortly before you go to bed, then in the morning look at your tongue in the bathroom mirror. You may see a white furry coating on it. This is an example of one type of *ama* staring back at you.

quite right." We can understand this in terms of what an accumulation of *ama* is doing to the physiology. Perhaps this is why the appearance of a seemingly unexplainable illness is often the harbinger of depression.

All machines build up residue, and if they are not cleaned they will not work properly or they will completely break down. In this respect, our physiology is no different. The regular use of Ayurvedic purification techniques to clean the physiology of *ama* is therefore part of the regimen for vital living.

Ama relates to the three archetypes of depression in different ways.

Airy Depression is distinguished by high anxiety. Mental and emotional *ama* are the culprits, underlying physiological imbalances that are manifested as worrying, racing thoughts, and continually creating fear-based scenarios in the mind. An imbalance in Vata dosha predisposes a person to sleep disturbances, which in turn impede proper functioning of the physiology. We need sleep to purify our physiology. Without it, physical, mental, and emotional *ama* builds up. People with a Vata

Depressing Gunk Dampens Happiness

Please answer the following questions:

* How's your appetite: keen or dull?
* Are your waste products (urine, feces, sweat) normal, regular, freely flowing, and without strong odor?
* Do you feel bloated?
* Is your skin lustrous and supple?
* Is your breath fresh?
* Are your teeth strong?
* Are your joints popping and cracking?
* Do your muscles become sore and achy for unknown reasons?
* Do you have visual fatigue?
* How's your sense of taste and smell?
* Is your vision and hearing as keen as it used to be?
* Do you frequently feel cold and clammy or hot and uncomfortable?
* Are you sleeping well?
* Do you feel refreshed when you wake up in the morning?
* Do you feel active and energetic?
* Does your brain feel foggy?
* Do you feel emotionally frazzled and fatigued?
* Do your relationships feel meaningful?
* Is your day's work fulfilling?
* Do you feel stuck in life?
* Have you been feeling depressed lately?

The common thread that runs through these questions is *blockage*. In all areas of your being—from sight and sound to energy and elimination—obstructions may exist. Your answers to these questions can give you a good estimate of the level of toxic accumulation in your system. These by-products impede the free flow of life force, or vital energy, and are a major cause of depression.

imbalance tend to always be on the move, even if this means spinning their wheels in place. Without the deep rest that sleep offers, their unfocused activity depletes their energy reserves. Consequently, fatigue often snuffs out their digestive fire, making their digestive capacity highly irregular and inefficient. Fatigue is a great generator of all types of *ama*.

Burning Depression is the archetype of depression least likely to be caused by *ama*. A distinguishing characteristic of high Pitta dosha is a high digestive capacity: the ability to burn through things, including *ama*. However, overdoing and excess emotional volatility are characteristics of people with a Pitta imbalance. Once depression gets a foothold in their physiology, they run the risk of accumulating physical, mental, and emotional *ama*.

Earthy Depression is the most concrete example of how *ama* triggers as well as perpetuates depression. Physical lethargy and emotional stagnation are characteristics of this archetype of depression. Earthy Depression is generally caused by *ama* at all levels of the physiology, created through a vicious cycle. For example, excessive eating or poor digestion causes a buildup of *ama* in the physiology. This *ama* then triggers a sense of heaviness at the physical and mental levels. The individual's response to this is to increasingly feel a need to slow down and to sleep, but this is actually the last thing the mind-body needs. In time, the physical lethargy leads to emotional withdrawal and social isolation. Feelings of loneliness and perceptions of rejection begin to overwhelm the mind, creating emotional and mental *ama*. This in turn causes even more imbalances in the physiology. The imbalanced individual may seek nurturance and comfort in overeating and excessive sleep. Oversentimentality and deep attachment, which also plague this archetype of depression, further feed into the cycle of physiological toxicity in the mind-body.

Transforming Life Experiences into Vital Energy

Consider the following questions to help you explore four major concepts.

1. **Emotions are guideposts**
   * Are your emotions trying to clue you in about some aspect of your being that requires attention?

- Are they telling you something about the way you are living your life?
- What happens when you listen to the messages they send?
- Do you make changes in your life accordingly?
- Do you feel better as a result?
- Would a systematic practice of self-referral help you to pick up the clues more astutely?

2. **Where attention goes, energy flows**

- Where are you placing your attention?
- What is draining your vital energy?
- Do you understand that a singular focus on object-referral contributes to the generation of physical, mental, and emotional *ama*?
- Do you engage in the process of self-referral?

3. **Problems can't be solved with the same mind-set that created them**

- Are you tired of carrying emotional baggage around, yet do you feel frustrated in your attempts to just let go of it?
- Would you consider that you might begin to change your mind-set by addressing the intense emotional fatigue you have accumulated from the replaying of old movies of your life?
- Are you willing to invest yourself in yourself by destressing and degunking your body so you can generate the energy and internal strength to create happiness?
- Which type of *ama* (physical, mental, emotional, or spiritual) is cementing your state of depression?

4. **Awareness heals**

- In what way has reading this book so far helped you to expand your awareness about depression and the restoration of wholeness?

8

Consciousness Becomes Us

> The real voyage of discovery lies not in seeking new
> landscapes but in having new eyes.
>
> —MARCEL PROUST

To untangle the roots of depression, we must dive into consciousness. Ayurveda is, after all, a consciousness-based system of health; it informs us that we are creatures of consciousness. At our most basic level, we are an expression of the universal intelligence that underlies everything in nature. In other words, consciousness is the essence of the mind-body. A basic tenet of Ayurveda is that interruptions in the flow of this underlying universal intelligence (consciousness) are at the root of all disease.

Our physiology, our mind-body, emerges from consciousness. Understanding this principle allows us to use the universe as a pharmacy. Through an understanding of consciousness, we come to appreciate the power that is generated by Ayurvedic interventions. Without this knowledge, the "muscle" behind the more subtle recommendations may be missed. For example, an understanding of consciousness helps us to realize that aromatherapy is about more than nice smells. Eating is more than consuming calories, and exercising is more than getting rid of them. Sleeping doesn't just put the body down for the count. Doing yoga poses accomplishes more than improving our flexibility. Finally, the impact of breathing techniques goes beyond the inhalation of oxygen and the exhalation of carbon dioxide. All of these interventions, in a subtle but potent way, manage the flow of consciousness into and through our physiology. However, the cornerstone of Ayurveda is meditation, because it directly connects us to consciousness.

Consciousness-based Ayurvedic interventions are full of the life force that revitalizes us. They rectify imbalances at the most essential and elementary level. The universal intelligence that they transport to the mind-body teaches it how to function in an optimal manner. Ayurvedic interventions connect our physiology to the ultimate natural source of vitality: universal intelligence. Practical interventions will be discussed in subsequent chapters. For now, however, let us examine the underpinning of it all: consciousness.

Consciousness and the Unified Field

What exactly is consciousness? This is a notoriously difficult question to answer. Generally the purview of philosophers and theologians, it has now also become a topic of discussion among neuroscientists and theoretical physicists.

For our purpose, a basic answer to this profound question is the following: Consciousness is awareness. It is the essential subjectivity of the mind. It is what lies beneath thought and feeling and is most intimate to our experience. It can also be defined as an energy field of potentiality and thus the underlying stratum of the natural world. Much like everything we see in the natural world, our physiology is a manifestation of this energy field of potentiality.

The Vedic sages referred to consciousness as *Veda*, a Sanskrit word meaning "all knowledge." According to them, pure consciousness underlies everything. To explain this point further, they frequently used the analogy of an iceberg. The entirety of the human being is represented by an iceberg: the body is symbolized by the tip; the mind is the slightly submerged portion; and consciousness is the expansive base underlying it all.

Like Albert Einstein, the Vedic sages cognized their theories in the depths of their minds. Consciousness, they realized, was not only a field of energy, it was the fountainhead of all energy fields. Modern scientific research has led physicists to agree with the Vedic sages. *Veda*, the ancient sages' term, is what modern scientists call the *unified field*.

Presently, demonstrating how the unified field functions—scientifically and mathematically—has become the holy grail of physicists who study string theory. It is considered extremely significant because it could potentially describe the laws of nature within a single, all-encompassing, coherent framework. Some scientists have even turned to the knowledge of the ancients for inspiration. Others have been struck by the parallels between their modern data and the cognitions of the sages. In fact, sage and scientist use almost identical words in describing the essence of the natural world. Quantum physicists and Vedic sages concur: Every "thing" is energy. The Vedic sages, however, described not only what the unified field is but also how it works.

The concept of the unified field is easy to understand if you think of plugging in your toaster, for instance. Every time you use an electric appliance you are availing yourself of energy that emanates from the electromagnetic field. Scientists have been able to access and harness the energy coming from this field, and you benefit from this knowledge daily. Imagine, however, that a field of energy thousands of times more powerful than the electromagnetic field exists. This is what is called the unified field.

The unified field holds the potential for all of the diversity we see in the natural world. The impulses that are generated from this fountainhead of energy bring about a sequential unfolding of the many layers of nature. In other words, the solid material objects that we observe around us are actually the result of fluctuations, or waves, that emanate from this underlying nonmaterial field of energy. Therefore, everything that our five senses perceive, including our physiology, is a manifestation of the vibrations from the unified field.

Our mind-body can best be described as consciousness in motion. Our physiology is constantly in a process of re-creating itself. It is in an ongoing energetic exchange with its immediate environment as well as the universe at large. This knowledge was a gift from the Vedic sages.

Now, in this century, physics is rediscovering what was once familiar to the ancients.

The understanding that consciousness is at the basis of everything in the natural world has the potential to revolutionize medicine. This is similar to the revolution in science that was brought about by advancements in molecular biology. Molecular science taught us to look beyond the cellular level, to infer how cells function by examining how molecules work. For example, a major advance in medicine came from molecular biology's understanding of the role of free radicals in disease causation. Likewise, advances in theoretical physics are helping us to look beyond the material to the nonmaterial—to consciousness.

Albeit with different language, today's physicists are describing ancient Vedic concepts. For instance, scientists point to the fact that molecules can be thought of as standing waves. Molecules appear solid and unchanging; in fact, at the subatomic level, they are simply fluctuations of the underlying quantum field. The conclusion of many physicists, chemists, mathematicians, and molecular biologists is that the body is not, as previously thought, a hunk of material. It is a pattern of vibrations that emanate from an underlying field of energy (the *Veda*, or unified field). Its atoms and particles are constantly in flux. All that remains constant is the underlying pattern.

In terms of treatment for depression, Ayurveda provides a way to address the quantum mechanical imbalances that precede and cause all disease. The sages understood how to utilize the vibrations that emanate from the unified field to promote wellness and to maintain physiological balance. They perceived the rhythms of nature in our body, and they developed the knowledge of how the human physiology is affected by energetic exchanges. These exchanges can be used to bring about health and well-being; this is the essence of consciousness-based interventions.

Consciousness: The Power Behind the Interventions

The manifest world is a creation of the unified field. As beings of consciousness, we extend our mind-body into the universe through our five senses, which have a direct link to the brain through the nervous system. Our brain in turn is the portal to the mind.

Ayurvedic interventions offer a practical means for directing this energetic exchange. By bringing awareness to what we ingest through our senses and how we metabolize what we ingest, these interventions are medicinal. Being consciousness-based, they not only affect the body (the tip of the iceberg) but also function as scaffolding to uphold the mind and fortify the spirit.

The basic modes of Ayurvedic interventions are described briefly below. They will be explored further in part II.

Aromatherapy

The nose is the gateway to the brain. The olfactory cells are connected to the hypothalamus, the master control center of the brain that oversees hormonal responses. Particular aromas carry subtle messages to the limbic area of the brain, which surrounds the hypothalamus. Since the hypothalamus is involved in the processing of emotions, aromas therefore influence our emotional brain.

Moreover, aromas can potentially trigger vivid memories because they also affect the hippocampus, one of the main areas of the brain where we maintain our memories; think of the hippocampus as a sort of photo album.

Aromas are a consciousness-based therapy because they carry medicinal vibrations from the natural world into our brain. Used therapeutically, aromas can help us to maintain or reestablish our vibratory balance.

Nutrition

Eating does more than fuel the body by supplying enough calories to keep it moving. Likewise, herbs and spices are not merely culinary garnishes; they do more than entice our taste buds. These gifts from Mother Earth are packets of universal intelligence. The energetic qualities in food, herbs, and spices serve as conduits of knowledge to our cells. Nature is orderly, and its products are designed to impart coherence into our physiology. What we consume should nurture us at the macromolecular level and, more important, at the energetic level.

Exercise

You won't find the Vedic sages huffing and puffing at the gym. Recreation is the name of their game. Overexercising induces an inflammatory state in the physiology. It also adds stress and strain, thereby exhausting the mind-body. Chronic exhaustion inevitably leads to disease.

Exercise should be a form of recreation that simultaneously re-creates our physiology. It removes blockages (*ama*) at the physical, mental, and emotional level and restores the flow of energy, which allows for cellular regeneration to occur.

Cardiovascular exercise is certainly good; however, according to Ayurveda, exercise should have a deeper purpose than simply building muscular strength. Restoring balance to the mind-body is a by-product of a good exercise regimen.

Yoga

Yoga poses promote neuromuscular integration. Through this highly refined type of movement, we affect the state of our nervous system, and this in turn affects us at the level of the mind. Yoga integrates the mind and the body. While strengthening our physical core, yoga poses invigorate us from the inside out. They improve the flexibility of both the body and the mind. Other exercise techniques may come and go, but yoga postures have withstood the test of time.

Breathing Techniques

How we breathe is a metaphor for how we live. With every breath we take, we are informing our brain about the state of our being. This is why breathing is considered a practice in neurorespiratory integration. Whereas it is difficult to break life patterns through personal will alone, these techniques are a practical means of reeducating our physiology on how to function more healthily.

Breathing exercises put us in the director's chair, so to speak, helping us to be in charge of the way we live. Simultaneously, by improving our awareness of how we breathe, we can gauge how we are feeling. More than the mere exchange of oxygen and carbon dioxide, breathing involves an energetic communication with our physical environment. It regulates the flow of energy through our seamless energetic system.

Sleep

Sleep might be even more important than nutrition. The Vedic sages considered it the nurse of all creatures, and modern science agrees. Rest is the foundation for liveliness; fatigue creates a pathway for depression. Deep physiological purification occurs at the cellular level while we sleep. More and more, scientific research is uncovering the inherent value of sleep.

Meditation

Meditation connects us to cosmic consciousness. Scientists who have studied both Vedic knowledge and quantum physics tell us that we are capable of direct contact with the unified field. The systematic practice of some meditative techniques cleanses our mind, our "door of perception." Meditation can infuse our physiology with the qualities of consciousness: liveliness, coherence, silence, creativity, and dynamism. Regular meditators experience many physiological changes because some meditative techniques access and harness the energy of the unified field.

The Science Behind the Sages: Life Is a Vibe

Candace Pert, Ph.D., is a renowned neuroscientist and pharmacologist who is best known for her discovery of opiate receptors in the brain. Her scientific expertise has also contributed to advances in psychoneuroimmunology, which studies the links between the mind and the body. It is well accepted in the medical community that the body contains biomolecular sensing devices (receptors) that receive messages via specific chemicals (ligands), but Pert expanded the knowledge.

The linkage of receptors and ligands was thought to occur in the way that a key inserts into a lock. Now this mechanical analogy has been revised to reflect Pert's experimental data. Ligands attach to receptors by sharing a distinct *molecular vibration*. As the Vedic sages proclaimed and quantum physicists have explained, vibration is the essence of function.

Pert also demonstrated that these receptors are not localized in a particular organ, as was once thought, but are distributed throughout the body. The ligand-receptor system is not, for example, unique to the nervous system and the brain. Whereas it was once assumed that neurotransmitters were localized in the brain (hence the name), we now know that nodal points exist throughout the body. There's speculation that these nodal points in effect decide what messages to send to the brain for further processing and what messages to ignore.

Your mind does not reside solely in your brain. Thoughts and feelings travel in the form of chemically encoded molecules from body to brain and vice versa. This fact led Pert to realize the inseparability of the mind and the body.

For instance, a major neuronal nodal point exists in the intestines. Therefore, saying that you have a "gut feeling" may be more than just a figure of speech. Gut feelings reflect a scientific fact. Your gut indeed has a mind of its own. This could explain why pharmaceutical antidepressants, which are aimed at the brain, often have such a strong adverse effect on the gastrointestinal system.

Equally important is the knowledge that the mind-body is not, as previously thought, an exclusively electrical communication system governed by firing nerve cells. Our cells are bathed in a vibrating sea of molecular chemicals. Thoughts and emotions are molecules of information, ready to change the landscape of the mind-body. The paradigm that Pert has proposed is that the body is a multidirectional network of communication. To this the Vedic sages would add that consciousness underlies it all.

Airy Depression: Taking Hold of the Cosmic Anchor

Arial, our case study of Airy Depression, is by nature an enthusiastic, optimistic person. A clever, hard-working individual, she was delighted when she received a promotion. She was so involved with happily clapping for her life, however, that she lost hold of her cosmic anchor.

Let us explain to you what we mean by a cosmic anchor. There are two aspects of life: the relative and the absolute. The relative aspect refers to our everyday experience, such as our jobs, our relationships, and our other activities in the world. This aspect of life is constantly changing. It is what we worry about, what makes us anxious and keeps us awake at night. This is the aspect of life that we are engaged in when we are in a state of object-referral.

The absolute aspect refers to the unchanging parts of life, those things that remain untouched by the winds of change. It encompasses what we cannot see but can experience as our abstract nature—consciousness. The absolute is accessed by engaging in the process of self-referral. Although the relative and the absolute aspects of life are always available to us, we often fail to place our attention on the experience of the absolute. We sometimes fail to even intuit its existence. It is, however, the acknowledgment of the absolute aspect of life that provides an anchor for us, stabilizing us in the relative world.

Amid all of the changes that were occurring in such a short period, Arial's attention was exclusively focused on the relative aspects of life. Her husband had to find a job in the city to which her new position was taking them. They had to find new schools for their children. Arial had to meet her staff and adjust to a more challenging job with higher expectations. She had to redefine herself in the context of her new life. Because she was stuck in a state of extreme object-referral, worrying became her default response to all of the above.

Arial's mind indulged in the creation of fear-based scenarios. Throughout our day, thoughts bubble up that reflect the state of our physiological balance. For example, if we are anxious, our thoughts reflect this feeling and the underlying imbalance. The mistake that was made by Arial's intellect was to identify with her thoughts. She began to believe that her thoughts were depictions of reality. According to Ayurveda, this is indicative of an imbalance in Vata dosha.

Imbalances indicate disruptions in our connection to consciousness. These physiological disruptions set a domino effect into place. With her awareness restricted, focused singularly on the relative world, Arial began to make an increasing number of lifestyle mistakes. Her anxiety was a cruel jailer. It limited her perspective, making her feel that she had no time or opportunity to behave in a manner that would promote her well-being. She neglected to nourish her mind and her spirit. Her thoughts, emotions, and behaviors all became manifested in her physical body. Energetically depleted, she became depressed.

Meditation was the antidote for Arial's depression. It gave her the deep rest that insomnia had robbed from her. Now she was able to sleep, which helped her mind-body to heal. Her nervous system became stable, and she felt grounded and in control once more. Meditating helped Arial to connect with the underlying field of potentiality, universal consciousness—the unchanging aspect of life; this in turn fueled her with energy that enabled her to change her mind-set. As a result, she gained perspective on the changes she was experiencing.

Aromatherapy was also an aid to Arial. As her mind-body moved into balance, she used specific aromas to create certain emotional and psychological states. For instance, lavender helped her body to relax at night. Rose and jasmine helped her to stay calm and centered during the day. Orange eased her fears. Each essence brought a specific medicinal vibration from the natural world into her brain.

Burning Depression: A Fiery Head and a Deflated Heart

The actions of Barbara, our case study of Burning Depression, were like flaming arrows. Her drive, determination, and stamina helped her to always hit the mark. She was repeatedly successful at reaching her goals. For many years she sailed though life, relying only on her keen intellect to guide her decision making and to help her discern the subtleties she encountered in interactions with colleagues and friends.

For Barbara, life was a puzzle that had to be figured out. Emotions were for dummies who did not understand the rules of the game. Over time, her intellectual life stopped giving her the emotional fulfillment she desired. She burned out. Unfortunately, it was not until she became deeply depressed that she realized that she had been maneuvering through her days with a fiery head and a deflated heart.

Barbara had no awareness of the inseparability of body, mind, and spirit. The body, especially her brain, was all that mattered to her. She considered entertaining emotions to be a waste of time. She did not realize that unrecognized emotions were creating blockages in her physiology, disrupting her connection to universal consciousness.

The body, the mind, and the spirit are one seamless energetic system. If, like Barbara, we restrict our awareness to a single aspect of our being, we cut ourselves off from the totality that is our nature. This disconnection breeds disease. Emotions become stuck within the physiology, preventing the free flow of universal intelligence throughout the mind-body.

Yoga postures helped Barbara to realize that her body was not a hunk of material but a pattern of vibrations that emanate from an underlying field of energy. The physicality of the yoga postures awoke Barbara to emotional sensations. The integration of these sensations paved the way for her development of awareness. She began to experience wholeness: the unity of all aspects of self. Her life force, no longer blocked by stuck emotions, could manifest as renewed vitality and unbridled creativity.

Other Ayurvedic interventions gave her a way to address the particular imbalances that preceded and caused her physiological distresses. Barbara easily learned how to use the natural world to maintain her mind-body in a state of doshic balance. She relished her new experiences and began to use her emotions as well as her intelligence as guideposts to help her navigate through life.

Earthy Depression: Letting Consciousness Flow

Ed, our case study of Earthy Depression, was unable to let go of the past, enjoy the present, or welcome the future. His attachment to the familiar created a longing for the "way things used to be." His oversentimentality got in the way of the development of his consciousness.

When change threatened to disrupt his status quo, Ed became depressed. He reacted to this condition by trying to soothe himself with food and sleep. His depressed mood was directly related to his inability to handle experience—to digest life. Ed's internal world was filled with remnants of an unprocessed life: feelings of rejection lingering from a love lost in his youth; the emotional emptiness following the healthy separation of a grown child leaving home; the insecurity and loss of identity ensuing from retirement. Undue attachment to predictability in life generates *ama* in every aspect of the being—physical, mental, emotional, and spiritual.

Change is an inevitable fact of life, yet Ed was constantly fighting it. Unable to stop the waves of change in his life, he became overwhelmingly sad. Consequently, the heaviness of his heart led him to behave in ways that blocked the free flow of consciousness through his physiology.

At this point Ed was so stuck that it was difficult for him to detach from his emotions long enough to develop an objective perspective on his situation. His breathing pattern reflected his emotional state; it was a concrete illustration of the way he was living life. Yet even though Ed could not view his depression objectively, he could analyze his breathing patterns with clarity. This insight was illuminating for him. Regularly practicing breathing exercises rekindled a light of hope for Ed. With each breath he took, he retrained his nervous system and infused his body with energy. As an exercise in neurorespiratory integration, breathing was a practical means of reeducating his physiology. With each breath, Ed released the regrets of his life.

Breathing exercises were the first step in mobilizing Ed's mind-body for change. However, consciousness cannot flow through a physiology that is gunked up with *ama*. Ed needed to begin a rigorous exercise program to enhance his digestive fire. Exercise allowed him to resolve the problem of *ama*. By moving his body, he infused a feeling of lightness and strength into his mind.

Connecting to Consciousness

The following questions review three of the key concepts presented in this chapter. The questions are geared toward enhancing your awareness. Answering them will draw your attention to aspects of your life that might need unification and revitalization.

1. **You are part of the natural world and in constant exchange with your environment.**

   Think back to a time when you were out in a natural setting.

   * How do you feel when you are near a body of water?
   * How do you feel when you are exposed to the sun?
   * How does the wind affect you?
   * How does it feel to walk in the moonlight?
   * How does a walk in the woods make you feel?
   * Do you have an awareness that the rhythms of nature are programmed into your physiology?
   * Do you spend some time outdoors every day or week?
   * How well connected to the natural world do you think are you?

2. **As beings of consciousness, we extend our mind-body into the universe through our five senses.**

   Think about the kind of information you are gathering with your five senses.

   * What are you feeding your mind through your senses?
   * What types of sounds surround you most of the day?
   * What type of visual stimulation do you find entertaining?
   * What textures attract you?
   * Did you know that there are six tastes in the natural world (sweet, salty, sour, pungent, bitter, and astringent)?
   * Which of the six tastes predominates in your diet?
   * Did you know that your sense of smell has a direct link to the brain through the nervous system?
   * Did you know that you could use your sense of smell to help you to manage your emotions?

3. **The goal of Ayurvedic interventions is to bring the vibrations of the natural world into our physiology.**

Aromatherapy

* Have you ever experienced an emotion or a memory that was triggered by a certain smell?
* Did you know that aromas can be used medicinally because they will help to reestablish your vibratory balance?

Nutrition

* Have you ever considered foods as packets of universal intelligence?
* Did you know that food products are designed to impart coherence into your physiology?
* Are you aware of the effects of food on your body, mind, and spirit?

Exercise

* Did you know that the wrong type of exercise for your physiological needs can trigger imbalances?
* Have you ever exercised to the point of energetic depletion?
* Have you ever felt lighter, happier, and more energetic after an exercise session?
* Did you know that appropriate exercise restores the flow of energy that allows cellular regeneration to occur?
* Do you use your exercise program to restore balance to your mind-body?

Yoga Postures

* Did you know that yoga postures have a direct impact on all the organ systems in your body: the nervous, endocrine, reproductive, digestive, immune, skeletal, and lymphatic systems?
* Did you know that yoga asanas (postures) manage the flow of energy in your body?
* Have you ever tried yoga?
* Do you think that yoga would be a helpful exercise for you?

Breathing Exercises

- Did you know that by improving your awareness of how you breathe, you can manage your emotions more efficiently?
- Did you know that breathing puts you in direct energetic communication with your physical environment?
- Are you aware that you regulate the flow of energy through your breath?
- Have you ever noticed a change in your breath in response to a stressful situation?

Sleep

- Did you know that sleep nourishes the body more than nutrition?
- Did you know that sleep offers physiological purification at the cellular level?
- Did you know that sleep deprivation is a primary precursor of depression?
- Are you aware of differences in your mental clarity and emotional well-being after a night of deep restorative sleep?

Meditation

- Did you know that meditation is a mental technique?
- Did you know that meditation can directly connect you to cosmic consciousness?
- Did you know that meditation purifies the physiology of stress?
- Did you know that meditation infuses the qualities of consciousness (liveliness, coherence, silence, creativity, and dynamism) into the physiology?
- Do you meditate or do you have a plan to learn a meditative technique?

Ayurveda

- Did you know that all Ayurvedic interventions aim to reconnect you with the vibratory essence of consciousness?
- Did you know that wholeness—integration with consciousness—yields health?
- Did you know that the by-product of health is happiness?
- Are you as enthusiastic about the positive results of Ayurveda as we are?

PART II

Creating Happiness

9

Meditation: Transcending Darkness

> In the depths of winter, I finally learned that
> within me there lay an invincible summer.
>
> —ALBERT CAMUS

The mind can't maintain a mood on an abstract basis. That is, we cannot feel unhappy, angry, depressed, or joyful without our mind finding some way of explaining why that mood occurs. Because we make the mistake of attaching feelings of depression to a reason, we often make a second mistake: thinking that things in the external world must change in order for us to feel better. This simply isn't so. To quote Charles Dickens: "Men who look on nature and their fellow men, and cry that all is dark and gloomy, are in the right; but the somber colors are reflections from their own jaundiced eyes and hearts. The real hues are delicate, and need a clearer vision."

It is the internal world that is calling for change, and meditation is the most effective technique by which to accomplish internal change. Through regular meditation, we secure the systematic practice of self-referral and infuse our awareness with the intelligence that underlies and governs the universe. The systematic practice of self-referral not only anchors us but also broadens our horizons. As a result, we view life with more depth and breadth. Meditation is the main agent of vitality that helps us to undo depression.

The Many Ways We Can Explore Our Being

Biofeedback, concentration meditation, cognitive restructuring, guided imagery, hypnosis, mindfulness meditation, the relaxation response, progressive muscle relaxation, sensory deprivation techniques, transcendental meditation, qigong, activity-oriented meditation, primordial sound meditation, tai chi, mindfulness-based stress reduction, walking meditation, Vipassana, Ninjutsu, Zen meditation, Buddhist meditation, Christian meditation techniques, kundalini meditation, Kriya yoga, self-inquiry meditation, Tratak meditation, and cathartic dancing meditation—there are so many choices! The list goes on and on. How do we make sense of the many meditation techniques that are available to us?

Meditation techniques differ in significant ways. Some use concentration or pointed attention on internal experiences such as bodily sensations, feelings, thoughts, or memories. Other techniques focus on external stimuli such as visual images, sounds, or musical melodies. Still others rely on the person's reasoning abilities.

How the various techniques are performed also differs. Some must be done actively, by calling upon mental force and determination, whereas others require passive receptivity and a sense of effortlessness. Some techniques come as a package, attached to a belief system; others are simply mental tools that are designed to relieve stress.

Thus there are many ways in which we can explore our being. In Zen Buddhist practices, concentration is directed toward experiencing one's breathing pattern, or one's conceptual attention is focused on paradoxes (called *koans*) that defy intellectual resolution. Taoist practices concentrate on the circulation of subtle energy throughout the channels of the body. Some yogic traditions focus on generating and dispersing energy through centers in the body called *chakras*. Still other forms use the repetition of special sounds called *mantras*; the repetition can occur internally or be heard externally, depending on the tradition. The chosen sound may or may not have meaning.

The many forms of meditation differ in their procedures, contents, objects, beliefs, and goals. Mindfulness meditation is done by bringing the mind to focus on what is happening in the present moment while simply noticing the mind's usual chatter without judgment. One can also be mindful of physical sensations. Integral yoga emphasizes attending to a sense of seeking and remembering calmness. Kriya yoga uses techniques of concentration on breath and on God. Christian Centering Prayer uses a word of love to stimulate receptiveness to God within. Meditation practices in the Theravada Buddhist tradition emphasize the dispassionate observation of the impermanence of whatever is being meditated on: sensations, thoughts, or even the self.

Are we making a mistake if we consider all of these diverse practices as being essentially the same? Research reveals that different techniques have very different effects, depending on the nature of the practice. For example, the techniques that emphasize active breathing may yield a positive outcome for respiratory health, whereas the techniques that focus on the utilization of mental faculties may improve brain activity and clarity of thinking.

Yet the notion that all forms of meditation are the same—that meditation is generic in essence—has generated a great deal of confusion. The assumption that all meditation techniques lead to the same end has caused the proliferation of many meditative techniques. Scores of these are scientifically untested and unproven in their efficacy. Basically, they have relied on the reputations of the more established meditation traditions. When these techniques don't prove to be effective, judgment falls on all forms of meditation.

Under the guise of meditation, a plethora of techniques have left people wanting more. This is how people have come to conclude that meditation does not work for them or that they just can't meditate. All we are saying is that different procedures offer different results and, consequently, should be rigorously evaluated on an individual basis. In light of this, how do you navigate through the many choices and pick a meditation technique that works for you?

The Transcendental Meditation Technique

In spite of all the meditation techniques that are available, we strongly recommend the Transcendental Meditation technique (TM). We realize that different forms of meditation work for different people, but our primary reason for recommending the TM technique is that it has been rigorously evaluated for efficacy. In addition, unlike some forms of meditation, the TM technique does not require adherence to any belief system—there is no dogma or philosophy attached to it, and it does not demand any lifestyle changes other than the practice of it.

Since this book is about depression, we wish to highlight a meditative technique that has been shown to create physiological changes in the mind-body. If we are to move from a depressed state to a happier state of mind, we must make a psycho-physiological shift, and we need a meditative technique that will assist us in making this shift. While the TM technique is an easy, natural, and effortless mental technique that takes the mind past thought and emotion to a place of restful alertness, it is also a purely scientific technique that produces scientifically verifiable results. This, and our personal experience, is what convinced us of its value.

If practiced regularly, the TM technique will inevitably yield positive results. Research has shown that this technique works no matter what the expectations of the practitioner are. It's a bit like holding a tennis ball in your hand and then letting it go—the ball will fall to the ground whether you believe it will or not. In the same way, the TM technique will affect your physiology whether you expect it to or not.

Let's allow the scientific research to speak for itself. There are many scientific studies, conducted over a period of several decades, that demonstrate that the TM technique reliably yields the benefits described below.

What Is Transcendental Meditation?

The TM technique is a mantra meditation. A mantra is a sound that can be heard externally or internally. In the case of the TM technique, it is heard internally. According to experts on meditation, for a mantra to be effective, it must resonate with the baseline biorhythms of the central nervous system. This is because the mantra works on the physics principle of resonance. Resonance is the phenomenon whereby one vibrating object causes another object to vibrate without direct contact. For example, if you strike a tuning fork, you can start the vibrations of a similar tuning fork just by placing it next to the first fork.

Researchers have offered a neurological theory to explain why a mantra must be carefully selected. The mantra enters the central nervous system via the brain's speech area, located in the temporal lobe where memories are stored. The mantra seems to represent a direct input of ease and order through which gentle and simple repetition reaches the innermost aspects of our brain and being.

This mantra, or simple sound, takes us through the layers of the mind to a place of inner silence and creates the experience of feeling alert and rested at the same time. In order to understand this, compare the mind to the ocean. Like the ocean, on the surface level of the mind exist waves representing mental activity, and as we go into the deeper layers of the mind we experience quiet and peace. The deepest layer of both the ocean and the mind is a place of deep quiet. The TM technique gives the experience of this level of the mind and this is why it is referred to as transcendental. Through this meditative technique we transcend thought and emotion and we experience the peacefulness that underlies our being. The meditative experience is pleasant. However, we do not meditate for the experience itself but for how the practice affects us holistically. There are physiological correlates to the practice of the TM technique. Through our practice we begin to feel better emotionally and think more clearly because our physiology is functioning in a more optimal manner.

Learning Transcendental Meditation

Can you learn the TM technique from a book? Although this technique is natural and easy to learn and practice, it *does* require instruction by a trained teacher. To become a teacher of the TM technique one must attend a six-month residence course. Meditation is both powerful and subtle. It is truly a marvel that a mental technique that moves the mind from the gross layer of active thought to more subtle realms can be taught at all. The process of learning the TM technique is delicate and must be performed by a trained instructor who teaches in a prescribed manner. The resources section offers information on how to find a qualified teacher.

Following are the steps to learn the TM technique:

- **An introductory meeting.** In this discussion, a TM teacher will explain the scientific underpinnings of the technique and exactly what it can do for you.

- **A preparatory discussion.** This session gives the teacher an opportunity to explain the mechanics of the TM technique. The focus is on the specific explanations of how the technique works, how it differs from other techniques, where it comes from, how it is taught, and why it is taught in this way.

- **A personal interview.** This is a time to ask questions and, if you have decided to learn the technique, to set up an appointment for your first session.

The technique is taught over a period of four consecutive days, two hours each day. On the first day you will receive instructions for the technique. Over the next three days you receive further instruction and answers to any questions you may have. These meetings give you an opportunity to discuss your experience and to discuss practical details of the practice. You will also explore the goal of the TM program, which is a stress-free life, with full use of your mental and physical potential.

The Benefits of Transcendental Meditation

Transcendental meditation has the following proven benefits.

Dissolving Deep-Seated Stress If asked about the cause of depression, the Vedic sages would point to stress that is lodged deeply in the nervous system. Yes, public health enemy number one tops the list again. Stress is the main cause of the physiological imbalances that predispose us to all of the archetypes of depression. Stress is basically gunk in the nervous system—or, as the sages would say, "It's *ama!*" Stress puts blockages in our physiology, thereby impeding the flow of life energy, dampening the digestive fire, and generating *ama*. Stress at the mental and emotional level distorts perception and inhibits all manner of expression.

A considerable number of studies have demonstrated that the TM technique removes existing stress from the physiology. For example, in a study of posttraumatic stress disorder (PTSD) in Vietnam veterans, meditation was instrumental in restoring mental and physical health. Other studies have shown that this practice improves an individual's ability to handle stress. Practitioners of the TM technique have consistently lower levels of cortisol and other stress-related hormones.

Providing Deep Rest Depression often robs our ability to get deep rest. Insomnia is the hallmark of Airy Depression, for example. The internal tornado that builds from a Vata imbalance keeps the individual's nervous system from settling down, making nights a nightmare of wakefulness. In Burning Depression, sleep comes easily but ends abruptly. Early morning awakenings are a hallmark of this type of depression. On the other hand, Earthy Depression illustrates the fact that not all who sleep receive rest. Oversleeping and napping only add to the lethargy that is experienced.

Electroencephalography (EEG) studies reveal that the TM technique produces a unique state of consciousness, different from the waking, sleeping, or dreaming states. This state of consciousness produces a profound rest that is much deeper than sleep. A state of restful alertness is how it has been described by neuroscientists who have analyzed the workings of the brain during a TM session. Physiological changes occur spontaneously, helping the mind-body to regain balance. Not only will you be able to fall asleep more quickly and maintain sleep, you'll sleep better. Research shows that the TM technique is an effective treatment for sleep disorders.

Alleviating Anxiety Anxiety is epidemic in all industrialized countries. Could this be why the rate of depression is also rising throughout the world? Anxiety and depression do go hand in hand, especially in the case of Airy Depression. Anxiety is an impediment to the full expression of health, creativity, and intellectual functioning. Medical authorities estimate that 60 to 90 percent of all physical illness is aggravated by mental tension and anxiety.

Neuroscientists inform us that the experience of the TM technique is exactly the opposite of the experience of anxiety. Regular meditation has a stabilizing effect on an agitated physiology. This balancing act is immediate in its effect as well as cumulative in its impact. Anxiety causes psychological rigidity and blocks the flow of energy in the mind and the body. A reduction in anxiety allows our intelligence, energy, creativity, and happiness to flourish.

Expanding Awareness By practicing the TM technique, we acquire a wide-angle lens with which to view life. Expanding awareness opens the "shutter" in the mind's eye. When we have a panoramic view of an event, our understanding is enhanced. This deeper viewpoint gives us more flexibility in the face of change, allowing the stress of life's transitions to roll off our backs more easily.

The TM technique has been shown to increase physical, emotional, and psychological resiliency. This means that we can get out from under whatever we perceive is keeping us down. Expanded awareness dons us with a protective cloak against depression.

Are You Contemplating Learning to Meditate?

We urge you to find a practice that suits you. Consider the following questions when deciding on a meditation practice.

Which meditation techniques have you tried?

Did you find the technique to be easy to do?

What do you want to get out of your meditation practice?

Do you require simplicity or complexity in the technique you undertake?

How much time are you willing to devote to the practice?

What will it take for you to make meditation a regular part of your routine?

Do you want a technique that is attached to a philosophy or a belief system?

Meditation as Medicine: Feeling Great the Natural Way!

A study published in the *Journal of Clinical Psychology* in 1989 investigated more than a hundred stress management and relaxation techniques to determine if they reduce anxiety with equal effectiveness. This meta-analysis, which compared nearly two decades of stress-related studies, found that the TM technique reduced anxiety more than twice as much as any other technique. Furthermore, when only those studies with strong research designs were considered, the TM technique was shown to reduce anxiety more than four times as much as all of the other techniques.

A meta-analysis of studies on self-actualization noted that the effects of the TM technique were much greater than the effects of concentration practices, contemplation, and other similar techniques. Thus, the TM technique is one of the best methods for undoing the factors that cause depression. Let's look at how it improves integration of the mind-body.

Internal Locus of Control

It has been said that the only constant in life is change. Flexibility is the quality that gives us strength in the face of change. It facilitates adaptation and allows us to more easily make life transitions. Flexibility of body, mind, and spirit helps us to handle the curveballs life throws at us and the stresses inherent in everyday living.

A study was conducted to investigate the effect of practicing the TM technique on an individual's internal locus of control. This parameter has been associated with flexibility, psychological adaptability, low anxiety, and the ability to effectively extract and make use of information from a complex environment. Compared with a control group of nonmeditators, the subjects practicing the TM technique demonstrated a significantly greater internal locus of control.

An internal locus of control gives individuals insight into the connections between their behavior and the environment as well as foresight about the consequences of their actions. Researchers have theorized that since the TM technique stabilizes one's internal sense of self and improves the integration of thought and action, the meditator naturally feels a greater sense of control over life. This in turn promotes the ability to be flexible and handle unpredictability with increased ease. Changes in perception then occur naturally.

Physiological Adaptability

TM enhances the ability of the nervous system to adjust to change. Regular practice of meditation engages the physiology in a daily cycle of deep rest followed by activity. Studies have shown that during the phase of deep rest, the entire physiology reaches a state of profound relaxation that is marked by a natural change in heart rate, breath rate, and breath volume. Oxygen consumption markedly decreases, informing us that the physiology is minimally at work. This state of deep rest increases balance in the autonomic nervous system.

Even more happens in the brains of meditators. EEG measures the electrical energy that is generated by nerve cells in the brain. Studies show that the brain wave patterns that emanate from the different parts of the brain become more synchronized. This indicates an increased orderliness of brain function and implies that the different parts of the brain are working together as a coherent whole. Other studies have shown that this improved brain functioning (coherence in thinking) becomes more permanent with increased regular meditation.

Practice of the TM technique also stabilizes the nervous system. This stability continues to be maintained even after the meditation session ends. The researchers explain that meditation reduces the noise level of the nervous system, thereby freeing more energy for perception, thought, and purposeful activity.

Psychological Adaptability

Practitioners of the TM technique also experience a direct influence on their psychological processing. Meditating enhances and develops our ability to adapt to events and new situations. The tyranny of recurrent bouts of depression ends when we develop positive traits that disallow the seeding of a depressive mood.

A study analyzed the effect of the TM technique on the development of self-actualization. As defined by this study, self-actualization includes the following qualities: an open, receptive, and caring attitude;

cheerfulness and good humor; a predominance of positive thinking; spontaneity and freshness of appreciation; self-sufficiency; loss of fear of death; and an acceptance of self, nature, and others.

The subjects who practiced the TM technique for an average of six weeks showed a significant increase in self-actualization, compared with a group of nonmeditators. The level of self-actualization was highest for long-term (average forty-three months) meditators, indicating that the benefits of the TM technique are cumulative.

It can be concluded from these scientific results that the TM technique effects integration and growth in all directions. When the nervous system is refined, the personality of the meditator unfolds naturally in the direction of self-actualization.

There is ample research showing that meditators engage in more positive relationships. These studies show an increase in self-reliance as well. This makes sense, because self-reliance gives a greater ability to have positive relationships. The better we feel about ourselves, the more we have to give—and the basis of positive relationships is giving. As self-sufficiency increases, having good relationships becomes the frosting on the cake.

Purification

It is through deep rest that we awaken the physician within. Given the opportunity, the physiology *can* re-create itself. This is why sleep is of vital importance. Regular sleep patterns can help to remove the marks left behind in our physiology by the wear and tear of everyday stress. One study has shown that after forty hours of sleep deprivation, a group of subjects practicing the TM technique recovered much more quickly than a control group of nonmeditators.

Dissolving deep-rooted stress, however, requires more profound rest. TM offers this opportunity. During meditation, the physiology is in a deep state of rest—much deeper than it is during ordinary sleep. This deep state of rest increases the efficiency of the physiology's natural purification processes. The purification process begins during the meditation session and continues after the session ends.

As the body purifies, its functions normalize. Consequently, to analyze the effect of meditation on the purification of the mind-body, researchers have studied recovery from stress. Some extraordinary events trigger enormous stress. After the Vietnam War, for instance, many soldiers returned home exhibiting symptoms of PTSD. An investigation of the effects of the TM technique showed a reduction in the symptoms of severe stress: emotional numbness, insomnia, anxiety, family problems, and depression. The meditators simultaneously improved significantly on several other psychological and social measures. The TM technique enabled these veterans to respond more effectively to demanding life situations.

Purification of stress from the nervous system positively affects the mind. As meditators begin to shed negativity, they make room for positive thoughts and emotions. Meditators experience an increase in self-confidence, tolerance, orderliness of thinking, and self-esteem. This is partly because the TM technique reverses the effects of anxiety, which is associated with the impairment of functioning in almost all areas of life: physiological, perceptual-motor, intellectual, and emotional.

Integration and Personal Growth

Health exists when every cell in the human body is functioning coherently and to full capacity. Happiness is the by-product of this condition. Happiness is dependent on the refinement of physiological function. The integration of body, mind, and spirit is the essence of personal growth.

A series of studies have demonstrated that the TM technique brings about personality changes in personal growth and self-integration. In one study, subjects practicing the TM technique showed significant positive improvement in the following traits: self-directedness, time competence, self-actualization, spontaneity, sensitivity to one's needs, self-acceptance, and the capacity for warm interpersonal relationships. Most impressive of all is that these improvements came about after only two months of practicing the TM technique.

The Chemistry of Happiness

Modern research has shed light on the impact of chronic stress on hormones and brain chemicals. Distinct neurochemical mechanisms have been found to be responsible for the effects. For example, individuals under chronic stress show a generalized impairment in the brain and in the endocrine system. Chronic stress affects what scientists call the hypothalamic-pituitary axis (HPA). The hypothalamus is the master controlling region in the brain, and the pituitary gland is the master controlling gland of the endocrine system.

Depressed individuals also show this pattern of impairment in the HPA. During a depressive episode, the levels of adrenocorticotropic hormone (ACTH) and cortisol secretion increase. The levels of serotonin, norepinephrine, dopamine, and other biochemicals fluctuate as an adaptive response to the changes in the HPA. Another affected biochemical is melatonin, a hormone associated with sleep. Also, when serotonin is substantially reduced by acute and chronic stress, there is an increase in the activity of the locus coeruleus, a part of the brain that affects anxiety, anger, fear, and frustration.

From tranquilizers and sleeping pills to alcohol and marijuana, many classes of drugs temporarily inhibit activity in the locus coeruleus, thus reducing anxiety, anger, fear, and frustration. Nevertheless, the effect of these substances is only transient at best, and their side effects are negative. The drugs themselves are stressors on the physiology and cause further derangements at every level of the mind-body.

The TM technique, on the other hand, has a positive effect on the brain and the endocrine system. Studies suggest that the practice of the TM technique increases serotonin levels; more important, it also reduces cortisol levels. Since the cortisol level indicates the working state of the HPA, we can deduce that the TM technique decreases the hyperactivity in the HPA that has been brought on by chronic stress. In this manner, the TM technique serves as an effective treatment for depression.

Getting a Flavor of the TM Experience

The scientific research we present in this chapter is based on the Transcendental Meditation technique as taught by Maharishi Mahesh Yogi. This technique has its origins in the Vedic tradition of ancient India but was introduced to the Western world by Maharishi Mahesh

Yogi. The title *Maharishi* means "great teacher." Maharishi was a student of physics and a spiritual man who possessed a deep desire to help people reach their full potential. His contribution to society was to revitalize an ancient meditative technique and to encourage scientific research into its efficacy.

Practicing the TM technique requires learning it from a qualified teacher. One reaps the benefits of the practice by meditating for twenty minutes twice a day: in the morning and in the late afternoon or early evening. At first, some people believe that they will not have time to fit this practice into their daily schedule. Most people quickly learn, however, that practicing the TM technique gives them time instead of taking time away. This is because, through regular practice, individuals experience an increase in inner calm and renewed energy. Because they feel less overwhelmed and more on top of things, they accomplish more with greater ease.

A great benefit of this technique is that it will fit into your lifestyle. It can be practiced anywhere, such as on a train or a bus, in your office, or in your home. The mind naturally settles down when one begins to think of the mantra, so the practice will not be hindered by external noise.

When we practice the TM technique, we sit quietly, close our eyes, and begin to think of the mantra. We do not concentrate on the mantra nor do we attempt to stop other thoughts from continuing to enter the mind; we gently favor the mantra. The gentle repetition of the mantra allows the mind to experience increasingly more subtle levels of the thinking process until thinking and emotion are transcended.

The purpose of the mantra is to give the mind a vehicle to transcend not only the mantra itself but the entire thinking process. The resulting experience of the TM technique is one of profound inner silence, with the mind wide awake yet perfectly still.

Any description of the very lively, yet restful experience that occurs during the practice of the TM technique is bound to come across as abstract. It is like trying to describe the taste of a strawberry. The taste is very real, but one must actually taste this fruit to realize the fullness of the experience. It is the same with the TM technique. Only regular practice of it can give you the full flavor of the experience.

Undoing Depression: Balancing the Elements of Being

The TM technique allows for the expansion of consciousness that enables us to have increased awareness of the effects of our lifestyle. This awareness helps us to change. Because the TM technique gives us a feeling of fulfillment and calmness, it also gives us hope.

Severely depressed people believe they will never feel better. The initial dive from the surface level of the mind into transcendental consciousness gives an experience that helps us to know it is possible to change how we experience ourselves. Even if depression doesn't immediately dissipate, a depressed individual now "knows" a different way of feeling is possible. A glimmer of light is what a desperate person needs to feel hopeful, and hope is the beginning of the move toward a new way of being.

With the expansion of consciousness comes a feeling of fulfillment, and this enables us to become more objective about our circumstances. Depressed people often speak about feeling overwhelmed by problems. Through its many positive effects, the TM technique imbues us with a stronger sense of objectivity. Objectivity in turn gives us a greater ability to solve problems, and as problems are solved, we feel a sense of empowerment, and this dissipates depression.

Here's how regular practice of the TM technique helped to alleviate the three types of depression: Airy, Burning, and Earthy.

Gaining Tranquility

After she learned of her promotion, Arial flew into a habit of overactivity. Her hectic lifestyle further added to her exhaustion until anxiety gained a foothold in her physiology; after all, we all lean in the direction of our imbalances. Anxiety is indicative of an exhausted nervous system and the hallmark of an Airy Depression.

When Arial began to experience anxiety, she attached this feeling to a number of worries. She had trouble sleeping at night, and she spent her days racing around, trying to satisfy everyone—her children, her husband, and her boss and coworkers. Drowning in her anxiety, she wondered how she could *not* be anxious when she had so many reasons to be so.

Anxiety indicates the presence of emotional *ama* in the mind-body. Arial felt as if she had lost her grounding and her sense of being cared for. She spoke of feeling out of control and lonely and as if all burdens rested on her shoulders.

Anxiety breeds increased anxiety, and the TM technique creates a physiological experience that is the opposite of anxiety. It disrupts the circularity of anxiety by giving the physiology deep rest and the experience of inner calmness. Through meditation Arial renewed her energy level and regained her internal locus of control. She began to feel on top of her life instead of being buried by everyday events. In addition, she reconnected with her inner self—that aspect of her being that remained free of anxiety. She transcended the mental static that constantly replayed her anxious worries and moved beyond this surface level of the mind to a deeper level.

The rest she gained from her practice imbued her body with strength and increased her psychological adaptability. Arial was no longer thrown off course by everyday events. She was instead able to adapt to new situations. The experience of the meditation moved her past mental and emotional reruns and allowed her to experience herself as stable. When we are rested and calm, we handle the stresses inherent in daily living better and build a protection against anxiety.

Building Self-Awareness

People suffering from a Burning Depression experience anger and frustration. Barbara's boss referred her to anger management classes, and she had overheard colleagues at work refer to her as the "dragon lady." Her overall experience of self was hot and fiery. Initially, Barbara had no idea that she could be depressed; she did not see a problem within herself. Her idea for making her life better was to have other people change their ways of thinking and operating in the world. Barbara's mental and emotional energy was directed outward toward her external world. She lacked self-awareness and a sense of her internal world.

Self-awareness exists on a continuum. Most of us have at least a modicum of awareness regarding our physical, mental, and emotional states of being. The majority of us have some awareness of how we affect others and are affected by others. However, when anger overtakes us, as it did with Barbara, we can have a significant loss of self-awareness in every aspect of our mind-body, and this eventually affects our being and lifestyle.

According to Ayurveda, a lack of fulfillment underlies the emotion of anger. We all have desires. When our desires are blocked, we feel thwarted and we express this frustration as anger. Resentment, hostility, and jealousy often accompany anger. Resolution comes when we increase self-awareness.

Awareness allows us to be intimate with ourselves. It brings knowledge of all aspects of our being. If we are aware, then we know what foods affect us and we can consume those foods that bring health and stay away from those that are not good for us. Barbara had an ulcer, yet she was continually consuming spicy foods. She was unaware that the foods she was choosing to eat were exacerbating her physical condition.

Barbara's lack of awareness extended to how she affected her colleagues. Her brain registered the social interaction, but she was not able to evaluate her role in relationships. The internal anger Barbara possessed overwhelmed her ability to understand her more subtle emotions as well as the emotions of others. With limited self-awareness, she was not able to experience the full development of her emotional potential. The Transcendental Meditation technique was a tool that helped Barbara to develop self-awareness because it broke down the confining walls of her inner life. It released negative emotion without incurring additional stress in the process.

Barbara was deeply stressed from a lifetime of identifying with her work. For many years her internal sense of self was related only to her success in the workplace and to her status in her company. Through her practice of the TM technique, Barbara's perceptions became increasingly refined and she became able to evaluate herself from her own information and inner awareness. No longer did she feel that she was being constantly evaluated and judged. As her physiology became more stable, Barbara became self-actualized and better able to rely on her inner nature than to base her self-esteem on her perceptions of the opinions of others.

Through meditation Barbara did not lose that which was so important to her—her competitive edge. On the contrary, when we meditate, the physical, mental, and emotional aspects of our being become integrated and we achieve personal growth. Barbara became better able to see the big picture instead of simply relating to only the career aspect of her life. Her creativity and self-esteem were enhanced through the practice of the TM technique, and because of this, she performed more effectively in the workplace.

Infusing Lightness

The physical *ama* that clogged Ed's physiology weighed him down. He felt heavy, hopeless, and helpless. His depression overtook every aspect of his life. Ed could barely move from one place to another. He leaned in the direction of his imbalance by overeating and oversleeping, and in this way he created increased physiological imbalances.

The personal experience of self is our touchstone with reality. Ed's reality was his depression. He was so mired in the depths of his depression that he believed he would never feel better. Because he had no hope, he possessed no motivation to begin to exercise or to change his eating or sleep patterns. Even though the primary source of Ed's depression was physical *ama*, the mental technique of the TM technique helped him to begin to make necessary changes.

We know that we all relate to our reality, and the first step in overcoming depression is to change the internal experience of self—to expand awareness. Experiencing ourselves as calm and fulfilled is the opposite of feeling depressed. Practicing the TM technique showed Ed that there was a different way to feel. This gave him a glimmer of light, and this was all he needed to feel hopeful. Hope allowed him to become more objective about his circumstances, which gave him an ability to solve problems, and once he began problem solving, he gained a feeling of empowerment. Taking one step at a time, Ed was able to make the changes necessary to overcome his depression.

The TM technique fosters psychological purification. It does not concern itself with negativity of any kind, so the purification occurs effortlessly. Purification of the mind-body is necessary because over time we build up stresses in vulnerable areas of our physiology. These stresses create toxicity in the physiology. The type of toxicity that builds up depends on the particular vulnerabilities of the individual. How and where the toxicity accumulates—whether in the physical, mental, or emotional aspects of our being—can depend on genetic or situational factors. Regardless of the etiology, we all need to make time for physical, mental, and emotional purification on a regular basis. Meditation ensures that this process is attended to.

Ed possessed physical and mental *ama*. When he retired, he became stuck in a rut. He could not adapt to his new role. He dealt with this through overeating and oversleeping. Eventually, the toxicity in his physiology hijacked his total being and he became unable to function. Ed's strengths, which were his steady and stable way of being, were actually getting in his way. He needed to purify both his mind and his body in order to realize his inner strength and to gain flexibility in the face of change.

Practice of the TM technique allowed Ed to experience deeper levels of his mind. The deeper level of the mind is pure consciousness or the intelligence that underlies nature. Pure consciousness is the basis of all progress. Turning inward through meditation brought Ed back to himself. He began to recognize a plethora of emotions and was able to use these emotions as guides to help him navigate his way through life. Increased self-awareness and the release of deep-seated stresses helped Ed to realize his overall potential and to pull himself up from the mud of depression.

Gauging the Benefits of Meditation

Meditating is like brushing your teeth: you must do it daily if you want to have its benefits for life. We wouldn't think of going about our day without brushing our teeth, yet we think nothing of neglecting to "polish" our consciousness through the process of meditation.

We believe that people fail to engage in a systematic and regular meditation practice because they haven't found one that suits them. Perhaps they have tried to meditate, but they were expecting—and did not find—immediate rewards. If you are not meditating regularly, it is time for you to evaluate why.

All we know, at any given time, is our personal experience. This is our only reality. When we begin an efficacious practice, we begin to change. We are usually not even aware of the changes until others mention that they have noticed differences in us. The changes happen rapidly but subtly. The experience can be compared to sitting in the bathtub. One does not know that the water is getting cooler until it feels cold. We don't notice subtle degrees of change until the change becomes pronounced. However, be assured that through meditation you will change, and once the changes begin they continue to manifest.

With an efficacious practice, change will happen in all of the parameters of our life and in all aspects of our being. The effects of a regular practice of meditation are subtle yet profound. In the beginning it is sometimes, but not always, difficult to gauge progress. Over time, for every meditator, the benefits become obvious.

The following five questions will help you to choose a practice and determine how it is progressing.

1. Do you have a meditation practice?
   - Do you engage in a meditation practice regularly and systematically? If not, what keeps you from it?
   - Do you believe that you do not have the time?
   - Do you need external support from a trained teacher?
   - Does the idea of meditating feel overwhelming to you—like yet another thing to do?
   - Does your technique require you to engage in a behavior that is difficult for you, such as concentrating, emptying your mind, or sitting still for long periods of time?

2. Is your meditation practice serving you as an agent of vitality? You will know if your meditation practice is connecting you to consciousness if it has the following effects:
   - It is helping you to expand your awareness.

- It is infusing you with energy and vitality.
- It is purifying your physiology at the physical level. For example, are you getting fewer colds or flus? Do you have an increased level of physical energy?
- It is purifying you at the emotional level. For example, do you sense that old hurts and angers are healing? Are you better able to let things go?
- It is purifying you at the mental level. For example, are you finding that you can think more clearly? Are you coming up with creative ways to solve problems? Have your racing thoughts slowed down or stopped altogether? Are you able to concentrate better?
- It is purifying you at the social level. For example, do you feel an increased sense of enjoyment in being with other people? Are you able to handle interpersonal conflict with steadiness and a clear head?
- It is purifying you at the spiritual level. For example, do you have an ability to view life with a panoramic lens? Are you better able to live in the present moment, to savor life?

3. Are you more resilient in the face of stress?
4. Is meditating giving you the deep rest your physiology needs to function well?
5. Is your meditation something you look forward to because it is easy to do and effortless?

Using the Mind to Relax the Body

The brain, which is so often accused of being the principal cause of depression, can actually be used to uproot the problem. This is possible because your physiology works like an ecosystem. A positive intervention at any point can infuse health and vibrancy to the totality. Although the following mind-body exercises do not offer the ability to transcend thoughts and emotions, they are enjoyable techniques for relaxation. Consider the following three exercises simply as a glimpse of how we can use our brain to relax our body.

Mind-Body Exercise 1: Prana Is Good Medicine

1. Sit comfortably and quietly.

2. Place your palms turned upward on your knees.

3. Relax your jaw, and touch the tongue to the roof of your mouth behind your teeth.

4. Observe your inhalation and exhalation just as they are.

5. In the quiet of your mind, attach *So* to your inhalation and *Hum* to your exhalation.

The power of this exercise rests on understanding the symbolic meaning of this exercise. *So* refers to the Divine; *Hum* refers to the I. When we breathe in (*So*), we are inhaling life (prana) and bringing the goodness of the Universe into us. When we breathe out (*Hum*), we are exhaling our limited individuality (ego), that which no longer serves us so we can make room for more prana. Prana is, after all, divine medicine.

Mind-Body Exercise 2: Evaporating Stress
You will need the following:

- A facial steamer (or vaporizer) or a bowl of steaming hot water

- A timer

- An essential oil of your choice. Our suggestion is that you try an uplifting scent like peppermint, lemon, or eucalyptus for a quick pick-me-up. If you desire a calming effect, consider scents like lavender, sandalwood, or rose.

Instructions

1. Once the facial steamer is ready to be used and you have put a couple of drops of essential oil in the water, set the timer for ten to fifteen minutes. This will allow you to delve into this exercise without worrying about time.

2. Sit comfortably and quietly.

3. Touch your tongue to the roof of your mouth, behind your front teeth.

4. Let your belly soften (yes, give yourself permission to pouch out your belly)—this is a key step. Relaxing your belly will allow your diaphragm and lungs to expand.

5. Enjoy the warm vapor as it enters your nostrils.

6. Enjoy the feel of the warm vapor as it makes contact with the skin of your face.

Take it a few steps further:

7. Allow your lungs to do their thing—breathe—with no effort on your part.

8. Allow your brain to do its thing—think—with no effort on your part.

9. Allow your heart to do its thing—beat inside your chest—with no effort on your part.

10. Your job is simply to pay attention to the sensation of the warm vapor.

11. Notice the sensation of your breath coming into your body (inhalation) and leaving your body (exhalation).

12. During inhalation, your belly should expand, as if creating space for the chest to welcome the air into the lungs.

13. During exhalation, your belly should retract naturally, as if pushing up on the chest to help expel the air out of the lungs.

14. Notice if you are able to take a long and deep breath.

Take it a few steps further:

15. Drop your shoulders, roll your neck gently, and stretch the muscles of your neck.

16. Inhale the warm vapor and follow it into your nose and down the back of the throat. With your imagination, continue its path down the windpipe and into the lungs. As the lungs expand and the diaphragm contracts, your belly should gently push out.

17. Pause for a second or two.

18. Exhale.

19. Now actively relax the muscles of your belly so that your breath can enter your lungs with even more ease.

Take it one step further:

20. If you have mastered the steps above, consider increasing the length of inhalation and exhalation. Be sure to pause in between the two for a comfortable length of time.

There are many benefits to this mind-body exercise.

* It will improve your breathing. By increasing circulation to your sinuses it will improve your breathing in general. This will help you prepare to do the breathing techniques suggested in chapter 11.

* The warm vapors soothe and clean the skin as well.

* You are receiving the benefits of aromatherapy. Depending on the essential oil you choose, the scent will send a distinct message directly to your brain.

Mind-Body Exercise 3: Feeling the Support of Nature

You will need the following:

* A small book that can be placed on your belly

Instructions

1. Lie flat on the floor (not the bed).

2. Notice which parts of your body are making full contact with the floor.

3. During inhalation, your belly should expand, as if creating space for the chest to welcome the air into the lungs.

4. During exhalation, your belly should retract naturally, as if pushing up on the chest to help expel the air out of the lungs.

5. Notice if you are able to take a long and deep breath.

6. Imagine your body melting into the floor. With each inhalation and exhalation allow yourself to melt more and more into the floor. Let the floor support your weight.

7. Notice how inhalations cause your back muscles to press against the floor. Realize that your breath is massaging your muscles from the inside out.

8. Let the pleasurable sensation of your back muscles being massaged motivate you to breathe deeper and deeper.

9. Once you have melted into the floor, place the small book on top of your belly button. Observe the small book rise and fall with each inhalation and exhalation.

10

Breathing: Letting Your Life Force Flow

Whenever I feel blue, I start breathing again.

—L. FRANK BAUM

How we breathe is how we live, it's been said. How we breathe tells the story of our emotional life. Have you ever noticed what happens to your breathing pattern when you feel anxious, stressed, or happy? Developing an ongoing awareness of how we breathe can teach us a great deal about the impact of events on our internal state of being. This is because the brain, the nervous system, the heart, and the lungs all function in unison. Distinct breathing patterns can be identified to match particular moods. For example, notice the shortness of breath induced by a constricted state of mind, one filled with fear and apprehension. A moment of stress can take our breath away.

Changes in the breath are not restricted to negative experiences, however. Consider laughter. A genuine deep belly laugh floods our cells with happy brain chemicals. It forces us to breathe with abandon, deeply and fully, so we release stagnant energy. After a belly laugh, we feel purified, lighter. Perhaps we even feel prompted to view life from a different perspective. The belly laugh has brought us a breath of fresh air, clearing the way for new thoughts.

Breathing involves a coordinated functioning of the nervous and respiratory systems. Consequently, it is referred to as an exercise in neurorespiratory integration. A single breath calls for an intricate interplay of the brain, the nerves that extend throughout the body, the heart, and the lungs. If we put our breath under our voluntary control, we can reset our neuronal networks. In other words, we can use our respiratory system to teach our nervous system how to function; hence, the ability to foster the integration of the mind and the body is at the tip of our nose. We can teach our brain how to perceive life rather than be under the tyranny of our perception. In this way, breathing is an instructional tool for living.

It is a goal of Ayurveda to teach us how to live with expanded awareness, to understand the workings of our mind-body. A wonderful opportunity exists for doing this by learning how to breathe with voluntary intent. Ayurvedic breathing techniques give us a great opportunity to achieve increased mastery of our physiology.

When we are depressed, our breath changes, and this further perpetuates the depressive mood. The Vedic sages knew that the subtle act of breathing serves as an agent of vitality, because it promotes well-being and happiness. Through neurorespiratory integration, we have the capability to assist our physiology in responding to life events. When we manage our breath, we regain control of our emotional responses. We can learn to intentionally blow off steam, take a sigh of relief, and breathe away stress—by integrating mind and breath.

Prana Is Good Medicine

Breathing techniques are potent. Integrating the performance of our respiratory tract with that of our nervous system has an impact on our digestive, immune, circulatory, and endocrine functioning. Neurorespiratory integration influences all bodily functions that operate under involuntary (that is, unconscious) control. Learning to regulate our breath is a major step in regulating our physiology: decreasing blood pressure, slowing heart rate, altering nervous and circulatory pathways, lowering stress-hormone levels, and orchestrating the creation and release of brain chemicals. In fact, these powerful techniques, when used properly and on a regular basis, help us to exert voluntary (that is, conscious) control over our mental and emotional states.

There is even more to a breath than the oxygen that meets the nose, however. Breathing mobilizes our vital energy, our essence. According to the Vedic sages, breath is a conduit of *prana*, the Sanskrit term for "primordial impulse." This is the vibration of life itself and connects our individuality with the cosmos. *Prana* is the vital life force that reigns over the physical, mental, emotional, and spiritual aspects of our being. It is what defines us as living, organic beings.

Reclaiming our vital breath is essential to undoing depression. Breathing is as important as digestion in the regulation of energy in the mind-body. The quality of our breathing influences our energy level, and our energy level has a direct impact on how we feel. Vital breathing infuses life into our seamless energetic network. If breathing is hindered, the body doesn't receive the bursts of vital energy that it needs for happiness to penetrate the veil of depression.

How we metabolize our experiences is revealed to us when we become aware of how our breath changes in response to life's circumstances. Healthy breathing involves the same steps as does the healthy processing of food or experience: ingesting, digesting, assimilating, and eliminating. Through the balanced and efficient acts of inhaling and exhaling, we continuously nourish and purify the physiology.

Consider how you feel when you hold your breath. Physical discomfort and emotional unrest quickly ensue while you are waiting to exhale. Notice the wave of relief that overcomes your body and your mind when you release your breath. Similarly, refusing to inhale has the same effect. The lesson imparted by this observation of the breath is that interrupting the natural balanced flow of vital energy causes distress. Breathing teaches us to fully take in, break down, and absorb that which nourishes us and to release what no longer serves us.

We must learn to breathe fully in order to live fully. We are born into this world with the ability to breathe naturally and effectively. Infants and young children spontaneously take vital breaths. It is not surprising that young beings unabashedly take in all that life has to offer with unmitigated enthusiasm and curiosity. Unfortunately, with difficult life experiences come restricted breathing patterns accompanied by a curbed enthusiasm for new experiences. Rather than maintaining the easy abdominal breathing done by infants, as adults we learn to breathe primarily with our chest. This type of breathing inevitably increases the stress and tension levels in our body. Our task is to unlearn this pattern and to restore our rightful state of vitality by relearning what we knew as infants.

Breathing exercises offer access to our physiology's natural healing pharmacy. With regular practice, these techniques provide a healthy substitute for a glass of wine or antianxiety medication. Like a strong cup of coffee, breathing exercises can energize by strengthening the brain and the nervous system, but without the deleterious side effects of caffeine. Breaths dissipate brain fog. Better than any antidepressant, whether synthetically or naturally produced, a vital breath can blow the blues away.

By increasing the oxygen flow to the brain, breathing techniques also increase blood flow and nourish brain tissues. This is basically how breathing techniques resolve a depressive mood. Specific techniques can be employed to address more unique imbalances in the physiology. Let's look at how specific breathing techniques work to resolve the different archetypes of depression.

Airy Depression: Calming the Winds of Change

Arial felt anchorless in the world. Anxiety accompanied her depressive mood. Her responses to a series of abrupt changes in a short period triggered a derangement in Vata dosha. Her nervous system was deeply affected. Insomnia, hypervigilance, constant worrying, and hyperactivity were indicative of her state of physiological imbalance.

How was Arial breathing? Watching her as she talked about her sadness, we noticed that her chest seemed to close in on itself, as if it were guarding her heart. As she expressed the sadness she was experiencing, her belly became rigid, and slow sips of breath entered through her mouth. When she was asked to describe her daily routine, erratic spurts of air shot out of her mouth. Arial's breathing patterns were a noticeable sign of how her physiology was functioning.

Our breathing patterns reflect our suffering. Will alone cannot change the way we feel, but we can will ourselves to breathe differently. In doing so, we change our physiology, triggering the transformation of our mental, emotional, and physical health.

Shallow breathing was a symptom as well as a cause of Arial's anxious state of mind. Choppy, irregular breathing causes an inadequate exchange of oxygen and carbon dioxide, which in turn causes the heart to pump faster to oxygenate the blood. Such an increase in heart rate enhanced Arial's experience of anxiety. With her heart pumping, her thoughts racing, and her emotions out of control, her vitality simply evaporated from her physiology.

As the force of her anxiety grew, the efficacy of her breathing diminished. Caught in a tornado of mental agitation, Arial was literally unable to catch her breath. Her shallow sips of air were not giving her physiology the support it needed. Nor were they triggering the release of biochemicals necessary for her nervous system to function in a calm and healing mode.

Gaining awareness was a key step for Arial. It was most important that she become cognizant of her breathing patterns. She quickly realized that she was in the habit of breathing through her mouth, especially when she was feeling anxious. Arial learned that this was an ineffective way to breathe. She was not taking in enough oxygen (nourishing her cells) or expelling enough carbon dioxide (purifying her cells) to maintain her physical health. Nor were her breathing patterns promoting positive mental health and dispelling anxiety.

The first step in training Arial's nervous system to function in a calm and healing mode was to teach her to breathe through her nose rather than her mouth. The mouth is for eating and speaking, and the nose is for breathing—this is according to both the Vedic sages and modern scientists. Mouth breathing, at best, fills only the upper lobes of the lungs. Mouth breathing has the same effect as gasping for air: it sends a message to the brain that the physiology is in a state of stress; the physiology then responds by going into overdrive.

When air enters through the nose, it affects the part of the brain that sends a message of relaxation to the nervous system. A deep full breath also ensures that oxygen is being delivered to the lower lobes of the lungs. As the lower lobes expand to accept the gush of air, stretch receptors are activated. These receptors trigger the release of biochemicals that ground one's mental torrents yet invigorate the physiology. This is a great antidote for a physiology that is overcome with anxiety and exhaustion.

The second step was to improve Arial's breathing efficiency. For this, she learned a specific breathing exercise called Three-Part Breathing. (See the description later in this chapter.) This technique fully ventilated all of the lobes in her lungs, ensuring an adequate exchange of oxygen and carbon dioxide. The rhythmic intake and release of air also induced a sense of emotional calm and physical stability. With Three-Part Breathing, Arial nourished her cells and vented her emotions.

Another technique that Arial learned is Alternate-Nostril Breathing. (See the description later in this chapter.) She reported that this technique lowered the noise level in her head. In fact, scientific research has determined that Alternate-Nostril Breathing improves the bilateral functioning of the brain. Arial quickly realized that she could use this exercise to prepare herself to do mental work; even a few minutes of doing this exercise primed her thinking abilities.

Arial began and ended her day with five minutes of these calming breathing exercises. The benefits of the practice were quick to manifest. Almost immediately she noticed that she could call on her ability to breathe deeply and fully throughout her day to manage her emotions. Getting caught in traffic became an opportunity to practice these exercises rather than a reason to panic.

However, there is more to this story. Since the physiology comprises a network of interdependent systems, inefficient breathing can set the stage for depression as well as other physical ailments. For instance, when breathing is shallow or irregular, the organs do not work to their full capacity. Shallow breathing decreases the blood flow to the organs in the abdomen, thus compromising all digestive functions. It is common to find that people who are anxious and depressed also have digestive problems.

Arial's depressed appetite mirrored her sad mood. Her nonexistent desire for food reflected her weak digestive fire. When she did eat, bloating and constipation occurred. Once she began practicing the breathing techniques, her digestion improved. This improvement was directly related to increased blood circulation to her abdomen.

The muscles around the solar plexus overlie our intestines and other digestive organs. When we breathe deeply, we cause these muscles to press up and down on our organs of digestion, which creates a gentle stimulation. Deep breathing also ensures that the diaphragm, a muscular sheet that is partly attached to the liver, fully expands and contracts. As the diaphragm moves up and down, the liver and other internal organs are mobilized. This action causes stagnant blood to move from the liver and the intestines to the heart and the lungs, where it can be purified.

Eventually, as Arial's breathing gained fullness, she learned a more advanced breathing technique called the Humming Breath (see the description later in this chapter). The humming creates a vibration that is soothing to the nervous system while at the same time invigorating the glands in the region of the neck, especially the thyroid. Arial noted enthusiastically that the breathing exercises she was doing were profoundly helpful: "I understand that these exercises affect me physically. Certainly, they calm and energize me. I feel better, eat better, sleep better, and think better."

Burning Depression: Diffusing the Smoke

As part of Barbara's imbalance in Pitta dosha, intensity and pressure marked every aspect of her being. At the same time, she was burning to cry because she perceived her competitive edge slipping away from her. A wall of anger and resentment served as a dam to hold back the flood of sadness and disappointment. "The dragon lady," as Barbara laughingly referred to herself, needed a way to dissipate her excess physical and emotional heat.

How was Barbara breathing? She perceived herself as being held back, and her breathing reflected this internal perception. It was as though her lungs were trapped like prisoners inside her rib cage. Her breath was pushy, as if her lungs were expanding in an attempt to blow down the sequestering walls. The depth of her inhalations was impressive at times. Nevertheless, the energy she drew in did not appear to flow throughout her physiology. This lack of energy flow was responsible, in part, for her headaches and the constant tension in her neck and back. Pain is, after all, the body's signal that an energy blockage exists in the physiology. Barbara's breathing pattern was similar to the way she was operating in life: pushing her way through things, with her foot stuck on the accelerator.

Logical and practical, Barbara took an interest in breathing techniques after she learned about the ills that come from inefficient breathing. Barbara needed to find a natural, comfortable breathing pattern that would diffuse the excessive heat she felt in her mind-body and soothe her feelings of irritability and frustration.

It was important for Barbara to focus on lengthening her exhalations, so she practiced inhaling through her nose and exhaling through a straw. As her exhalations lengthened, her inhalations became deeper. Barbara noticed that this breathing practice was effective in diminishing the buildup of tension in her body. She no longer felt as if she were wearing a suit of armor.

Barbara then learned a breathing exercise called Breath of Victory (see the description later in this chapter). Breath of Victory expels the excess internal heat that is created by unnecessary mental friction. It balances the heart and the lungs, cools the physiology, and dissipates internal constriction. It reduces wear and tear on the physiology by improving respiratory efficiency, decreasing inflammatory processes, and reducing cellular oxidation. It is no surprise that Olympic athletes are coached in this manner of breathing as part of their training.

Breath of Victory enhanced Barbara's ability to be successful by helping her to function at maximum capacity. In time, she noticed that she naturally shifted into this breathing technique whenever she found herself becoming aggravated, be it on the tennis court or at work. Triumphantly, Barbara exclaimed, "I can go the extra mile without the burnout!"

Barbara also learned a technique called Cooling Breath (see the description later in this chapter). This breathing exercise quickly relieves the physiology of excess heat and is therefore a great summertime breathing exercise, but it also helps us to tolerate the hot, dry, artificial heat that is emitted in buildings during the winter. Cooling Breath helps us to keep a cool head, even after we have been sitting for many hours at the computer, "heating" our minds with mental activity.

The technique functions like a pressure valve, allowing the gradual and controlled release of internal pressure (like the kind that builds up when anger swells).

Cooling Breath brought Barbara two gifts: First, it gave her yet another tool to help her achieve physiological balance. Second, because she found herself frequently availing herself of this technique, she developed a greater awareness of how affected she was by her external environment.

Earthy Depression: Stoking the Internal Fire

Ed needed to liven up. He wanted to do so, but he did not know how. Weighed down by his sadness as well as his flesh, he did not see a way out of the profound depression he was experiencing. An imbalance in Kapha dosha had transformed him into a couch potato. His digestive fire was so low that he was unable to digest either food or experience. Ed's physiology had become a storage space for physical, emotional, and mental *ama*. This gunk was clogging up his mind-body, blocking the flow of his life force, and making joy unattainable.

How was Ed breathing? On inhalation, his belly drew inward, and on exhalation, it relaxed outward; this is the reverse of a healthy breathing pattern. Ed's extreme lack of motivation was evident in his breathing pattern. Watching him, we could see that his body collapsed with every breath. He appeared to be holding his breath when he talked, which made his voice sound like a whisper. Unable to mobilize his energy, he felt paralyzed and apathetic.

Ed needed to move and be moved. He had learned that invigorating action increases the depth of breathing. The therapeutic goal was to help him experience the reverse: that consciously deepening the breath invigorates the physiology.

Bellows Breath (*Bastrika*, in Sanskrit) is an empowering breathing exercise (see the description later in this chapter). The name refers to the tool that a blacksmith uses to enhance a fire. By igniting one's metabolic fire, Bellows Breath melts away *ama*, the gunk that hinders the free flow of vital energy throughout the physiology.

Bellows Breath was instrumental in boosting Ed's energy level. A few rounds of this technique first thing in the morning nudged Ed to get moving. Throughout the day, whenever he felt the onset of lethargy, doing this breathing exercise gave him a natural lift. As he performed it several times a day on a regular basis, Ed began to notice an increase in his general level of energy. The exercise fanned his digestive fire, causing his metabolism to burn more intensely, so he began to lose weight. Naps after meals became a thing of the past. When the digestive fire is high, we digest efficiently, and after eating a meal we feel energetic rather than groggy.

The second exercise that Ed learned was Head-Shining Breath, or *Kapalabathi* in Sanskrit (see the description later in this chapter). Ed was eager to learn a breathing technique that promised to clear the cobwebs from his head and make his brain shine as bright as it did when he was not suffering from a depressive episode. So efficient was this technique that the engineer in him wanted to know how it worked.

Bellows Breath and Head-Shining Breath both balance Kapha dosha. They work by quickly oxygenating the blood. Rapid exhalations propelled by strong abdominal contractions dispel stale air from the lower lobes of the lungs, allowing for oxygen-rich blood to take its place. The strong abdominal contractions also strengthen the abdominal muscles and massage the internal organs.

In terms of depression, Bellows Breath and Head-Shining Breath stimulate the network of nerves in the abdominal cavity that regulates digestion and metabolism. These exercises trigger the release of two stimulating substances: epinephrine and norepinephrine. The latter, you may recall, is one of the brain chemicals that is deficient in an Earthy Depression. Increasing the levels of this biochemical in the bloodstream uplifts mood and improves physiological performance in every way.

Breathercise for Life

The following "breathercises" (breath exercises) are simple, proven techniques that can be easily implemented at any time or place. They will raise your energy level when you are depleted and calm your physiology when you need to focus or relax. They will do this by helping you to regulate your physiology. Eventually, you will be in the driver's seat—pressing the accelerator when you need invigoration and putting your foot firmly on the brake when you need to catch your breath (literally and otherwise!).

Please note that the following breathercises build on one another. The assumption is that you have mastered Three-Part Breathing before going on to Alternate-Nostril Breathing, Humming Breath, Breath of Victory, or Cooling Breath. Head-Shining Breath and Bellows Breath are advanced techniques that require you to have command of full diaphragmatic breathing before attempting them.

Three-Part Breathing

This is a cleansing and balancing breathing exercise. It involves consciously filling three different areas of your lungs. Start by filling the lower parts as you watch your belly expand, move up through the middle chest region, and finish in the upper spaces with a gentle lifting of the collarbone. Shift your intention as you direct your breath, and you will notice a deeply releasing, expanding effect as tension dissolves from the body.

Instructions

1. Stand or sit erect with a straight spine.
2. Inhale steadily through your nose.
3. Fill the lower part of your lungs. Your belly will push out as it expands.
4. Fill the middle part of your lungs. Your lower ribs, breastbone (sternum), and chest will push out as they expand.
5. Fill the highest part of your lungs. Draw in the abdomen slightly as your collarbone expands.
6. Exhale twice as slowly as you inhaled. The belly will naturally contract as it returns to its natural position.
7. Complete your exhalation by letting the abdomen draw slightly inward and upward.

What will this breathercise do for you?

- Increase calmness
- Enhance detoxification of blood-borne toxins through the lungs
- Enhance oxygenation of the blood, which benefits the liver and other organs of digestion
- Reduce physical tension in the abdomen, chest, and back
- Increase intake of vital energy (*prana*) from the air

Alternate-Nostril Breathing

According to the Vedic sages, there are approximately seventy-two thousand tubelike channels traveling through the body called *nadis*. This ancient concept correlates well to the modern notion that nerves function like channels carrying electrical impulses throughout the body. It is of vital importance to keep our energetic pathways clear of obstructions if we are to maximize the flow of *prana* to our mind-body. This breathercise is essential in calming a racing mind and an accelerating heart rate.

Instructions

1. Sit with your spine erect and spend thirty seconds doing Three-Part Breathing.
2. When you feel ready, close your eyes and take a deep breath. Hold it for as long as you feel comfortable.
3. Place your right hand up to your nose and close your right nostril with your thumb.
4. Inhale slowly and deeply through your left nostril.
5. Once your inhalation is complete, allow it to remain in your lungs for a few seconds.
6. Open your right nostril by removing your thumb from it while also closing your left nostril by placing your forefinger against it.
7. Exhale completely through the right nostril.
8. Repeat this cycle for approximately two minutes, or longer if you are comfortable.

An example of Alternate-Nostril Breathing

What will this breathercise do for you?

- Coordinate functioning of the two hemispheres of the brain
- Improve thinking and concentration
- Induce mental clarity
- Balance Vata dosha

Humming Breath (*Brahmari pranayama*)

In Sanskrit, *Brahmar* means "bee." This breathercise is called Brahmari because a buzzing sound, similar to that of a bee, is produced. The buzzing sound causes a resonant vibration in the head and neck. This vibration in turn creates a soothing effect on the physiology by stimulating the parasympathetic nervous system, which induces muscular, physical, mental, and emotional relaxation.

Instructions

1. Sit in any comfortable position with the spine and the head held erect for a minimum of one minute. Gently close your eyes and bring awareness to your body. Keep your lips together, your jaw relaxed, and your teeth separated slightly.

2. Cover your ears by either plugging them with your index fingers or pressing your earflaps with the palms of your hands while keeping your elbows pointed outward from your sides.

3. Partially close your glottis (the back of your throat) as you inhale through both nostrils, making a high-pitched humming sound that comes from the back of your throat. At first it may sound like a snore. (Note: As you get used to controlling the flow of air through the glottis, you may want to just focus on taking in a full, deep breath and then build up to making a humming or snoring sound. The emphasis of this exercise is on the exhalation.)

4. Exhale slowly, emitting a sound like a humming bee.

5. Focus your awareness on how the vibration of the sound reverberates through your head and neck.

6. Practice for a couple of minutes, building up to ten to fifteen minutes. Take resting breaths in between as needed.

   What will this breathercise do for you?

* Help reduce stress and anxiety by activating the parasympathetic nervous system
* Clear and vibrate the head and neck
* Invigorate the glands in the throat area, especially the thyroid gland
* Balance hormonal secretion
* Trigger serotonin release
* Help release tension in the head and neck, thereby preventing and relieving headaches
* Tone the nervous system and dilate the blood vessels in the brain, increasing blood flow
* Help address insomnia

Breath of Victory (*Ujjayi* Breath)

This breathercise is similar to Three-Part Breath. The major difference is that this technique involves slightly constricting the back of the throat during inhalations and exhalations.

Instructions

1. Inhale through your nose while slightly constricting your epiglottis (throat) as if making a gentle "e" sound.

2. Exhale through your nose as you maintain the slight constriction in your throat. (Your breathing should sound like a gentle ocean wave.)

What will this breathercise do for you?

- Increase the efficiency of the vessels that carry blood to the lungs and the heart
- Create a calming influence that dissipates anxiety
- Clear the mind of stress. (In fact, this breath comes naturally to you when you want to compose yourself in the face of a sudden stress.)

Cooling Breath (*Shitali* or *Sitkari*)

This breathercise is beneficial for people with an imbalance in Pitta dosha. It physically cools down the physiology that has been exposed to high temperatures. It also works to remove heated emotions and agitated thoughts. It creates space in the mind to receive a cool breath of fresh air. When this breathing exercise is done through a curled tongue, it is called *shitali*; if the tongue is not curled, it is called *sitkari*.

Instructions

1. Sit with your spine erect.
2. Observe the natural incoming and outgoing process of your breathing for a few minutes.
3. Curl the sides of your tongue, creating a circular pattern. If you can't curl the sides of your tongue, press your tongue against your teeth and skip steps 4 and 6.
4. Extend your tongue outside your mouth.
5. As you breathe, gently bring the air in through the central passageway of your tongue. Imagine you are drinking in the air through a straw (your curled tongue or your slightly opened teeth).
6. As the final part of your inhalation is reaching completion, bring your tongue inside your mouth and close your lips.
7. Hold your breath for as long as is comfortable.
8. Release the breath through your nose gently and slowly.
9. Repeat this cycle up to ten times.

What will this breathercise do for you?

- Decrease Pitta dosha
- Remove heated emotions and agitated thoughts
- Create space in the mind to receive a cool breath of fresh air

Precautionary Note: The strong abdominal contractions required for doing Head-Shining Breath and Bellows Breath are contraindicated if you are menstruating or pregnant. Additionally, because the abdominal contractions increase the pressure inside your thorax, it may exacerbate respiratory or cardiovascular conditions, so proceed with caution. Individuals with hiatal hernias, abdominal disorders, or herniated (slipped) disks that are actively causing pain should refrain from doing these exercises as well. Ideally, these exercises should be done one hour before a meal or two hours after a meal.

Head-Shining Breath (*Kapalabathi*)

This breathercise sparks the fire in your mind-body and cleanses the entire system, not just the respiratory passages. Flooding the physiology with *prana*-filled oxygen, it uplifts emotions and invigorates the body.

Instructions

1. Spend a couple of minutes doing Three-Part Breathing so that you are taking in full, deep breaths. This will create space in the upper body in preparation for this exercise.

2. Sit with your spine erect. Throughout the exercise keep your face and neck free of tension, but maintain your torso strong and steady. The focus of this exercise will be a forceful pumping motion (abdominal muscle contractions) in your navel area.

3. Exhale actively through your nose by snapping your belly toward your spine (contract your belly).

4. As your abdominal muscles revert back to their natural position (expand), you will inhale air passively through your nose. In other words, your body simply receives the breath as a result of the natural expansion of your abdominal muscles.

5. Be sure to inhale fully before taking another active inhalation.

6. The exhalations should come every two or three seconds. The important thing is to focus on contracting the belly forcefully in order to create a full active exhalation.

7. Repeat for one to three minutes.

What will this breathercise do for you?

* Ignite digestive fire
* Stimulate the vagus nerve: the cranial nerve that has a strong and general impact on the physiology, especially the heart and the digestive system
* Increase physical and mental endurance
* Increase resistance to stress through the probable release of "feel-good" hormones such as oxytocin and prolactin
* Reduce addictive impulses
* Release toxins from the mucous membranes of the lungs
* Increase output of epinephrine and norepinephrine
* Balance the autonomic nervous system

Bellows Breath (*Bastrika*)

Bellows Breath consists of a series of rapid, powerful, diaphragmatic rounds of breathing and is an excellent tonic any time your energy begins to flag. It is similar to Head-Shining Breath with the exception of the pace. Unlike in Head-Shining Breath, in this breathercise, you are asked to exhale at a pace of one breath per second for one minute at a time.

If you experience slight light-headedness from this practice, it is a signal that your physiology has not fully acclimated to the high levels of oxygen that this exercise is infusing into it. If this is the case, stop, rest a few minutes, and try again. Ayurveda always recommends that you work within your comfort zone. A minor tingling sensation may also occur because this exercise increases nerve tone. The tingling will subside in time.

Instructions

1. Sit with your spine erect.
2. Inhale forcefully through your nose and expand your belly.

3. Exhale forcefully through your nose by snapping your belly toward your spine.

4. Take swift and powerful inhalations and exhalations of even lengths that last about one second each.

5. Do not pause between inhaling and exhaling. (You should sound like "the little engine that could.")

6. Continue this practice by doing cycles of ten breaths.

7. Rest by doing Three-Part Breathing for a couple of seconds.

8. The total practice time should be three to five minutes.

Eventually, the goal is to practice this exercise at a pace of one breath per second for one minute nonstop. In this case, two or three one-minute rounds should suffice with a short break in between each round.

What will this breathercise do for you?

* Ignite digestive fire
* Stimulate the vagus nerve: the cranial nerve that has a strong and general impact on the physiology, especially the heart and the digestive system
* Increase physical and mental endurance
* Increase resistance to stress through the probable release of "feel-good" hormones such as oxytocin and prolactin
* Reduce addictive impulses
* Release toxins from the mucous membranes of the lungs
* Increase output of epinephrine and norepinephrine
* Balance the autonomic nervous system

Myths That Take Our Breath Away

Myth 1: Relaxing your belly makes it bigger. Relaxing your belly when you breathe won't weaken your muscles and cause you to have a sloppy girth. On the contrary, when we let the belly expand and contract freely, we promote weight loss. This added bonus happens because letting the belly move in rhythm with the breath allows the blood to circulate freely to fat cells, driving in nutrients and flushing out toxic waste products. In addition, the abdominal muscles, like all other muscles, must completely relax between contractions in order to function properly. We encourage you to let go, let your breath move your belly, and experience both the relaxation and the contraction phases of the breath cycle. As you do this, you will be breathing away your depression—and helping your physique.

Myth 2: Holding in the belly supports the back. The breath is actually a tool that massages the spine. The gentle expansive force that is created when you breathe tractions the spine: each inhalation and exhalation expands and contracts the bones of the spine, generating movement and creating space between them. This process reduces the likelihood of pinched nerves, bone degeneration, and arthritic conditions. Allowing the abdomen to move when you breathe promotes a healthy back. The cushions between the vertebrae work like shock absorbers and function like sponges. They remain thick and healthy by absorbing fluid. Since there is no direct blood supply to the disks after approximately the age of twenty, the only way to make fluid enter the disks is through physical movement. When we breathe expansively, we not only perk up our spirit, we enliven our backbone.

Strong abdominal muscles stabilize the spine. Abdominal muscles should be used, especially when lifting, to support the back. However, keeping the abdomen contracted all the time increases the tension and stiffness in the lower back muscles; if you suffer from back pain, it can increase your pain levels. The diaphragm attaches to the front of the lumbar vertebrae, so any constriction in this important breathing muscle will immediately be reflected in the function of the spine. Allowing your abdomen to move when you breathe is the most effective way to keep your back healthy.

Check Your Breathing Pattern

How we breathe is how we live, so let's check on how you are doing. Sit quietly and notice your breath. Bring your awareness to your breathing pattern and answer the following questions:

Are you inhaling through your nose or through your mouth?

Through which nostril are you predominantly breathing?

Does your abdomen expand during inhalation?

Do you feel as though a wave of *prana*-filled air enters and exits your body?

The answers to the above questions will help you to determine the health of your essential breath. Natural breathing occurs like this:

1. Breath enters through the nose.

2. The abdomen actively expands during inhalation and passively contracts during exhalation.

3. There is a steady rhythmic flow to the cycle of a breath; it travels through the whole body like a shimmering wave, leaving a sense of relaxation in its wake.

This is the way Mother Nature intended for us to breathe. If, however, you have acquired an inefficient breathing pattern, you can easily unlearn this. By placing conscious attention on your breath, you will be able to restore your natural and healthy breathing pattern.

11

Exercise: Moving Your Spirit

If we could give every individual the right amount of
nourishment and exercise, not too little and
not too much, we would have found the
safest way to health.

—HIPPOCRATES

The Vedic sages considered exercise to be an agent of vitality. Not only did they understand the power of moving your body, they also knew how to maximize movement's antidepressant benefits. Modern scientists echo their beliefs and assert that exercise is indeed an antidote for the blues. Consider the following scientific data:

- Exercise can lead to a steady decrease in depression. A study of depressed women measured the impact of exercise. The interventions included the following: (1) aerobic exercises, (2) relaxing exercises, and (3) no exercises. Only the women in the group that practiced aerobic exercises improved their mood.

- Exercise has greater long-lasting effects than medication. A study compared the impact of antidepressant medication, exercise, and a combination of medication and exercise on depressive

143

How Much Exercise Is Enough to Feel Better?

There is confirmation that twenty minutes of moderate exercise will boost your mood. Researchers studied people who exercised for different lengths of time. With ten minutes of exercising, the individuals experienced less depression and felt less confused. At twenty minutes there was greater relief, and at thirty minutes the relief was no greater than for twenty minutes. The conclusion: twenty minutes of exercise will lift your spirits, but if you have limited time, you will benefit from a quick ten-minute walk.

symptoms. Sixteen weeks into the study, all three groups showed similar improvements. Six months later, however, the exercise-only group was doing better than the other two groups. Less than one-third of the medication-free exercisers had depressive relapses, whereas more than half of the patients in the medication group and the combination medication-exercise group had relapses.

- Anxiety is significantly diminished while exercising; this effect continues for the next several hours.
- A meta-analysis of anxiety-reducing exercise studies has shown that twenty minutes of exercise is sufficient to induce the natural tranquilizing effect.

Shaking Off the Blues: Motion, the Magic Potion

There is no doubt that moving will shake up your spirit and oust depression from your physiology. The Vedic sages knew that exercise, as an agent of vitality, helps us to ward off depression in the following ways:

- Exercise ignites your metabolic furnace.
- Exercise helps to optimize mental and physical digestion. It increases your brain's ability to create and utilize serotonin,

dopamine, and norepinephrine, among other vital chemicals that affect lucid thinking. It increases the availability of all other body chemicals, such as hormones and enzymes. Exercise massages your internal organs, making them more efficient in their performance.

- Regular and appropriate exercise keeps *ama* (toxins) from becoming lodged in the mind-body.

- Deeper breathing and increased heart rate lead to greater blood flow. All vital organs, including the brain, benefit from improved oxygenation. Fully oxygenated blood provides more nutrients to the cells and clears more toxins from the system. Oxygen is the key ingredient in the generation of energy by the cells.

- Exercise promotes the free flow of the natural intelligence that underlies physical processes.

According to Ayurveda, stress hinders the flow of natural intelligence. Western scientific research has shown that exercise increases body temperature and thus induces a more relaxed physiological state. The correct type and amount of physical activity boosts our ability to respond to stress. It makes the stress hormone, cortisol, available for the body to use as nature intended: for the short run, in small amounts, and for protective purposes. Cortisol becomes a problem only when it is secreted continuously and for extended periods. In that case it functions to suppress the immune system.

If a new drug came on the market that helped depression as much as exercise does, people would be clamoring for it. A truly natural antidepressant, physical movement (exercise) changes the profile of chemicals in your brain and your body. It causes mood-brightening brain chemicals—such as serotonin, dopamine, and norepinephrine—to be released in a balanced and well-orchestrated way. If you choose an exercise program that fits your physical needs, there are no side effects, only the benefit of making you feel physically strong and mentally stable.

Moving our body moves our spirit. Exercise infuses lightness, strength, and vitality into the body, mind, and spirit, according to the Vedic sages. Modern science agrees: a daily infusion of oxygen—twenty minutes of exercise—helps to counteract the ills of depression. Why, then, do many of us dread exercising? Why is it so hard to get moving, especially when we are feeling down in the dumps? The problem lies in finding a positive way to integrate movement into our daily life. This is where the modern concept of exercise has gone awry.

You won't find the Vedic sages huffing and puffing at the gym. According to Ayurveda, exercise offers more than cardiovascular and musculoskeletal health and burning excess calories to lose weight. Exercise should never be punishment for enjoying the delights of food. Rather, it is intended to re-create the flow of energy in the body and thus aid the body's regenerative processes.

Our physiology is changing constantly. The process of cellular turnover never stops; cells are continuously re-creating themselves. Exercise helps this natural process to take place in an optimal manner by priming the entire physiology.

A health-promoting exercise program will activate our internal fountain of joy. Both Galen, the father of modern medicine, and the Vedic sages advise, "First do no harm." Applying this adage to a truly effective exercise program means the following:

* Plan on having "playouts," not workouts. If you don't enjoy it, you will not do it.
* Instead of "no pain, no gain," make your motto "no pain, much gain."
* Use your awareness about your internal needs in choosing your exercise program.
* Choose exercises wisely; the objective is to create and maintain your individual doshic balance.

Arial's Story: Trying to Run Away from Depression

Speedy, restless Arial is light on her feet and limber in her body. Her natural proclivity is to engage in physical activity. She especially loved running, because it gave her a reprieve from the stress that was incarcerating her mind. Unfortunately, wherever Arial ran, her depression followed.

Arial began experiencing insomnia. Over time the bouts of sleeplessness increased. In addition, she noticed that her joints felt cold and dry, and ached throughout the day. Believing that exercise would be an antidote, Arial boosted her daily run from three miles to five. Unfortunately, her anxiety and feelings of restlessness increased in intensity as well, as if trying to catch up with her. She was wiped out by her exercise routine.

Arial was suffering from an imbalance in Vata dosha. Her symptoms were telltale signs that Vata was aggravated, and her exercise program was doing more harm than good. It is human nature to lean in the direction of our imbalances, and the more wiped out Arial became, the more she saw increasing her exercise routine as a solution. When she understood the dangers of overexercising, she slowly but steadily began to cut back on the type, amount, and intensity of her pattern. Arial started doing slow-paced jogging and brisk walking. If done in moderation, both have a calming effect on Vata.

Two Ayurvedic principles aptly describe what was wrong with Arial's exercise program: (1) we all lean toward our imbalances, and (2) like increases like. From this perspective, Arial likes running because it fits with her internal sense of self: being in a hurry, feeling restless, and wanting to accomplish things quickly. At the same time, running and moving quickly threw her further out of balance, into a chronic state of anxiety. The internal mirrors the external, and vice versa.

For Arial, over time, high-paced strenuous activities like running increased a physiological imbalance in Vata dosha. In other words, running stressed her already frayed nervous system. Consider the effect of this on her mental capacity. When she was in balance, Arial had a quick mind and an energetic way of being; out of balance, however, her thinking became somewhat erratic and impulsive. Over time, her anxiety manifested as increased forgetfulness and difficulty concentrating. This condition created fertile ground for making mistakes, which snowballed into insomnia, racing thoughts, worry, anxiety, fear, the feeling of not being good enough, the feeling of being out of control, and deep sadness. Nevertheless, addicted to the quick release of stress that exercise gave her, she was unaware of the deleterious effects that running was having on her physiology.

An imbalance in Vata dosha causes one's physical energy to come in bursts. Individuals with this imbalance are in danger of pushing themselves beyond their physical capabilities. They often lack the stamina for rugged continuous exercise, such as long-distance running or competitive sports. If they push themselves past the point of fatigue, they are in danger of creating an exhausted physiology, which is a precursor of depression.

It was important for Arial to develop an awareness of her body's capacity and not to overexert herself. She needed to listen to what her body was saying and not push past the breaking point. It had been common for her to exercise until her muscles burned and trembled and she began to sweat profusely and breathe heavily.

The body appreciates acts of physical kindness. Light aerobic exercise and activities that emphasize balance and flexibility, such as yoga and Pilates, settled Arial's nervous system. Her mind-body was soothed, and her Vata dosha became balanced.

Seek Rhythm Rather Than Vigor

A Vata imbalance manifests as an anxious depression. This archetype of depression corresponds to the Western scientific notion of a serotonin-deficient depression. Nervousness, sleeplessness, and excessive worry are the hallmark traits of an Airy Depression. Vata energies are the easiest to disrupt, but fortunately they are also the easiest to rebalance.

As we saw with Arial, when it comes to balancing Vata, vigor is less important than rhythm. If you see yourself in Arial's story, don't overexert your body or overstimulate your mind. Seek activities that embed rhythm into the physiology. Take heed of the following serotonin-boosting activities.

Do anything outdoors that is relaxing and enjoyable, such as:

* Moderate-paced walking
* Biking
* Canoeing
* Hiking
* Golfing

Do anything indoors that involves rhythmic, soothing, and gentle motion, including:

* Simple stretching
* Gentle yoga

> ### Three Serotonin-Boosting Principles for the Racing Body and Mind
>
> 1. Engage in gentle, rhythmic, or repetitive movement.
> 2. Maximize the opportunity to be out in a setting near nature and water.
> 3. Maximize your exposure to heat: generate it internally or use warm clothing.

- Pilates
- Tai chi or qigong
- Light aerobic activity (about twenty to thirty minutes daily)

How Overexercising Can Lead to Burnout

The exhaustion that is experienced from a long history of overexercising can not only drive Vata dosha out of balance but also impact Kapha dosha. As a self-preserving mechanism, the body hijacks the racing mind. In an effort to rebalance the physiology, the mind-body shuts down in order to get the rest that it needs to recover from exhaustion, be it mental, physical, or emotional. Consequently, it is common for a person to experience a bout of Earthy Depression after an extended period of Vata Depression. Kapha dosha compensates for the imbalance in Vata dosha, infusing the mind-body with heaviness. It is no surprise that the person flops listlessly on the couch.

Excessive exercise can also overheat the physiology, leading to a Pitta overload. Like a fan turned on high in front of an open fire, Vata can either blow out the flame or disperse the fire. Unfortunately, since we lean in the direction of our imbalances, a person with excess Pitta mentally reacts by becoming overly competitive, even with themselves. They set ever higher performance expectations, run extra miles, and pump heavier weights. The internal flames eventually begin to burn not only the mind but also the body. Inflammatory diseases frequently develop, such as ulcers, colitis, boils, and heart disease. At this point, the natural intelligence of the mind-body moves to correct the imbalance.

Because Kapha is the dosha that cools the physiology, it rises as a natural physiological response when the mind-body is faced with burnout through excess Pitta. As Kapha rises, a person begins to feel like a wet blanket. Sadness and lethargy become constant companions. Because of the lack of energy, goals aren't accomplished with the usual rate of efficiency. In response, waves of anger and irritability roll in. It's important to understand that becoming a couch potato is the mind-body's way of recovering a healthy state of being. With Ayurvedic interventions the root cause of the depression can be remedied.

Barbara's Story: Burning Down the House

On good days, Barbara finds the intensity of her work, the deadlines and the pressure, intoxicatingly good. Driven to succeed, she brings determination to all her endeavors—exercise included. She often feels bored by physical activity that lacks challenges. Walking, for example, is most unattractive to her. A fierce tennis match or a head-banging round of squash is more her style.

Exercise was initially a way for Barbara to let off steam, but the workouts turned hotter as she carried her resentment and irritability to the gym. The more frustrated she felt at work and at home, the more intensely she worked out. Barbara was burning her body to the ground. She was getting migraine headaches more frequently. Her skin was irritated, and she developed unexplained rashes. Her eyes were more red and irritated than usual. From the Ayurvedic perspective, these are all symptoms of an imbalance in Pitta dosha.

Barbara's Burning Depression was creating great difficulty for her. It was thwarting her success in her personal and professional life. Resentful people do not have a very good chance of succeeding in the workplace, and early-morning awakenings don't help one to be on top of things during the day.

A Burning Depression is marked by frustration and irritability at every level of the being. From the Western medical perspective, an excess of Pitta dosha translates into an increase in dopamine and a decrease in serotonin. Barbara's aggressive exercise program was further elevating dopamine and depleting serotonin. Her body was chronically tense.

Convincing a person with a Pitta imbalance that physical activity can undo depression is not usually difficult. Like Barbara, most require exercise in order to feel good. The difficult part comes in persuading them to find a way of moving that involves only pleasure and not an attempt to reach a predetermined goal.

Pushing too hard or getting caught up in the heat of competition are the typical downfalls of individuals with aggravated Pitta. They tend to like sports because of the skill level required and the competition involved. Their drive and single-mindedness can be such that they may not even be aware of their competitive nature.

Barbara's challenge is to exercise leisurely, to learn not to push but to enjoy the process instead. However, the concept of taking it easy is hard for her to incorporate into her lifestyle. The idea of having fun for the sake of it was elusive to her. The fun was in the windfall of winning. Bringing awareness to these tendencies is a key factor in a dopamine-lowering, serotonin-boosting "playout." Monitor your level of enjoyment and intensity. If what you're doing is not easy and fun, stop doing it; switch gears to something else or drop the intensity level.

A good exercise program for Barbara would involve water, which pacifies Pitta dosha. Indeed, Barbara found swimming to be excellent for relieving tension and toning the physiology. At first it was difficult for her not to drive herself to do a set number of laps every time her body sank into the water. Eventually she learned to focus on enjoying the process rather than on being completely goal-oriented. As she became more balanced (judging from the cessation of her symptoms), she could tell herself that having fun and getting good exercise

Four Dopamine-Lowering, Serotonin-Boosting Principles

1. Maximize the opportunity to be out in a cool natural setting, preferably near water.
2. Minimize drive, competition, and high intensity in your chosen sport.
3. Schedule fun time into your daily activities.
4. Minimize your exposure to heat.

was more important than winning—and one day she could even make herself believe those words!

Other recommended activities for Barbara include anything that is relaxing, enjoyable, and preferably cooling, such as the following outdoor activities:

- Swimming
- Moderate-paced walking or hiking
- Low-intensity rowing or canoeing
- Windsurfing
- Horseback riding
- Mountain biking
- Golfing
- Noncompetitive winter sports

Recommended indoor activities include anything that involves gentle, repetitive motion, such as the following:

- Moderate aerobic activity
- Moderate-intensity yoga
- Tai chi or qigong

Ed's Story: Shake Your *Buddhi*!

At the peak of his physical health, Ed had a strong and sturdy build. As a teenager he ran cross-country and did very well, winning several awards. He was often not at the head of the pack in the beginning of the race, but his natural endurance and muscle strength paid off, so he frequently moved ahead during the race and crossed the finish line first. Ed recalls feeling invigorated when he worked up a good sweat, and his physiology definitely benefited from hard, sustained exercise. It made him feel good!

Ed liked cross-country running, but it was the team spirit that pushed him to keep coming to practices. On his own, he would not take up running as a pastime. After Ed married and had children, he began to have difficulty finding time to exercise. Besides, he felt too tired to get moving.

A Kapha imbalance over a prolonged period is likely to manifest as a lack of energy and motivation, social withdrawal, a loss of interest in the world, difficulty concentrating, and trouble remaining focused and alert. We oversleep, but it only makes us more tired. The individual overeats in an effort to gain energy, but weight gain is all that seems to happen. Eventually, the added pounds weigh one's mood down even more. Feeling dependent, clingy, and stubbornly set in one's ways, the individual has a hard time getting going. A Kapha imbalance causes a person to literally sink into the earth—with too little energy or motivation to pull oneself out of the damp ground in which one is mired. This is the picture of the classic Earthy Depression.

To undo Earthy Depression, one needs activities that rock one's world. Such activities trigger the branch of the nervous system that activates the physiology. Stimulating exercise would inevitably shake Ed's *buddhi* (which means "mind" in Sanskrit), shaking up the mental dullness and physical stagnation he was experiencing. A rush of adrenaline jump-starts the physiology.

Ed needs to embark on the fast track to resolving his Earthy Depression. This archetype of depression is the only archetype that profits from vigorous exercise. Physical activity that pushes beyond the Kapha-imbalanced person's comfort zone is good. Heat burns *ama*, so breaking a sweat encourages the detoxification of the physiology. (This assumes that a person is physically fit enough to exercise without causing injury to the body.)

Lack of movement and exercise is the surest way of enhancing a Kapha imbalance. One of the first symptoms of a Kapha imbalance is a lack of motivation to move the body. The best way to break this cycle is by stimulating one's senses and one's mind. For example, we suggested that Ed listen to stimulating music—fast, strong-beating, dance music—to motivate him to walk. Ed made going to the sauna part of his regular routine. If an individual with a Kapha imbalance feels that he or she can only muster motivation to watch television, we suggest that he or she watch exercise videos—this will at least get the person's mind thinking about exercising. People are also excellent motivators. Ed enjoyed walking with friends and turned this time into a social activity. The company stimulated him to get moving.

> ## Five Norepinephrine- and Dopamine-Increasing Principles to Rock Your World
>
> 1. Move (and keep moving). Run or do fast-paced walking.
> 2. Do anything that makes you break a sweat *every day*.
> 3. Do some vigorous, stimulating, strength-training activity.
> 4. Participate in competitive sports or hang out with competitive people.
> 5. Have dry rather than moist heat in your environment; use a sauna rather than steam.

Recommended activities, preferably done in a group setting, include the following:

- Vigorous aerobic exercise to stimulating music
- Running
- Fast-paced walking
- Weight training
- Competitive team sports
- Any exciting outdoor activity, preferably done in dry heat

Excessive Exercise and Free Radicals

Cutting-edge research in the field of exercise physiology validates the wisdom of the Vedic sages. The quality and quantity of exercise must be suited to the physiological needs of the individual. Incorrect exercise can create an inflammatory state in the body and lead to physiological burnout.

Overexertion causes free radicals, which are highly reactive forms of oxygen molecules that eat away at other molecules. Free radicals are not all bad—some are necessary and serve as part of our defense against germs. However, an excess of free radicals can cause extensive damage to our cells and even to our DNA.

Free radicals are caused by many factors besides overexertion, including mental stress, overexposure to the sun, ingestion of tobacco and alcohol, and pollution. A major health benefit of being in shape is that through moderate exercise we reduce the number of free radicals. However, overdoing exercise—straining the physiology—accelerates metabolic processes and generates excess free radicals.

Overexercising may produce fine muscles and may even help with cardiovascular health, but it does not assist the entire physiology in moving toward optimal health; in fact, according to Ayurveda, it is dangerous. There are many benefits from exercising at 50 percent of one's capacity, such as eliminating excess free radicals. Another important benefit is that people tend to exercise more regularly when they are not straining themselves. Exercising at 50 percent capacity usually means that you will enjoy your exercise and will feel lively long afterward—not exhausted.

The Danger Signs of Overexercising

It seems to us that many Americans are inclined to exercise either not at all or too much. As much as we want you to begin to exercise regularly, it is also important that you know when to stop. There are six signs that you have gone too far with your exercise regimen:

1. Panting or shortness of breath

2. Unusually heavy perspiration

3. Undue fatigue

4. Dizziness

5. A heartbeat faster than your target range

6. Pain in your chest, back, or arms that remains even after you slow down your pace

See your doctor immediately if you experience any of the above danger signals during or after your exercise session. It is also a good idea, especially if you are in poor physical condition, to consult with your doctor before beginning a new exercise program.

Walking Away from Depression

When the universe is your pharmacy, your medication could be a couple of paces away. Recall that in essence, we are a pattern of vibration—consciousness in motion. As such, we are in a constant state of energetic exchange with our environment. Walking away from depression entails getting a daily infusion of nature's healing vibrations. Depending on the type of imbalance you have, profound therapeutic interventions include making a habit of walking daily out in nature, especially in the early morning. The natural world comes alive in the early morning; when we walk outside at this time, our physiology comes alive as well. Walking in nature in the early morning infuses into our bodies the vibratory qualities of liveliness that are inherent in the natural world at that time of day.

However, if you are unable to go for even a short early-morning walk, please don't give up on walking altogether. You can begin to park farther away from work or take time at lunch to go outside and walk. You've heard of taking time to smell the roses. When we become mindful, we feel better because we take the time to properly ingest with our senses the world around us. When you walk, *do* smell the roses—notice nature around you; enjoy the sight of a tree, birds, or flowers; and look up at the sky. Even in a city you can see the sky, and looking up at the sky will take your attention away from everyday worries to a different, larger dimension.

If you walk every day, especially if you walk every morning, you will find this activity to be extremely uplifting for your emotional life. The suggestion to take time to notice nature while walking is not New Age mumbo jumbo. It is clinically accurate advice. What we place our attention on grows within us. If we place our attention on the beauty of the world around us, we enhance our own inner peace and beauty.

Timing Is Everything

Research studies have determined that exposure to morning light has an antidepressant effect. In fact, morning light was more effective in producing clinical improvements in depressed individuals than either midday or evening light.

Here's what Ayurveda knows: A walk in the early morning, preferably between the hours of 6 and 10, is an antidote and a preventative for depression. Why is timing of the essence? Like everything else in the natural world, the doshas impact the quality of the energy that is experienced at different times of the day. Between the hours of 6 and 10 a.m., Ayurveda explains, the natural world is marked by a heavy lethargic quality typical of Kapha dosha. Walking in the early morning infuses lightness and liveliness into the mind-body because physical activity during this time of day balances the sedentary and heavy qualities associated with this dosha. In addition, experiencing the rising of the sun gives energy to the body and the mind—recall that through our senses we bring in the vibratory nature of the world around us.

Modern scientists propose that depression can be counteracted by the antidepressant effect of a phase advance caused by exposure to morning light. Studies suggest that exposure to morning light has a direct effect on the production of serotonin. The production of this neurotransmitter, in turn, correlates with the production of melatonin in the body. A morning walk might light up your life by brightening your day and helping you to snooze at night.

Your Exercise Program: What's Love Got to Do with It?

Physical movement forges a connection between awareness and your physiology. Especially if your activity is done outdoors, exercise can attract nature's rhythms into your mind-body. However, all is for naught if the type of physical movement you are undertaking is not suiting your physiological needs. A good way to assess this is to shed light on your relationship with exercise:

Have you become estranged from your body?

* Is there no regular exercise program in your life?

- What has caused you to have a bad relationship with exercise?
- Was there a time in your life when physical activity was effortlessly incorporated into your day?
- Was it a "no pain, no gain" mentality that burned you out and squelched your motivation?
- Did you abandon exercise because you did not believe you had the time to spare? Look a little deeper—it usually is never about the time. When you love what you do, you make time to do it.

Are you getting the love you want from your current relationship with exercise?

- Do you enjoy your current exercise program?
- Do you look forward to it with pleasurable anticipation?
- Do you look forward to this time because it is a source of recreation?
- Is exercise a drudgery, something you must discipline yourself to do because you've been told it is good for you?
- Are you putting in more energy than what your exercise regimen is giving back to you?
- Is your exercise regimen increasing your enthusiasm for life?
- Is your physical activity toning your muscles and lubricating your joints? Or are your aching muscles and squeaky joints trying to tell you something: that you may be pounding your body into the ground?
- Is your relationship to your exercise program a match made in heaven?

If you have become estranged from your body and have determined that your exercise program is not a match made in heaven, we suggest that you review the general Ayurvedic principles in this chapter. Focus on a program to bring balance to the dosha that is most immediately in need of attention:

- If you are experiencing anxiety, balance Vata dosha.
- If you are experiencing frustration and irritability, balance Pitta dosha.

* If you are experiencing emotional and physical lethargy, balance Kapha dosha.

It is common for people to experience a mixture of symptoms. If this is the case for you, address the most prevalent concern. If you can't discern which emotion is most prevalent, the rule of thumb is to address Vata dosha first. The reason for this is that the nervous system is under the purview of Vata dosha, and an optimally functioning nervous system is essential for the regulation of the entire mind-body.

The ancient Vedic text on Ayurveda, the *Charaka Samhita*, states the following about exercise: "From physical exercise one gets lightness, a capacity for work, firmness, tolerance for difficulties, elimination of impurities, and stimulation of digestion." The following questions can guide you in assessing the health benefits that you derive from your exercise program:

* Is your physical activity helping you to feel less energetically congested?
* Is it helping you to not let the everyday travails of life get you down?
* Are you feeling stronger in body, mind, and spirit?
* Is it bringing clarity into your thinking?
* Has your immunity improved?
* Has your ability to digest food improved?
* Are you sleeping better at night and waking up rejuvenated?
* Are you feeling less depressed?

Adopting Ayurvedic guidelines for finding an exercise program that helps to bring balance to your mind-body should lead you to answer yes to the majority of the questions listed above.

12

Yoga: Posing for Life

Lack of activity destroys the good condition of every
human being, while movement and methodical
physical exercise saves it and preserves it.

—PLATO

Perhaps you have seen pictures of people doing yoga and they
were twisted like pretzels. You may have thought, "I could never
do that! I'm not flexible." Even if you can't twist like a pretzel (most of
us can't), you certainly *can* do yoga.

Yoga untangles the intertwined roots of depression through the
healing power of awareness. Yoga postures allow us to place our
awareness on the body. This attention is like water to a plant. It provides nourishment and liveliness to the physiology and refreshes as it
rejuvenates.

Physical, mental, and emotional disorders are effectively treated by
the practice of yoga. Increasingly, interdisciplinary scientific research
attests to this. Once again, the Vedic sages and modern scientists agree
that by bending, inverting, twisting, and stretching we can undo the
stranglehold of depression. By naturally inducing the release of mood
brighteners and brain-stabilizing biochemicals in the physiology, yoga
postures relieve the many symptoms associated with a depressed state:
anxiety, lethargy, and sleep problems.

Ayurveda recommends the daily practice of asanas (the Sanskrit word for poses) to develop an awareness of energy flow, remove blockages, rebalance the doshas, and strengthen our connection to cosmic consciousness. The asanas extricate the mind-body from the tenacious grip of depression. Yoga is a key agent of vitality because with one graceful motion after another, it accomplishes the following:

* Addresses the root of the problem of depression by replenishing our energy reservoir

* Awakens the physician within by activating our innate physical, mental, emotional, and spiritual healing capability

* Promotes the integrative functioning of the mind with the brain, the body, and the breath

* Promotes neuromuscular integration—the ability to use our muscular and skeletal systems to influence the working of our nervous system, and vice versa

Yoga poses are concrete and practical instruments for physiological reconstruction. Within the solid mass of flesh and bones we call our body is a network of channels that transports energy and natural intelligence. The life force—the energy extracted from our digestion of thoughts, emotions, and food—moves through these channels. The musculoskeletal system holds together the bundle of channels, but it is our posture and our breath that direct the flow of energy throughout the network. A yoga practice puts a plug on the energy drain caused by our overactive mind and body in response to the stresses of life. In essence, it revitalizes us—it fills us with life energy!

The Energetic Flow behind the Poses

Yoga poses are indeed an exercise system, but they are so much more than that. Research has shown that they are a form of medicine, dissolving many problems and helping good health to flourish.

Yoga poses work in a holistic way, affecting us at the most basic physical level but also creating mental and spiritual well-being. Yoga addresses structural imbalances in the body such as bone, joint, or muscular problems. This ancient practice has also been shown to have a positive effect on the respiratory, immune, endocrine, digestive, and cardiovascular systems. By helping us to maintain a healthy body, the practice of yoga sets the stage for a fuller manifestation of the spirit. Our consciousness shines best through a healthy body that is brimming with vitality. Yoga asanas facilitate the management of our vital energy.

Each asana has its own structural effect on the physical body. In general, standing poses increase strength and energy, whereas sitting poses provide stability in the spine and create flexibility in the legs. Forward bends affect the branch of the nervous system that triggers a relaxation response, creating a pleasant calming influence. Back bends, on the other hand, affect the branch of the nervous system that stimulates us. They also increase spinal extension and create strength in the back muscles. Hence, a yoga session provides a full tune-up for our physical body. Nevertheless, this represents merely the starting point of the healing process.

There is indeed more to a pose than the physical effects that emanate from exotic contortions. Asanas attend to the body so that the mind-body can begin to mend. The real power of the poses lies in the attention we place on the physical sensations they generate. Awareness heals the body, and intention mends the spirit. If done properly, the poses create doshic balance, and balance equals health and happiness. Yoga poses have an extraordinary potential to unleash the healing forces of the physiology. When we direct our body into a pose, we orchestrate the movement of energy throughout our seamless energetic system. The result is integration. A regular yoga practice integrates—brings into union and coordinated functioning—the physical, mental, and spiritual aspects of the being.

Recall that according to the Vedic sages, the physical body is a manifestation of consciousness. Think of your body as a crystallization of the mental, emotional, and behavioral patterns created by your mind. It is not an exaggeration to say that our life story is recorded in our mind-body. In other words, long-term patterns of feeling and behavior determine the form of the body and the distribution of energy through the physiology.

How we feel on a psychological level is reflected in how we move on a physical level, and vice versa. This is evident in our everyday life. Our body language reflects our sense of self and how we use our energy.

What a story a slumping body tells about its overburdened mind! A forceful stride with the chin jutting out indicates mental determination and courageous drive. Posture is indeed a reflection of emotion.

What if we could work in reverse—that is, intentionally strike a pose to create an emotion? This is what yoga asanas help us to do. Certain poses give us a feeling of strength and power, whereas others create calm and still others stimulate and excite the physiology. In our consciousness exists all knowledge; unfortunately, the stress we incur in daily life creates a barrier to our positive internal experience and all the contentment, compassion, serenity, love, and strength that is our birthright. Through the practice of yoga asanas we pull these powerful positive aspects of our consciousness into awareness.

The various energies of the body are similar to the different sections of an orchestra. The asana is like the conductor, waving a baton, gesturing to the musicians the directions for creating the symphony. As the conductor's attention moves from section to section, the energy that emanates from his or her gestures changes. Musical tone and harmony are created in response to the conductor's movements. When we practice yoga, we become the conductor, synchronizing our internal energies.

The mental power behind the gestures of the orchestra conductor is as important as the motions; likewise, the impulse or attention behind the asana is as important as the asana itself. In other words, depending on how we direct our attention, the same asana can take us to different places. The energetic influence of an asana depends on such factors as how quickly we do the posture, the degree of force we exert, and, above all, how we breathe during the posture.

To achieve maximum benefit, yoga postures should be performed as exercises in mindfulness. The attention focused on the body will determine how liberating the practice is for our consciousness. If awareness is not engaged during the asana, then the practice may limit its effects to the physical level—to stretching and toning muscles, increasing spinal flexibility, and lubricating the joints. This is good in and of itself, but why stop here? The ultimate healing power lies in consciousness. Where attention goes, natural intelligence flows. It is common for people to report that happiness springs forth from the heart during a yoga practice. Eventually, this feeling will stay with you outside of your practice.

The Poses

Yoga postures were inspired by the natural world. The Vedic sages seemed to want to harness certain qualities, and they did this by incorporating what they saw into physical postures. Each pose brings into our awareness a positive aspect of consciousness. Through a regular yoga practice we incorporate these beneficial qualities and subsequently carry them through to our everyday life.

Triangle pose allows us to experience the state of equanimity that is possible when we connect the three aspects of our being: body, mind, and spirit.

Mountain pose puts us in touch with our self-confidence.

Tree pose affirms that the winds of life cannot topple us when our feet are firmly grounded on the earth.

Cobra pose brings alertness to our awareness.

Warrior pose infuses us
with the strength to help us
overcome fear.

In Tortoise pose, our back muscles create a
physical shield so we can safely experience our
inner world.

Child's pose takes us back to the
nurturance experienced in infancy.

Two series of poses—Sun Salutations and Moon Salutations—are described later in the chapter.

A pose is just a pose, however, unless we understand the consciousness behind it. As we noted in the previous section, the energy and attention that we put into the pose is as important as doing the pose itself. This requires that as we practice the poses, we are aware not only of the technicalities of the postures but also of the mental and emotional states that they create within us. Through our intention and attention we expand our awareness, and in this way the poses serve as tools for uprooting depression from the mind-body.

Architecture, whether of a building or a body, serves as a blueprint for the organization of consciousness. The open spaces, the cloistered structures, and other design features will influence how the building is used—how energy will be distributed throughout the place. In much the same way, yoga poses leave their energetic imprint on the body. The posture is the architecture that influences the internal design pattern. Even though we cannot see how the architecture of the posture affects our internal space, we can experience its effects. We do this through the mental, emotional, and physical sensations it evokes. Just as a building should be designed to enhance its stated function, the body must be fine-tuned to allow for the free flow of natural intelligence. By doing yoga, we re-create our internal design, knocking down oppressive walls so that joyous feelings can congregate in the inner sanctum of our heart.

The Yoga-Ayurveda Connection

Ayurvedic principles easily explain the healing capabilities of yoga. According to Ayurveda, we develop disease because of two factors: (1) imbalances in the orchestrating forces of nature—the three doshas—that govern our physiology, and (2) blockages to the free flow of our life-energy.

Both yoga and Ayurveda have as their goal the creation of better health and, ultimately, the attainment of union with the self, with the spirit. Yoga exercises are a tool for experiencing a more settled state of mind through the development of self-awareness.

There is no limit to the degree of self-awareness a person might attain. The mind is an ocean, and through meditation and yoga we are able to dive through its depths. Think of your mind as constructed in layers, with the top layer holding the busyness and static incurred in living everyday life. As you delve deeper through the layers of the mind, you will experience an increased degree of inner silence and calmness. As your mind becomes quieter, your intuition will grow. Experiencing increased inner calmness will help you to become centered, and this will carry you through challenges and obstacles. This is the state of a healthy person, someone who has established mind-body union. In Sanskrit, the word for healthy is *swastha*, meaning "established in the self" (referring to the cosmic self). Happiness, according to Ayurveda, is a by-product of health.

It is the goal of all Ayurvedic interventions to assist us in achieving a state in which the physical body, the senses, the mind, and the spirit are fully integrated, functioning in unison. Practicing yoga poses is central to this state of being. Yoga is, in fact, considered the ideal Ayurvedic exercise because it rejuvenates the mind, improves digestion, and removes the stress incurred in the process of daily living. Yoga thus addresses the three key Ayurvedic principles for health maintenance: restoration of energy, enhancement of digestion, and purification of the physiology.

By dissolving physical stress and calming the mind, yoga asanas are an essential preparatory step for meditation. We know how to prepare appropriately before every event or activity; being unprepared dampens an experience. Meditation is no different, and performing asanas is a worthy preparation for that activity.

Yoga poses address a major concern of Ayurveda: detoxification. The postures, with their associated breathing techniques, cleanse the internal organs of toxins. People who attend a yoga class on a regular basis begin to dislodge the *ama* (impurities) in the body, but if they maintain nutritional habits and a lifestyle that encourages the creation of *ama*, then all they are really doing is moving the gunk around. The yoga practitioner needs to know how to enhance the detoxification process through the nutritional and lifestyle practices recommended by Ayurveda. Yoga and Ayurveda are therefore interdependent; they enhance each other's goals. The physical and the spiritual reflect and affect each other.

Yoga Poses and the Doshas

As a science of health, Ayurveda teaches us how the doshas rule our lives and shows us how to channel them for our greater good. Ayurveda gives us the knowledge; yoga helps us to put it into action. The practice of yoga hinders the onset of disease by managing the doshas. The stretching, contracting, stimulating, and soothing nature of the poses keeps the doshas in their proper place, proportion, and flow. Through yoga the doshas remain forces of health rather than triggers for disease and depression.

Specific asanas affect the doshas in particular ways. By impacting Vata, Pitta, and Kapha—the principles that coordinate physiological functioning—the asanas have a profound effect on the physiology at a most fundamental level. Yoga poses have the potential to bring balance to one or more aspects of the mind-body; they keep our physical structure and energy in harmony. The poses undo disturbances in the doshas, and the proper circulation of energy throughout the physiology is thereby ensured.

The doshas, as we have explained, govern every aspect of our nature. They go awry through offenses against wisdom. Sometimes, even when we know better, we behave in ways that compromise our internal balance: eating heavy food late at night, eating before the previous meal is digested, overexercising, or underexercising; these are all examples of behaviors that will cause imbalances. Any time we live our lives out of sync with the rhythms of nature, we compromise our internal balance.

Each dosha has a primary area of function in the body. The primary site of Vata dosha is the large intestine; of Pitta, the small intestine; and of Kapha, the lungs. By understanding this, we come to understand how yoga poses keep the doshas in balance. In general, this is how the poses aid in balancing the doshas:

- Forward sitting bends balance Vata dosha by putting pressure on the lower abdomen, thereby releasing tension from the large intestine. This action relieves distension in the colon.

- Forward bends and twists are beneficial for balancing Pitta dosha. Twists accomplish this by putting pressure on the small intestine, and forward bending pushes the energy downward and out of the body. These types of asanas also improve circulation in the trunk of the body. As a result, they promote the cleansing of the liver and the gallbladder. Since the liver is the body's main organ of detoxification, these types of asanas help the physiology to remove toxins from the system. In Ayurvedic terms, this means that they reduce heat (inflammation) and stress from the small intestine and central abdomen, therefore cooling (detoxifying) the blood and the liver.

- Back bends stimulate the chest area and the stomach, the domain of Kapha dosha, releasing the congestion and stagnation of energy in these areas. The process of moving energy up and out of the body is aided by deep breathing and increasing our heart rate.

The doshas also reign over our mental and emotional life. An imbalance in Vata dosha creates fear and anxiety, leaving one feeling ungrounded and unstable. An imbalance in Pitta dosha overheats the system, resulting in anger, resentment, irritation, and jealousy. The stability and solidity of Kapha dosha can, if unbalanced, congeal to produce a state of excessive emotional attachment and a feeling of stagnation.

The practice of yoga asanas mollifies all of these problems by grounding and calming Vata dosha, cooling Pitta, and lightening Kapha. If you support your physiology with a healthy lifestyle, then your regular practice of yoga will decrease mental agitation, dispel mental dullness, and promote clarity of thought and peaceful emotions.

Arial's Story: Calming the Winds of Change

A yoga practice for Arial would focus on slowing her down from head to toe—calming and soothing her overactive mind and stabilizing her body by planting her feet on the ground. It was important for her to understand that her physiology needed regular rest and relaxation. These concepts can be elusive, however, especially when one is caught in the torrents of excessive busyness. Besides, true relaxation is more than just resting. True relaxation involves balancing and restoring our internal energies. The restoration of equilibrium requires the release of pent-up energy. This is where yoga asanas and breathing techniques come into play.

Arial took to yoga like a bee to nectar. She likes to do new things, she enjoys movement, and she tends to be both physically and mentally expressive. Because of her gregarious nature and her need for structure, signing up for a class that met regularly worked well for her. She soon felt the benefits of the practice in her body. The cracking and popping of her bones and the pain in her neck and shoulders greatly diminished. The massaging action on her muscles and joints that her yoga practice provided released tension from these areas. From an Ayurvedic perspective, Arial's pain and discomfort signified a blockage of Vata dosha in those areas of her body. Yoga asanas alleviated the drying effect of Vata dosha in her back and bones.

To address the other symptoms of her Vata imbalance—primarily hyperarousal and insomnia—Arial instituted an Ayurvedic bedtime ritual to prepare her nervous system for sleep: doing inverted poses. Yoga practitioners report that the regular practice of inverted poses is calming to the nervous system and the mind.

From the Western medical perspective, this is because inverted poses cause blood to rush to the brain. When the extra volume of blood goes through the main blood vessels to the head, the carotid arteries, it stretches these vessels. The nerve bundles in the carotids register this stretching of the blood vessels. Since their job is to maintain stable blood pressure, they respond by sending messages to the heart to slow down its rate of pumping. They also send a message to the blood vessels in the extremities to open up in order to receive more blood. The result is that when you come out of the inverted pose, you feel an overall sense of relaxation and a slowing down of the heart rate.

The lesson that Arial carried over from her yoga practice to her life was *do* less, *be* more.

Vata-Pacifying Principles for Airy Depression

Bringing balance to Vata dosha requires creating warmth and serenity during an asana practice. A restorative practice is best. This can be cultivated by following some basic guidelines.

Mental Focus

- Maintain a smooth and steady rhythm.
- Hold each posture for a short amount of time.
- Move fluidly into and out of each pose by imagining that you are moving through a thick, viscous substance like warm mud.

Physical Focus

- Stay warm to prevent injury.
- Refrain from hyperextending.
- Create physical stability by focusing on the foundation of each pose.
- Rotate your legs inwardly and press the outer edges of your legs toward the ground.
- In standing poses, ground your big toe.
- Activate your muscles with every pose—imagine that your muscles are hugging your bones.
- Be aware not to deplete your physical energy.

Spiritual Focus

- *Do* less, *be* more—maintain presence of mind throughout the practice.
- The practice should leave you physically strengthened, emotionally nourished, and spiritually grounded.
- Let your breath guide your practice—focus on lengthening your inhalations.

Barbara's Story: Opening the Mind's Eye

Barbara's body tended to overheat with physical activity. She responded emotionally with irritability and reacted to the idea of doing yoga with apprehension. She claimed that she was strong but not flexible and that she didn't have the patience to attempt something she didn't think she would be good at doing.

For Barbara, an asana practice was instrumental in improving her self-awareness. An essential part of an asana practice is hearing the feedback from your body. Developing your awareness of how the postures affect you in the moment is the secret for healing. This is how internal awareness is developed. It is the key that opens the door to attunement with the inner self.

Barbara habitually pushed herself to her maximum capacity. She tended to overdo. It was important that she not become overdetermined about her practice. At first, she had a propensity to stick with poses she could do well, and she disliked those that she was not good at doing. These were often the very ones that would offer her the most benefit.

When practiced with awareness, yoga teaches us to eliminate striving and to remove the pressure that pushes us. It can be beneficial to push one's yoga practice to its maximum limit at times; however, it is equally important, if not more so, to enjoy the process of simply moving into a pose. It was important for Barbara to focus on the sensations evoked by the poses as she moved her body through the practice. During her practice, she acquired a sense of her internal energy flow.

Restorative poses helped Barbara with other manifestations of her Pitta imbalance, primarily migraine headaches and high blood pressure. We suggested that she practice these with her eyes closed and while wearing a head wrap. Doing poses that involved bending forward cooled Barbara's physiology and relaxed her. The head wrap helped her to turn inward, allowing her to focus on her inter experience of her mind-body as she practiced.

The lesson that Barbara carried over from her yoga practice to her life was learning to observe herself and others without judgment.

Pitta-Pacifying Principles for Burning Depression

A yoga practice for balancing Pitta dosha should encourage compassion, acceptance, and relaxed effort. Keeping cool is of the essence. Here are some basic guidelines.

Mental Focus

* Remind yourself that less is more!
* Have fun during your practice by not taking yourself or your poses too seriously.
* Soften your gaze or practice with your eyes closed.
* Smile.
* Allow freedom and creativity in your practice. Change it around. Avoid sticking to one style or series of poses.
* Focus on the physical sensations of your body, not your brain.
* Use the exhalation to release any heated emotions such as pent-up anger, frustration, and stress.

Physical Focus

* Keep cool in your mind and don't overheat your body.
* Practice in a well-ventilated space.
* Listen to your body and don't go past your limits—in other words, move your body until you feel the stretch but not the burn.
* Make sure that you have plenty of practice space around you.
* Exhale through your mouth if your body overheats (but always inhale through your nose).
* Use Breath of Victory (*Ujjai* Breath) when doing your postures (see chapter 10)
* Focus on lengthening your exhalations.
* Maintain an awareness of your breath as it moves through your body.
* Gently engage in side-twisting poses and chest openers.

- Maintain an awareness of the position of your ribs. Hug your ribs to your body and don't let them jut out.
- Practice at a moderate pace.

Spiritual Focus

- Avoid judgments and criticism of yourself.
- Remind yourself that yoga is not a competition.

Ed's Story: Lightening the Load of His Heart

Ed needs to be unburdened of physical, mental, and emotional *ama*. Yoga can be very helpful in doing this. It reduces physical *ama* by triggering the detoxification processes in the body. It also improves physical conditioning and promotes weight regulation. Yoga lowers stress by decreasing cortisol levels. This is important because from the Ayurvedic perspective, stress is the main generator of mental *ama*. In addition, Ed's response to stress is to overeat, which inevitably leads to the production of physical *ama*.

Yoga increased Ed's general awareness of the impact that his behavioral and food choices were having on his physiology. For example, when he ate an excess of sugar- and fat-laden foods, he felt the detrimental impact on his body during his yoga practice. With his increased awareness, he not only decreased the load of *ama* in his body but also stopped accumulating it. In addition, yoga's focus on attention to bodily sensations prevents the accumulation of emotional *ama*. Ed learned to distinguish when he was eating because he was hungry from when he was eating just out of habit or boredom.

In the morning, Ed regularly practiced Sun Salutations (see the description later in this chapter) to help him wake up and feel energized. He was instructed to put vigor into his practice in order to raise his heart rate into the aerobic range, giving him the stimulation he needed. Sweating was therapeutic for Ed. The skin is the largest organ of detoxification, and sweating eliminates toxins that would otherwise burden the liver and kidneys. Standing with his shoulders back and his chest out, he ended his yoga practice feeling revitalized.

Ed was especially delighted with his increased energy. Consequently, he was inspired to get moving in other aspects of his life, including his intimate life. Another unexpected benefit to his regular yoga practice was a marked improvement of his immune system. Without realizing it, Ed had lived most of his life with mucus plugging up his head and his chest. Once he began practicing yoga, his sinuses cleared up and he stopped catching colds. Seasonal allergies became a thing of the past. His ability to do breathing exercises also improved with the decongestion of his upper respiratory tract.

The lesson that Ed carried over from his yoga practice to his life was empowerment. One pose at a time, he eradicated his deep-rooted sense of helplessness.

Kapha-Pacifying Principles for Earthy Depression

A yoga practice to balance Kapha dosha should aim at stimulating the flow of energy, generating internal heat, creating opening spaces in the body, and creating a sense of lightness. This can be cultivated by following some basic guidelines.

Mental Focus

- Focus on creating expansiveness in the physical body and in your energetic field.
- Challenge yourself.
- Using your mind's eye (internal awareness), pay close attention to your body alignment.
- Keep your heart open—do this symbolically by keeping your chest out and your shoulders down, as if you were opening the door to your heart.

Physical Focus

- Practice at a vigorous pace and intensity.
- Practice in a warm space.

- Use a strong forceful breath during practice.
- Don't give up—when you are ready to release the pose, take one more breath.
- Maintain a sharp upward gaze, as if looking ahead to catch a glimpse of the future.
- Pause for a moment between your inhalations and exhalations.
- Keep moving.
- Have short resting periods between poses.
- Be precise in the way you do your poses (for example, extend your arm purposefully with fingers straight and strong).

Spiritual Focus
- Feel stable in your body and let your spirit soar.
- Let go—begin by giving up preconceived notions about yourself, such as what you can and cannot do.
- Welcome change.

Yoga Poses and the Body's Systems

Yoga poses have a tremendous effect on all the physical systems of the body. In addition, they create energy patterns that can change your energy field—and your life.

The Skeletal System

Bones are living tissues. They may appear static in form and strength, but the reality is that they can be strengthened through use or weakened through inactivity. Gravity plays an important role in bone health and development. This is why the weight-bearing aspect of yoga asanas triggers healthy cellular regeneration in the bones. In outer space, beyond gravity's pull, bones begin to decalcify and muscles weaken. Weight-bearing exercises stimulate the bone cells to regenerate, changing the architecture of the bones on an ongoing basis. In this manner the skeletal system is kept healthy and strong.

A good series of yoga poses mobilizes all the joints in the body. This has the effect of increasing blood flow to the area, which promotes the lubrication of the joints. Having aching joints is not a necessary symptom of aging. In addition, a regular practice of yoga asanas prevents and reverses osteoporosis.

Elongating the spine helps to prevent the drying out and degeneration of the intervertebral disks, which function as shock absorbers in the spine. The cartilage that makes up the spinal disks lacks an independent blood supply; consequently, it requires movement in order to mobilize blood from nearby vessels to receive nutrients. The traction and contraction that comes about from doing back bends, forward bends, and twists keeps the disks healthy by preventing them from dying out and degenerating. Cushioning each vertebra, as a disk does, protects the nerves that exit the spinal column from compression and impingement. This prevents sciatic pain and the phenomenon of appearing to grow shorter as you grow older.

The Muscular System

Yoga poses teach us how to use, tone, build, and balance the muscular system. Unlike most forms of exercise, an asana practice improves muscle strength; even more important, it improves flexibility. Muscle weakness contributes to many physical limitations. Arthritis and back pain—two of the major reasons that people seek medical attention—are directly affected by the health of the muscles that support the bones. Muscles that are strengthened and lengthened are less prone to injury than are short, tight muscles. Excessive tension within the muscles causes postural misalignment and inefficient use of energy.

Yoga philosophy states that the muscular system stores emotional tension and trauma. Yoga poses assist in the release of these stored emotional memories. An easy attention on the body allows the emergence of self-awareness and fosters the release of the old memories that are stored in the body. Although yoga poses are very physical, the practice involves a great deal of mental conditioning and development.

We learn to expand our awareness to all areas of the body while simultaneously directing our focus to specific parts. Losing excess emotional baggage lessens the load on the mind, making space for the experience of joy.

The Circulatory System

Good health, vitality, and immunity require keeping all bodily fluids moving well in veins, arteries, capillaries, the lymphatic system, and even in the bones, marrow, and spinal disks. Assisting the circulatory system in its pumping action on a daily basis is an essential component of a good health-maintenance program. Physical exercise also promotes the release of tension and the detoxification of the body.

Yoga poses have many unique circulatory effects. Many postures direct the flow of circulation to specific body parts, glands, or organs that would otherwise not receive stimulation. For instance, if not during a yoga session, when else do you invert your body? When else do you undo the effects of gravity?

Inversion poses bring increased circulation to the upper body. The benefits of moving blood against gravity are significant. This effect carries over to the lymphatic system, which is heavily responsible for proper immunity. The many compressing and squeezing actions in yoga postures keep fluids moving, preventing stagnation. Flooding the thyroid, pineal, and pituitary glands with oxygen and nutrient-rich blood keeps them at peak performance.

The Respiratory System

Yoga improves posture and breathing. Breathing capacity is affected by the strength and flexibility of the thoracic (chest) area. If your body is hunched over and your chest, ribs, and intercostal (between the ribs) muscles are stiff, there will be a physical limit to the amount of air you can inhale. You will also not be able to fully utilize your diaphragm, the large sheet of muscle that ventilates your body. This will greatly restrict your breathing abilities. This in turn impacts the nervous system, because one of the main ways to affect the nervous system is through the breath. Ventilating your body airs your mind!

The Digestive System

According to Ayurveda, the foundation of health lies in the organs of assimilation and elimination. Hippocrates said, "Let food be thy medicine." If sadness has depressed your digestive capacity, yoga will greatly increase your appetite and your ability to digest foods, because the asanas stoke the digestive fire and tone the intestines. Inverted poses, twists, and forward bends increase the flow of energy to the digestive system. Relieving compression in the spine improves nerve function to the digestive organs. Forward bends, twists, and abdominal lifts stimulate peristalsis (the coordinated movement of the intestine) and promote internal cleaning. They also revitalize the internal organs, such as the pancreas, kidneys, and liver.

The Endocrine System

Our energy level is closely determined by the fitness of the endocrine glands. Our hormones affect all aspects of growth, development, and function in the body. They are complex chemical messengers that transfer information and instruction between cells. For example, cellular functioning, our metabolic rate, and our reproductive ability all depend on the biochemical signaling that occurs between the different systems of the body. The burgeoning field of psychoneuroimmunology attests to the fact that the state of our endocrine system is reflected in the functioning of our mind and our immune system. Studies have shown that inversions, back bends, and twists have beneficial effects on maintaining the health of the endocrine system.

The Nervous System

The nerves of the spinal cord can be considered an extension of the brain. The nerves that travel through the spinal cord exit the spine through small openings. Without proper maintenance of the spine, the openings between the vertebral disks become smaller and can impinge upon the nerves of the corresponding muscles or organs. Weakness in the knees and leg muscles and the poor balance that is often associated with aging can be a sign that the electrical impulses from the spinal nerves have been compromised. This need not be so.

Yoga postures help to lengthen the spine, thereby creating space between the vertebrae. This maintains the natural intervertebral spaces, thereby preventing nerve pinching. Furthermore, in sitting and in standing poses we learn to direct and extend nerve energy out to our extremities, especially into the toes. This training keeps the nerve pathways clear and active so that the electrical impulses can travel efficiently. Learning to energize the nerves that activate all parts of the body improves mental capacity, attention, and mental power.

Letting the Body Move the Spirit

No one-size-fits-all approach is true, especially when it comes to how we perform poses. In this section we present two series of asanas: Sun Salutation and Moon Salutation. Sun Salutation is a series of twelve extension exercises that are done in a continuous flow. The energetic intention that drives the practice of Sun Salutations should depend on your particular doshic imbalance. Undoing Earthy Depression requires infusing vigor into each pose, bringing it into the range of a cardiovascular practice. In other words, aim to break a sweat. For Airy Depression, a gentle and rhythmic flow will impart order into the internal chaos. Sun Salutation is not suited for a Burning Depression; rather, a cooling practice such as Moon Salutation is recommended.

Solar Power: Harnessing the Energy of the Self

Following are directions for the Sun Salutation series. Start at the top center illustration and continue clockwise (see the next page).

1. **Salutation Pose.** Begin by standing with your weight distributed evenly over your feet. Press the palms of your hands together at chest level. Breathe easily for about five seconds.

2. **Raised Arms Pose.** Inhale as you bring your arms up over your head in a large circular motion. Keep your elbows straight and behind your ears with your palms facing each other. Move your tailbone down, dig your heels into the ground, and pull your navel in toward your spine. At the same time, arch your chest upward and extend your arms and head back.

The Sun Salutation.

3. **Forward Bend Pose.** Exhale and fold your body forward and down. Keep a soft bend in your knees.

4. **Runner's Lunge Pose.** Inhale as you step your left foot back. Bend your right leg into a 90-degree angle. Lift your chest and head, look forward, and press your hips down toward the ground.

5. **Downward-Facing Dog Pose.** As you exhale, step your right foot back to meet your left. Keep your feet hip distance apart. Lengthen your arms, shoulders, and torso into a straight line. Hold the sitting bones up as you lower your heels as close to the ground as possible. Your body will form an inverted V.

6. **Knees-Chest-Chin Pose.** Exhale and, bending your knees, lower your knees, chest, and chin to the ground. Keep your buttocks lifted.

7. **Cobra Pose.** As you inhale, slide forward. Keep your elbows close to your body as you lift your head, neck, and chest. Arch upward. You should bear no weight on your hands or arms. Allow your spine to keep you lifted.

8. **Downward-Facing Dog Pose.** As your exhale, raise your torso and hips up. Repeat Downward-Facing Dog.

9. **Runner's Lunge Pose.** Inhale and bring your left foot forward between your hands, lifting your chest and head. Repeat Runner's Lunge.

10. **Forward Bend Pose.** As you exhale, bring your left foot forward. Repeat Forward Bend.

11. **Raised Arms Pose.** As you inhale, bring your arms and torso back to an upright position. Repeat Raised Arms pose.

Exhale and return to Salutation pose.

Repeat the full cycle, this time extending the right leg during Runner's Lunge.

Melding with the Moon: Extinguishing the Flames in the Mind-Body

The Moon Salutation.

From the many versions of Moon Salutations (*Chandra Namaskar*), we have chosen to highlight the sequence taught by Kripalu Yoga. One full Moon Salutation includes both the right and left sides of the body. Start at the top center illustration and continue clockwise.

1. **Salutation Pose.** Begin by standing with your weight distributed evenly over your feet. Press the palms of yours hands together at chest level. Breathe easily for about five seconds.

2. **Half Moon Pose.** As you inhale, circle your hands overhead, interlacing your fingers and pointing your index fingers upward. Exhale. Inhale and shift your weight to your left foot and hip as you extend your torso and arms to the right. Exhale. Move back to center. Inhale and shift your weight to your right foot and hip and extend your torso and arms to the left. Exhale.

3. **Victory Squat.** Inhale. Take a step to the right, separating your feet. Keeping your feet wide apart, turn your toes slightly out. Soften your knees. As you exhale, squat, lowering your tailbone while simultaneously lifting your head. Keep your elbows bent, pointing your arms and fingertips upward.

4. **Five-Pointed Star.** As you inhale, straighten your legs. Lift your head but keep your chin down while extending your arms and fingers out at shoulder level.

5. **Triangle.** As you exhale, turn your right foot out. Keeping both legs straight and both arms at shoulder level, extend your torso to the right. Move your right arm down your leg and grasp either the shin or ankle of your right foot (or place your hand on the ground behind you) and raise your left arm toward the ceiling. Gently twist your torso as you turn your gaze upward.

6. **Runner's Stretch (Pyramid).** Lower both hands toward your right foot and fold your upper body over your right leg. You may bend your knee if you need to.

7. **Lunge.** Bend your right knee, bringing your hands to the ground on either side of your right foot. Press your tailbone down as you lift your head upward. Keep your left leg straight and strong.

8. **Extended-Leg Squat.** Bring both hands to the left of your right foot and press your tailbone down as you pivot to face center. Keeping your left leg extended, rotate it so that your toes point upward. Press your hands, foot of the bent leg, and tailbone downward and extend your head upward.

9. **Squat.** Bring your extended left leg back to center. Press your feet and tailbone downward. If you are easily able, bring your palms together at elbow level.

10. **Extended-Leg Squat.** Extend your right leg out and repeat Extended-Leg Squat.

11. Repeat Lunge on the left leg.

12. Repeat Runner's Stretch on the left leg.

13. Repeat Triangle on the left side.

14. Repeat Five-Pointed Star.

15. Repeat Victory Squat.

16. Repeat Half Moon.

End in Salutation pose.

Body Language: Analyzing the Pranic Meaning of Yoga Poses

The healing power behind yoga poses lies in your ability to use them as tools to infuse vitality into your physiology by directing the flow of energy to the areas that need it. The following exercise aims to heighten your awareness of the inner workings of your mind-body, to deepen your experience of the poses, and to shed light on your internal experience of yourself.

The question we want you to consider is this: What physical, mental, and emotional experiences do specific poses evoke in me? We will work here with the Triangle pose as an example. Because this is an exercise in self-study, there are no right or wrong answers, only experiences. Yoga poses are a practice in noncognitive self-awareness, in shedding light on the infinite consciousness that underlies our being. This is why yoga poses are considered consciousness-based interventions and a powerful agent of vitality.

Triangle Pose: Embodying the Stability of This Geometric Form
Instructions

1. Start with your feet spread 3 to 4 feet apart. Put your hands on your hips and face forward as you turn your right foot 90 degrees out to the right and turn your left foot 30 degrees in to the right. Maintain straight and strong legs and keep your weight evenly balanced between both legs. Rotate both legs outward as if opening them away from each other.

2. Inhale and lift your arms to shoulder height, then exhale while extending your arms out horizontally from your shoulder blades to your fingertips.

3. Exhale and extend your right arm so that the right side of your torso shifts toward the right. (The ultimate goal is for the right side of your torso to extend until it becomes parallel with the floor.)

4. Rest your right hand on either your ankle or your shin or on the floor behind you, depending on your flexibility. Raise your left arm straight above you, palm facing forward and fingers stretched. Be sure to keep your spine straight.

5. Breathe deeply for several breaths. Inhale and straighten up.

6. Exhale and lower your arms. Put your hands on your hips and pivot, exchanging the position of your feet. Repeat the pose on the other side.

Gaining Physical Awareness

Building awareness occurs one step at a time. Repeat Triangle pose, and this time, turn your attention to the physical patterns your body is creating as it goes into the pose.

1. How's your alignment? Notice whether your tailbone and the crown of your head are at approximately the same height.

2. Bring awareness to your spine—how is it holding up through this pose? Imagine it lengthening as you take in a deep breath, then observe what happens. What happens to your spine as you inhale and exhale?

3. Have you ever wondered why this is called the Triangle pose?

4. As you hold the pose, consider how many triangles are being created by your limbs. Can you identify them?

There are three triangles that are created during this pose.

Gaining Mental and Emotional Awareness

The mental and emotional realm is more subtle than the physical realm. Once you have gained confidence in your ability to do the pose, deepening your practice calls for gaining awareness of the sensations you experience while holding the pose. To guide you in this endeavor, consider the following questions:

1. Are your nostrils flaring and your heart pumping noticeably hard? Is your gaze soft or hard? Are the muscles in your legs shaking, making you feel unsteady?

2. Based on the way you are holding this pose, what inferences can you draw about how you sustain yourself through life? Do you hold a belief that you must stress and strain in order to accomplish the goal in mind, or do you let the flow of inspiration lead you to your goals? How would the latter be represented in the way you hold a yoga pose?

Reevaluate the three triangles created in Triangle pose.

The three triangles created in Triangle pose.

1. How well were you able to sense each of the three triangles?

2. Which triangle were you able to sense most clearly?

3. Do you notice how each triangle directs energy into a different plane?

   * Triangle 1, with the floor as its base, points upward, as if drawing energy from the earth and toward you.

- Triangle 2, formed by your leg, downward-pointing arm, and spine, points sideways, as if propelling your head forward.

- Triangle 3 has two concrete sides (spine and arm extended up) and one side that you have to imagine in your mind—this triangle opens you up to space.

4. What aspect of your being is sustaining the pose the most? Is it the physical (muscles and bones), your will and determination (mental and emotional), or your breath and imagination (the spiritual)?

5. Using your breath, expand your shoulder blades, lengthen your spine, and strengthen your legs as if straightening out each of the triangles. Repeat this process two more times. How does expanding your chest make you feel? How does bringing awareness to your heart affect your experience of the pose? Notice that it is your breath (the carrier of your life force) that causes this pose to energize, to come into being.

Gaining Spiritual Awareness

After releasing the pose, make a note of how the pose made you feel. Herein lies the metaphysical healing power of this pose: a triangle is the symbol of dynamic balance. It demonstrates the stability that is derived from bringing the different aspects of our being to conscious awareness. This pose helps us to identify the areas of stability in our mind-body and reminds us that stability in every area of our life promotes the expansion of our heart.

Consider the following metaphysical lesson: as this pose illustrates, in the course of life, although we may lead with our head, our ultimate power comes from the heart.

13

Sleep: Recharging Your Life Force

> Now I see the secret of the making of the best
> persons. It is to grow in the open air and to eat and
> sleep with the earth.
>
> —WALT WHITMAN

Sleep, according to ancient Ayurvedic texts, is an often forgotten blessing. These words lead us to believe that even thousands of years ago people were having difficulty getting to bed on time. Human nature, it seems, has not changed over the millennia.

We don't know what people in centuries past were doing when they stayed up at night. In today's world, however, we have endless temptations for work or play. Artificial light keeps us enchanted in a world of activity. Through technological advances, we can indulge in around-the-clock living.

However, one thing has not changed through the centuries: our human physiology. It continues to be in tune with the rhythms of nature. Our physiology will not succumb to our erratic behaviors. Its basic needs have remained constant. Sleep is, and always has been, a necessary source of nourishment for the physiology.

We can burn the candle at both ends, but this has a high price. Sleep is an agent of vitality; being deprived of it catches up with us immediately and is a major cause of depression.

If You Snooze, You Don't Lose

Temptations for fun abound, and achieving a reasonable standard of living means putting time and energy into productive pursuits. You probably work hard and like to enjoy leisure activities. In addition, the plethora of modern communication devices and the ability to easily travel from place to place avail us of a great many opportunities. When we want to live life to the fullest, sleep is often considered a thief of time.

Our modern culture supports an erroneous belief that if you snooze, you lose. It is common for us to cut back on sleep so we can pack more activities into our waking lives, but is this wise? The Vedic sages didn't think so, and modern scientific research validates their thinking. Sleep is indeed an often forgotten and unappreciated blessing. Our mind-body suffers untold ailments if we accumulate a sleep debt. Mild depression can be a signal, telling us that it is time to wake up to reality and sleep more. A bout of major depression, on the other hand, is our physiology's way of taking its due.

Studies have shown that we should sleep one hour for every two hours we are awake. This means that most of us need eight hours a night. Of course, some people need more and others need less. If we miss more than we require, the incurred debt has to be repaid, or else we pay. We are both the borrower and the creditor of our sleep debt. We have borrowed from existing reservoirs of energy, and the impact of the debt is lodged in our bodies. Eventually our physiology will become like an angry and relentless collection agency demanding payment. Without payment, interest is siphoned off through a variety of physiological ills—including depression.

The Price We Pay for Not Getting Enough Sleep

Success in life depends on our ability to be awake and aware; ironically, both wakefulness and awareness require deep, restorative sleep.

Nevertheless, throughout the centuries, every society has looked for artificial ways to keep the brain stimulated without sleep. Sigmund Freud, for example, supported the use of cocaine to this end—that is, until the deleterious effects of this drug, including its addictive qualities and its propensity to induce psychosis, made it unpopular. Currently, our society sanctions caffeine to keep us going. In extreme cases, other stimulant drugs are prescribed to suppress the symptoms of the sleep-deprived.

Human beings erroneously believe that sleep is a detriment to success. In truth, it is losing sleep that comes with a high price tag. Sleep deprivation impacts job performance and burdens the mind. It impairs memory and concentration, decreases efficiency in completing daily tasks, and thwarts one's ability to problem-solve. Without mental energy, creativity is blocked. Weariness of the body translates into emotions that drag you down. Your sleepless mind will hijack your body and your emotions at unexpected times. Proper sleep is a prerequisite for success in all areas of life.

Sleeplessness goes against the dictates of Mother Nature. According to Ayurveda, whenever we go against the natural flow of the biological world, we endanger our well-being and create doshic imbalances in our physiology. Since the doshas, as overarching principles, coordinate the proper functioning of the mind-body, doshic derangements are a harbinger of bad effects. There is nothing like a physiological breakdown to bring on depression.

Seen through the eyes of the exhausted, life is pale and weak. Tired people feel sick, unstable, sluggish, and unglued. The brain turns to mush. With unclear thinking, we misunderstand what we hear and misrepresent what we feel. The next thing we know, we are snapping at people, making bad decisions, and nodding off here, there, and everywhere. All aspects of life—relationships, creativity, productivity, enjoyment—suffer. Some of our sleepless friends even worry about early dementia when word retrieval fails them or they forget where they have put their keys for the third time that day. When you forgo recharging your body with sleep, you relinquish the vitality that is necessary to enjoy living.

If you snooze, you won't lose, nor will you become depressed. It is our belief that fatigue is the number one underlying cause of depression. Rest is a most powerful antidote for depression: it prevents and cures it.

The Benefits of Sleep

Your body undergoes myriad tasks while your eyes are closed and consciousness has escaped you. From the cellular level to the subtle spirit realm, sleep allows you to do the following:

Give your cells a refreshing bath. Sleep allows a change in the chemicals that bathe all of the cells of the body, thus enabling the process of renewal. Your pituitary gland, which is in your brain, produces a chemical called growth hormone. In children, this hormone promotes growth and development; in adults, it maintains our vitality by promoting the repair and renewal of tissues. If we are sleep-deprived, we deny ourselves these enriching benefits.

Rebuild your neural networks. When you sleep, your brain is able to relax and generate new thoughts. Information is stored in your long-term memory, and you will be better able to access that part of the brain when you are awake. The saying "Sleep on it and you'll see things differently in the morning" is based on hard facts. Basically, new brain patterns are created.

Strengthen your bodyguards. During sleep, the brain directs the body to heal and repair itself, rebuild damaged or worn-out tissues, and restore chemical balance. Natural killer cells are manufactured by your immune system. These cells are the "soldiers" of the immune system, ready to fight invaders at a moment's notice.

Clean up your act. During sleep, your physiology diverts most of its energy to the purification of your body. "Cleanup crews" collect and discard toxins and cellular debris (*ama*). During sleep your digestive fire burns off the *ama* in your system. Without *ama*, the drama of depression is gone. Unimpeded by gunk, the delivery channels in your body will carry your life force, or *prana*.

Give a lift to your spirit. Sleep provides the mental clarity you need to develop self-awareness. It adds depth to your thinking, allowing a greater appreciation of the richness of the abstract aspects of our lives—that which we can see only with our mind's eye. Spirituality is enhanced by a well-rested physiology.

Heal a broken heart. What sleep giveth, sleep debt taketh away. Sleep deprivation creates ill health. Whether you are chronically sleep-deprived or have just missed one night, the likelihood is that you will suffer the consequence of feeling daytime drowsiness. In order to stay awake, your body is forced to continuously activate your sympathetic nervous system. It is as if you are keeping your foot on the gas pedal and revving up the engine even when you are parked. The long-term effects of revving up the body are as follows:

- It raises blood pressure. As your blood vessels constrict, your heart is forced to pump harder.

- It puts your immune system in jeopardy. Your immune system can neither manufacture nor activate its highly effective sentinel cells if you are lacking sleep.

- It increases the blood levels of stress hormones, especially cortisol, so your body feels as if it is constantly under siege. This increase in cortisol makes you gain weight easily, especially around the waist, and you are unable to readily shed the excess padding.

- It causes you to feel sick and tired. Your body encounters difficulty in regulating its energy level because the long-term effect of stress hormones is to impede the efficient transformation of glucose into energy at the cellular level. Your pancreas is under physiological stress because it has to work beyond its normal capacity to maintain healthy blood-sugar levels by pumping increasing quantities of insulin. This predisposes you to diabetes and general ill health.

- It disturbs the electrical impulses that create the rhythmic beating of your heart. An unsteady heartbeat leads to inefficient pumping.

- It breaks your heart. It introduces the highest risk factors for heart disease: increased blood pressure, diabetes, irregular heart rhythms, and chronic sadness. Depression is closely related to heart disease.

Attuning Ourselves to the Rhythms of Nature

Our bodies work best if we go with our genetically programmed biorhythms. If our habits surge against the programming of nature, our physiology will rebel. Our body will feel as if it has become our enemy: assaulting us, triggering myriad problems, and obstructing our capacity for happiness.

As creatures of nature, we are innately receptive to the rhythms of the natural world. As critters of habit, our task is to align our lifestyle with the flow of our internal programming. Chronobiology, a branch of modern medicine, informs us that our bodies are finely tuned chronometers. Our temperature fluctuations, the production of our hormones and enzymes, and all of the body's neurological and endocrine functions follow internal rhythms that often mimic cycles in nature such as a circadian, or daily (twenty-four-hour), cycle. We also respond to lunar (thirty-day) cycles, solar (one-year) cycles, and the ebb and flow of the tides. These cycles greatly influence every aspect of physical functioning.

The concepts of chronobiology would not be new to the Vedic sages. The primary principle of Ayurveda has been that human physiology is an aspect of the natural world. Health will flourish if we allow the natural programming of our physiology to take the lead. We accomplish this by living in sync with the cycles of nature and by understanding the messages that are encrypted in the doshas.

As the saying goes, to everything there is a season and a time to every purpose under heaven. *When* we catch our zzzz's is just as important as how many hours of sleep we get. The notion that eight hours of sleep during the day is just as beneficial for the upkeep of the mind-body as eight hours of sleep at night should be quashed. The biochemistry of our body supports sleeping from 10 p.m. to 6 a.m. During this time, our hormonal cycle prepares our physiology to obtain the most restorative rest. It seems that Benjamin Franklin's advice was right: early to bed and early to rise makes a person healthy, wealthy, and wise—and to this we would like to add happy!

So primed is the body to rest by 10 p.m. that scheduling sleep at this time is often an antidote for insomnia. People who have insomnia have the most to gain from this information. They fear going to bed early, because they anticipate that they will toss and turn endlessly. In fact, the opposite is true.

Ayurveda and Western science agree that a 10 p.m. bedtime is optimal. It is during this time in the evening that the hormone melatonin rises and peaks in our body. This hormone prepares us to rest and nest. By lying down to sleep by 10 p.m., we allow ourselves to seize the opportunity that our biorhythms have provided for us. We ride this biological wave and ensure the kind of deep rest that dispels fatigue.

Depression and Sleeplessness: Which Came First, the Chicken or the EEG?

When you are depressed, sleep is amiss. We also know that sleep debt is a major contributing factor to depression. With regard to the broken brain (imbalances in the neurotransmitters), the question is this: Which came first—the depression or the sleep debt?

Sleep debt breaks the brain. The brain possesses stimulating bio-chemicals that prepare it for interaction with the world. If either the production or the synergistic functioning of these neurochemicals is altered, our emotional health is jeopardized. Like a theater director, sleep sets the tone for the performance of the molecules of emotion.

By impairing the production and activity of brain chemicals, sleep debt diminishes our emotional well-being. We lose our optimism. Our enthusiasm for the things we love is squelched. Resiliency is challenged when we need it most. If the balance of waking time and sleeping time is disturbed, our spirit begins to fade. Good spirits *do* come in a bottle, but sleeping at night is the healthier way for them to be engendered.

Sleep and Emotion

Deep in the brain stem there is a bundle of nerves that are exquisitely sensitive to the rhythms of nature. This bundle is called the reticular activating system (RAS). Its nerve cells receive messages from the suprachiasmatic nucleus (neuron clusters in the hypothalamus) about environmental cues such as light. The sleep-wake cycle is naturally set here. By interfering with the cues sent by Mother Nature, we throw a wrench into the works and disturb our sleep and our mood.

From the RAS, messages are sent to the rest of the brain about patterns of activity. The nerve cells in this area also interact with the limbic system, the emotional part of the brain. The limbic system has a concentration of neurotransmitters that are associated with mood: primarily norepinephrine, dopamine, acetylcholine, and serotonin.

The parts of the brain that affect physical and emotional activity are thus intimately related, probably because the capacity to react quickly to a challenge requires both a primed body and emotional motivation. By being in sync with our circadian rhythms and getting a good night's sleep, the RAS competently grooms our emotional brain. The flood of norepinephrine and dopamine that rushes through our bloodstream lifts our energy level and motivates our mind-body.

Sleep affects mood. Physical, mental, and emotional activity triggers the release of biochemicals from nerve cells, thereby depleting the resources that are available for the body. Sleep and the deep rest that some meditation techniques provide replenish the supply. Your body speaks to you through physical and emotional messages. Like the low-fuel light on the instrument panel of a car, the symptoms that accompany sleep deprivation are warning signals that you need to stop and refuel or suffer the consequences of running out of gas. Your body's natural intelligence is trying to tell you something: "Either help me or get out of my way!"

Now that we've described the problem, let's talk about solutions.

The Pill versus the Pillow

Every generation throughout civilized history has tried to bottle a substance that will energize the brain. There are all sorts of artificial substances that keep us going short-term. These include cocaine, caffeine, and prescription drugs. We want to have our cake and eat it, too: we want to feel good without taking the time to get the rest we need. Nevertheless, the only way to fully energize the brain is to follow nature's prescription and give the body as much sleep as it needs. Failure to do this is likely to result is a sleep-deprived body that will eventually succumb to depression.

It is not unusual for people with depression to take an antidepressant to get them geared up for the day and then a tranquilizer or a sleeping pill to help them relax in the evening and fall asleep at night. This is understandable, given the desperate need to function in the day and recharge one's energies at night. However, this turns the regulation of the sleep-wake cycle over to synthetic pharmacology, and we all know that that's not what we need. We all sense that within us lies a natural intelligence that is eager to awaken us and also put us to sleep. There has to be another way!

Dr. William C. Dement is the world's leading authority on sleep, sleep deprivation, and the diagnosis and treatment of sleep disorders. He is the past chairman of the National Commission on Sleep Disorders Research, and his work led directly to the creation of a new agency within the National Institutes of Health, the National Center on Sleep Disorders Research. In his book *The Promise of Sleep*, Dement writes the following:

> For now, the body's own natural chemistry is the most reliable, sustainable way to set the brain up to enjoy life. Without excessive sleep-debt to hold it back, the healthy brain is practically a vitality machine, creating the chemical environment necessary for vigorously engaging and conquering life's challenges. Artificial stimulants may be beneficial in the short term to level out the settings of the biological clock or to deal with emergencies. But, until proven otherwise (which may never happen), healthy sleep is the best long-term strategy for spurring brain activity and lifting our spirits.

Snoozing: The Natural Means to Awaken the Brain

When deciding whether to take a pill or hit the pillow, consider this: the majority of antidepressant compounds suppress REM sleep, the stage of sleep in which dreaming occurs. This has many consequences for the body.

Brain health and the regulation of neurochemicals depend on the physiology going through all of the discrete stages of sleep. REM sleep is essential for the consolidation of memory. One of the main symptoms of sleep deprivation is difficulty remembering. This is why students are urged to get a good night's sleep before an exam. Without sleep they will be less likely to retain the information they meticulously gathered while studying.

The purpose of antidepressants is to activate brain function. Essentially, they rev you up, making it difficult to attain the relaxation response required for sleep. Disrupting sleep architecture—the structure, or discrete stages, of sleep—can indirectly trigger sleep disorders.

Life Is a Mess When Sleep Is Amiss

Every aspect of human life depends on the awareness we bring to it. The more aware we are of our environment, the safer we are. The more aware we are of our thoughts and feelings, the better we handle our relationships. The more aware we are of our body—its needs and its reactions to our dietary habits and lifestyle—the healthier we are.

Awareness is dependent on proper physiological functioning, which in turn is dependent on proper rest. Sleep releases the impact of stress from the day. Sleep allows for the integration and growth of the nervous system. With deeper rest comes increased capacity.

The deleterious effects of sleep debt are not usually immediate. This makes it easy for us to be tricked into believing that burning the midnight oil doesn't matter, that it doesn't really affect our health—at least not long-term. How wrong we can be!

Sleep is a natural process that releases physiological stress. By rebalancing all aspects of body, mind, and spirit, sleep recharges your supply of vitality. Sleep impacts the quality of our consciousness and our ability to function in the practical world. It affects our awareness of the abstract values of life. This is why deep sleep is essential in the prevention and treatment of depression.

The combination of sleep and meditation is the best natural antidepressant. Sleep enables the integration of the nervous system, and meditation enhances this process. Together they help an individual to develop a greater perception of reality. The better we rest, the more keen our perceptions.

Millions of people have difficulty falling asleep or staying asleep. For these problems the Vedic sages have advice.

Sleep: Guidelines from A to Zzzz's

If you're serious about repaying your sleep debt to your physiology, Ayurveda can help you to maximize the payments. Sleep is improved if you pamper your nervous system. Do this by pacifying the dosha that most directly affects your nerves: Vata.

People frequently don't get the sleep they need because they do not see it as a priority when they have many things pressing on them:

everything from preparing for the next day's work to helping the kids prepare for theirs. We don't want to add to your burdens by giving you a complicated list of steps for how to fall asleep. Just approach sleep as you would romance, because, after all, sleep must be wooed, not willed.

Ayurveda offers practical guidelines for helping the body to prepare for sleep. You are certainly not going to do all of them; simply pick what catches your eye and flirt with it. If you choose what suits you and do it consistently, you will begin to be able to fall asleep more easily and maintain your sleep.

These recommendations are intended to help you repay the sleep debt your physiology has incurred. Depending on the extent of your sleep debt, you may need to follow these guidelines for a couple of days, a week, or even months until you feel better. Think of these guidelines as an investment in your physical, mental, and emotional health. The time you put into resolving your sleep debt will pay off as you regain vitality and embrace life with more zest.

Consistency Pays Off

- Maintain a regular daily routine: meditate, eat, and sleep at approximately the same times every day. Your physiology craves consistency. It needs to know what to expect and responds better to the structure you give it.

- Set a firm date with yourself to be in bed (lights out as close to 10:00 p.m. as possible). Consider doing this as much as possible until you resolve your sleep debt. This is an invaluable investment in the future of your health.

Commitment Counts

- Make a regular daily practice of meditating and doing yoga postures.

- Eat dinner as early as you can so you can to ensure the adequate digestion of your food. Go for a short walk afterward to facilitate the digestive process. Alternatively, eat a light and liquid meal, preferably soup or a healthful smoothie.

- As much as possible, do only light mental activity after dinner: avoid TV, focused work, intense conversation, and excessively stimulating entertainment.

Indulge Your Senses

The skin is not just an outer covering. It is the largest organ of your body. This organ relays information from the outside world to your inside world. Besides maintaining physical integrity, it allows for the integrated functioning of your mind-body because it is so intimately related to the nervous, immune, and endocrine systems.

* The simplest way to soothe your nerves is to do self-oleation. This simple procedure will yield many benefits. Instructions on how to do it and an explanation of how it pacifies your nervous system are in the next section. Self-oleation can be done before bedtime for a few weeks, until sleep improves.

* Lubricate your nasal passages with oil to ensure ease of breathing and to calm your mind. Your nasal passages are a link to your brain. By putting a few drops of oil in your nose, you are caressing your brain into slumber. Herbalized oils for use in the nose are available from Ayurvedic product distributors (see Resources). Look under the category of *anu thailam* or *nasya* for a nose oil to rectify your doshic imbalance.

* Befriend your brain with aromatherapy.

* Lull your mind to sleep with relaxing music.

Be Your Own Best Bed-Buddy

* Make the bedroom environment conducive for resting and nesting.

* Make your bed as comfortable as possible.

* Figure out the room temperature you need in order to trigger sleep.

Prepare for Your Date in Bed Hours Ahead

* Optimize digestion
  ○ Minimize eating between meals.
  ○ Avoid cold, frozen, or leftover foods.
  ○ Avoid or minimize meat.
  ○ Avoid drinking water with every bite.
  ○ Avoid eating too quickly or too slowly.

- Balance Pitta dosha
  - ○ Minimize intensely spicy or very oily food.
  - ○ Say no to alcohol.
- Balance Vata dosha
  - ○ Refrain from sleeping in the daytime.
  - ○ Monitor your mind's impressions by keeping a clean and orderly environment.

Oil: Royal Treatment for the Mind-Body

The ancient Ayurvedic texts describe the process of *abhyanga*, or massaging with oil, as having profound health benefits. In fact, it's been said that the expression "getting the royal treatment" refers to the days when the maharajas (Hindu princes) regularly received Ayurvedic massages from their servants. You too can treat your mind-body to this majestic sensual experience, knowing that there is Western scientific proof to back the assertions made by the Vedic sages.

Oiling the skin, which seems to have been a therapy of choice in ancient times, improves one's capacity to digest life by building strength and flexibility, toning the nervous system, enhancing immunity, inducing hormonal balance, and aiding in the detoxification of the physiology. Since the roots of depression can often be traced to an ailing physiology, regularly massaging the skin is a way of undoing depression. *Abhyanga* is thus an agent of vitality. The *Charaka Samhita*, the most authoritative ancient Ayurvedic text, states the following about *abhyanga*:

> Of one whose head is every day saturated with oil, headaches never appear, nor baldness, nor the effects of decrepitude; the hair of such a man does not fall off. The head and skull, in particular, of such a man acquires great strength. By anointing one's head with oil, one clears one's senses, and the skin of one's face becomes good; one gets sleep easily, and one feels ease in every respect. By applying oil every day to one's ears, one becomes free

from all disorder of the ear born of Vata, wry-neck, lockjaw, hardness of hearing, and deafness. As an earthen jar saturated with oil, a piece of leather rubbed therewith, or the axle of a car or cart from application of the same substance becomes strong and capable of resisting wear and tear, even so, by application of oil, the body becomes strong, the skin improves, and all disorders due to Vata are dispelled. Through such means the body also becomes capable of enduring exercise and fatigue.

The skin is not merely a physical barrier. Besides being the largest organ of detoxification, the skin plays an integral role in the functioning of your immune and endocrine systems. Oiling your body is designed to stimulate blood flow through the circulatory and lymphatic (where your body disposes toxic waste) systems, thereby strengthening the immune system; hormone receptors are also stimulated. Here are other benefits of oiling:

Calms the nervous system. Calming the nerves is beneficial to the mind. The process of oiling and massaging the skin increases the circulation of blood to the nerve endings. This accounts for its soothing effect. Massaging with warm oil brings about the relaxation response that is associated with the activation of the parasympathetic nervous system. Our physical and mental stamina improves as our digestive capacity is enhanced and restorative sleep becomes easier.

Stimulates the endocrine system. According to Ayurveda, there is a correlation among depression, aging, and the atrophy of hormonal glands. Optimal health maintenance requires the proper functioning of the glandular system. Daily massage increases blood circulation to these glands, thus retarding their deterioration.

Tones the muscular and skeletal system. By toning the muscles and lubricating the joints, massaging wipes away the daily wear and tear that they receive. Muscular aches and pains can often get in the way of our ability to rest. They adversely impact sleep, either by not letting the body settle down or by interrupting the process. The aches and pains of the body, by echoing the moans and groans of the mind, can often add to the spiritual malaise of depression.

Promotes detoxification. Oiling promotes the release of toxins from the physiology by priming the skin to do its job. Oiling facilitates the release of the toxins from both the cellular level and the circulatory system. By penetrating the pores and reaching deep into the layers of the skin, oiling loosens impurities and toxins. Oiling relieves depression because a toxin-filled body is more susceptible to depression given that toxins block the flow of energy throughout the physiology.

Sesame Oil

The properties of the oils used for *abhyanga* play a tremendous role in rejuvenation. Let's look at sesame oil as an example.

Sesame oil is 40 percent linoleic acid, a liquid unsaturated fatty acid. The chemical structure of sesame oil allows it to penetrate deep into the skin. It is an omega-6 fatty acid, which is essential for the growth, development, and maintenance of the nervous system. Linoleic acid can be readily ingested by the skin and incorporated at the cellular level.

Sesame oil is a powerful anticarcinogen: Laboratory studies have shown that sesame oil inhibits the growth of malignant tumors on the skin and in the colon. Sesame oil is teeming with antioxidant power, and heating the oil enhances its properties.

Once absorbed into the skin, sesame oil shields it from harmful ultraviolet light and enhances its ability to make vitamin D. A depletion of vitamin D can add to a depressed mood.

A Lesson in Oil Massage

There's an adage that it takes money to make money. Similarly, we believe that it takes time to make time. The time you invest in caring for your mind-body will result in your feeling more on top of life. An oil massage can take anywhere from three to twenty minutes, depending on how much time you have to invest.

First, find an oil that suits you. Sesame oil works for most people. It balances Vata, Pitta, and Kapha doshas and has many salutary properties, as we have described above. The oil must be cured and warmed to activate its effects. Be sure that any oil you use is organic and of the highest quality. Given the vital function of the skin as an organ, the Ayurvedic advice is this: if you wouldn't put it in your mouth, you shouldn't put it on your skin.

If you have a Burning Depression and sesame oil leaves you feeling physically hot or emotionally irritable, consider a cooling oil, such as olive oil or almond oil in the winter and coconut oil in the summer. You can also use herbalized oils (see Resources) formulated to bring doshic balance.

Preparatory Steps

1. You will be doing a full-body massage with approximately one cup of oil. It is best to place a large towel on the floor so you don't have to worry about the oil dripping.

2. Use a nonbreakable container; things become slippery when oil is involved.

3. Have disposable rags or heavy-duty paper towels on hand with which to wipe off excess oil.

What to Do

1. Warm the massage oil. Place the container in a hot-water bath for a few minutes to warm it to slightly above body temperature. Pour the oil on your body, starting with the head. Do not forget your ears, scalp, and feet. Be generous.

2. Massage the body.

3. Apply light pressure on sensitive areas such as the abdomen or the heart. Use more oil and spend more time where nerve endings are concentrated: the soles of the feet, the palms of the hands, the head, and the ears.

4. Use circular motions over the joints and straight strokes on your arms and legs. Use a clockwise rotation over your abdominal region (this is the direction in which the large intestine moves). On your upper torso, the motion should be toward your heart.

5. Allow the oil to soak in for five to ten minutes. When you are finished, wipe off the excess oil with the disposable rag or heavy-duty paper towel.

6. Shower. Do *not* wet your head before applying the shampoo. Putting the shampoo on first will remove the oil from your hair. Use a gentle soap so you don't strip the oil from your skin.

7. Perform the oil massage and shower approximately one hour before bedtime. Your sleep will be dreamy.

Sleep Serenade: How to Sleep Until Sunrise

Oil Yourself

Perform your oil massage on a daily basis for at least three weeks to determine its effect on sleep and resetting your biorhythms. Follow this with a warm bath or shower. If you find it difficult or too stimulating to bathe at night, then limit the application of the oil to your scalp and the soles of your feet. Spend several minutes rubbing the soles of your feet back and forth with the open palm of your hand. Either wash off the excess oil from your feet or wear old socks to bed to keep the bed from getting oily. (Consider pretreating sheets with vinegar and detergent before washing if the sheets are saturated with oil.)

Concoct a Sleeping Remedy

After oiling, prepare 1 cup of boiled milk with ¼ teaspoon of nutmeg and 2 pinches of cardamom. If you are intolerant of cow's milk, use goat's milk or take ½ cup of chamomile, lavender, or rose tea instead.

While sipping your milk or tea, listen to some soothing classical instrumental music for ten minutes.

Try Aromatherapy

In a saucer of warm water placed next to your bed, put three to five drops of aromatherapy oil (see the sidebar "Aromatherapy: Making Sense of Scents" on page 205). Try various aromas to find one that evokes a sense of tranquility, such as lavender, sandalwood, jasmine, or rose.

Have a Midnight Snack

Place half a glass of milk or a ripe pear at your bedside. If you awaken in the night and are not asleep again within ten minutes, partake of this snack. This has the effect of settling Vata dosha as well as cooling Pitta dosha.

Aromatherapy: Making Sense of Scents

The nose is an open gateway to the brain. When aromatic molecules hit the smell receptors in the olfactory bulbs in the nose, they swiftly convey messages to the nervous system. Olfactory stimulation affects the limbic system—a major center for the formation and processing of emotion and learning and for storing memories. Messages delivered to the limbic system through the olfactory bulbs generally evoke an instinctive emotional and often instantaneous physical response. It is for this reason that early in our infancy we learn to rely on our sense of smell to navigate our environment. Scents carry with them subtle yet powerful messages that influence the state of Vata, Pitta, and Kapha doshas.

Vata-balancing blends generally include sweet warming oils such as jasmine and lavender that soothe the mind and emotions and have a grounding effect on the mind-body. Adding half a cup of Epsom salts and a fistful of baking soda to bathwater can help remove aches and pains. The salt has heating properties that bring balance to Vata dosha, and the baking soda helps remove the lactic acid buildup in muscles.

Pitta-balancing blends soothe by infusing the cooling, calming energy of essential oils such as rose and sandalwood. Consider adding these essential oils to a lukewarm bath to shed excessive physical and mental heat from the body. Add a half cup of nonfat evaporated milk and a half cup of whole evaporated milk to the water for an extra soothing effect. Milk has a balancing effect on Pitta dosha.

Kapha-balancing blends are generally warm, spicy, and invigorating scents. They may contain vital oils such as eucalyptus, camphor, cedar, rosemary, and cloves. Consider adding these essential oils to your shower gel (use four to six drops per two ounces of unscented cleanser). A drop of eucalyptus clears congestion (a sign of Kapha accumulation) from the head and chest when used in steam therapy or in a diffuser.

Airy Depression: The Wind That Blows Sleep Away

Arial's body was exhausted—it was almost too tired from the tossing and turning she did every night. She began to fear going to bed. After only a few hours of sleep, watching the sun rise at the beginning of another workday merely added to her feeling of being overwhelmed.

Arial felt as if she had an internal fan blowing confetti inside her. She was on edge, anxious, afraid of what was around the corner. Thoughts came rapidly one after another, and letting go of them was difficult. She found refuge from her anxiety by running from one thing to another, keeping herself constantly busy. It was difficult for her to rest her body.

Not only did Arial experience continuous fatigue, she was frequently sick. She was definitely tired of being sick and tired. In the past six months she had had several colds and frequent problems with her digestive system.

Arial was so internally revved up that it was hard for her to rest. She is not alone: a recent study revealed that one-third of parents and two-thirds of older Americans have trouble going to sleep, which contributes to depression, anxiety, and lowered immunity.

Difficulty falling asleep is usually caused by an imbalance in Vata dosha. In particular, it indicates a problem in the aspect of Vata that correlates with the brain. An imbalance in this dosha causes a mental whirlwind, which in turn drains the brain of nourishment. In Western terms, it causes a depletion of neurochemicals.

It was imperative to address this problem with expediency, so we recommended that Arial take an herbal formula to help with insomnia. The ideal formula contains herbs such as Indian valerian, jatamansi, and ashwagandha (see Resources). These herbs work synergistically to balance, nourish, and calm the mind, the senses, and the nervous system. They improved the quality of Arial's sleep, enabling her physiology to repair the damage resulting from sleep debt. In addition to improving her immunity and reversing the damage caused by sleep debt, they also enhanced the coordinated functioning of her heart and her mind. This improved integration of emotion (heart) and thought (mind) brought Arial an increased sense of well-being and contentment. However, in order to relieve insomnia long-term, it was essential for her to make lifestyle adjustments.

For Arial, the most important therapeutic intervention was to stop ingesting mind-racing, body-stimulating substances such as caffeinated drinks. A creature of habit (as we all are), she had grown accustomed to beginning the day with coffee, and she looked forward to her afternoon sodas.

To maximize the quality of sleep—to catch and surf the wave of nature, so to speak—meant that Arial was to be settled in bed and ready to snooze by 10 p.m. We advised her to avoid actively trying to fall asleep. Instead, we recommended that she direct her attention to her breath. The general rule is to let sleep come to you, don't chase after it.

Arial needs regularity in her day. She had gotten used to eating on the run and sleeping whenever she could. Her body needs to anticipate sleep time by gathering cues from the environment. We suggested that she keep her bedroom dark. Darkness is necessary for the production of the hormone melatonin, which prepares the body for sleep. In order to minimize all sources of intense light, she was encouraged not to read, work on the computer, or watch TV for two hours before her designated bedtime.

Warm, heavy foods, such as soups and stews, balance Vata dosha. These are true comfort foods. We asked Arial to favor sweet, sour, and salty tastes. Believe it or not, in time, a sweet fruit juice instead of a caffeinated drink began giving her an afternoon boost. In addition, we suggested that Arial favor spices that bring warmth to the body. Nutmeg or cinnamon in warm milk at night was a tasty way to end the day.

Restorative yoga poses, meditation, and calming breathing exercises also went a long way in helping Arial to embrace sleep.

Burning Depression: Alert but Not Ready for the Day

After a long day of work, while preparing dinner, Barbara relaxed with a couple of glasses of wine. She spent the remainder of the evening finishing up her work, then went to bed around midnight. She was exhausted, so sleep came easily to her. After a few hours, however, her brain would spring into action. She would turn to look at her alarm clock, amazed to see that it had happened again: at 3 a.m. she was awake and alert but too tired to start her day.

During the day, Barbara experienced enormous mental pressure. Her internal conflict came from simultaneously feeling driven to succeed but thwarted in the process. Barbara felt a continuous undertow of irritability and frustration. These feelings became a reality in her behavior. Through her interactions—which were expressions of her internal feelings—she was actively undermining her personal relationships. In turn, these damaged relationships were adding to her depressed state.

Migraines brought her home from work early at least once or twice a month. Dermatological problems also haunted her. Barbara was embarrassed by her adult acne, which seemed to flare up with increasingly regularity. She noticed that stress seemed to encourage its onset at the most inopportune times. These symptoms only got worse when her sleep was truncated.

Difficulty maintaining sleep often results from a combination of both Vata and Pitta imbalances. When we approach life with great intensity, we eventually experience a buildup of energy that manifests as mental pressure. This mental pressure pushes on the mind-body like a wave beating against the walls of a dam. The mental wall that kept us asleep becomes lighter and less structurally fortified during the early-morning hours. Now the wave of mental pressure can break through the wall and wake us up. The mind awakens, but the body, still burdened by fatigue, fails to spring into action.

Minimizing caffeine and other stimulants was essential for the correction of Barbara's sleep problems. The half-life of caffeine is about six hours. This means that consuming caffeine even in the morning can still affect you in the evening and negatively impact the quality of sleep at night. We alerted Barbara to watch out for hidden sources of caffeine, such as chocolate, her favorite afternoon snack.

The alcohol that Barbara was drinking every night was toxic to her nervous system and her brain. Alcohol calms the physiology for an hour or two because it suppresses brain function. However, this suppression of normal performance results in a rebound wave of mental hyperactivity. Pushing Barbara out of slumber, this rebound hyperactivity jolted her mind awake but failed to joggle her body.

We advised Barbara not to overexercise. Studies have shown that twenty minutes of exercise daily is optimal for health maintenance. Exercise stimulates the sympathetic nervous system. After all, your body doesn't know that you are exercising for health reasons (it thinks that perhaps you are running away from a bear!). The stress response induced by excessive exercise does give us a mental and physical boost. However, this effect can be counterproductive for the purpose of being able to fall asleep.

We suggested that Barbara exercise in the morning. Revving up our physiology late in the evening throws our circadian biorhythms out of balance. Exercising in the morning effectively regulates our hormonal and neurochemical production. It sets the stage for our physiology to function optimally the rest of the day.

We also advised Barbara to eat her main meal at lunch and have a lighter, smaller dinner. She also moved dinnertime from 9 p.m. to 7 p.m. It is counterproductive to eat late in the evening. Food energizes our physiology, and an active digestive system interferes with the ability to relax and to slumber.

Finally, it was necessary for Barbara to cut down on her emotional responses to intensity. She accomplished this by monitoring her physical reactions to events throughout the day. It is natural to breathe more shallowly when we are focusing on mental work, so conscious attention to periodically taking deep breaths was important for her. When tension amassed, she also took short breaks to stretch. A daily walk became part of Barbara's lunchtime routine.

Earthy Depression: When Sleep Is Too Much of a Good Thing

The alarm jangled Ed into consciousness. As he opened his eyes, he felt a sinking feeling, remembering his depression and feeling its tentacles stretching out to strangle him. He heard Janice close the back door as she left for her morning walk. Ed rolled over, letting his head sink deeper into the pillow, and decided he just couldn't do it yet: he couldn't face the new day—perhaps a bit later. About 10 a.m. he woke up to hear Janice entreating him to rise and shine.

"Shine" he could not do, but with a heavy spirit and a guilty heart Ed hauled his body out of bed. He spent what was left of the morning moping around the house trying to find something to engage his interest. By lunchtime he had given up. The sad feelings were overwhelming. Eventually he found solace in the companionship of the TV. He retreated to the couch, where he dozed on and off.

The next thing he knew, Janice was nudging him to come to dinner. Four hours had passed. He woke up feeling groggy and ashamed. This only made him want to go back to sleep even more.

After helping Janice do the dishes he sat down to read a book but couldn't concentrate. His dinner was resting in his belly like heavy rocks. He drank a cup of coffee, hoping that it would help him to digest his food better. He knew that a walk would do him good, but he didn't have the energy. The television beckoned to him, and he couldn't resist the temptation to lie down again.

An hour later he woke up. He felt a little spry, and now there were some good shows on TV. When Janice walked though the living room to say good night, he replied, "I'll be right up." At around midnight, Ed craved a little something. He ate leftovers, then returned to the couch with a container of ice cream, which he consumed while watching reruns. Before he knew it, the ice cream was gone. Disgusted by the icky sweet taste that lingered in his mouth, he returned to the kitchen for a bag of potato chips.

At about 2 a.m., Ed made his weary way up the stairs to bed. He rested in bed for an hour, feeling dreadful and yucky. He had done it again.

The ultimate goal was to replace Ed's existing routine with another one. This requires a lot of motivation, which he doesn't have at this time. Ed needs to begin to feel lighter in his body first, before he can make the necessary changes.

In order to help him, we had to connect with his present state of mind. Although we might think that he could benefit from a boot in the bottom, what he desperately needed was nurturance. To this he would resonate. Rather than practicing denial and restriction, he needed interventions that offered him acceptance and expansion. He was motivated to try the Ayurvedic recommendations because they were easy to follow, but more important, they offered him comfort.

Depression was not just in Ed's head. At the root of his problems, we find a physiology replete with gunk, or *ama*. His sleep problem and depressed mood were cemented by this toxic buildup. Ed was caught in a vicious cycle: his behaviors generated *ama*, and the *ama* further promoted his feelings of depression and his unhealthy behavioral patterns. Fortunately for Ed, lessening the existing physical *ama* will alleviate the mental and emotional *ama*.

Excessive sleep indicates an imbalance in Kapha dosha. Reversing Ed's sleep pattern is the key to undoing the Earthy Depression he is experiencing. Until and unless this is accomplished, the heaviness in his heart will continue.

Ed began an *ama*-reducing Ayurvedic regimen. As soon as he woke up in the morning, he did breathing exercises that stimulated his metabolism by activating his sympathetic nervous system. These exercises (see chapter 10) blew away the cobwebs. Filling his lungs and delivering well-oxygenated blood to his cells made him feel good. Besides the breathing exercises, something as simple as opening the window to breathe in fresh air awakened his spirit. He was motivated to do this because it gave him immediate gratification.

Ed began to understand that his food choices were a response to an imbalance in Kapha dosha. We suggested he drink an *ama*-reducing tea throughout the day (see chapter 14). The mere action of sipping plain hot water has positive physiological effects for reducing *ama* by triggering the body to prepare for digestion. If there is no food present in the digestive tract, the digestive fire begins to break down the *ama* that already exists in the body. Spices like ginger, cumin, coriander, and fennel enhance this action. Without much effort, Ed's cravings were squelched.

Ed felt grungy. Garshan, an Ayurvedic dry massage, left him feeling meticulously clean. As if removing a layer of gunk from his body, this massage left his skin feeling light and tingly. Garshan (see sidebar "Garshan: The Brisk Massage That Rubs Away Depression" on the next page) stimulates circulation to all of the tissues of the body. It improves metabolism, thus facilitating the breakdown of *ama*. After doing Garshan, Ed was to do an oil massage with invigorating herbalized oils.

As his physiology became lighter, Ed was able to give up daytime napping. For several weeks he worked to get in sync with his natural biorhythms. He started by advancing his bedtime by a half hour every couple of days. Eventually he joined a volunteer group. The volunteering required him to be out and about all day long, thus ending his days spent on the couch.

Garshan: The Brisk Massage That Rubs Away Depression

Garshan brings lightness to the physiology and should be part of any *ama*-reducing regimen. Garshan takes only a few minutes and should precede oiling the body. By helping with the elimination of impurities, Garshan promotes weight loss and a reduction of cellulite—another good selling point. It energizes the body and braces you for the day. Garshan is ideally performed with a pair of raw silk gloves (but a loofah sponge or a skin brush also works well).

Here's what to do:

- Put on a pair of silk gloves.

- Massage the head first. Move down your neck and shoulder area.

- Using brisk and vigorous strokes, massage your body. Use long strokes over the long bones of your body and circular strokes over the joints.

- Use long horizontal strokes over your chest area, avoiding direct massage over the heart and the nipples.

- In the abdominal area, stroke twice diagonally and twice horizontally.

- In areas with a high concentration of fatty tissue, feel free to exert more force and spend more time as necessary.

Sleep's Promise of Health and Happiness

In our quest for wellness and prosperity, we focus on exercise and nutrition for the health benefits they provide. We use welcome supplements to give us energy so we can be alert and productive. Yet the main ingredient, the activity that is certain to provide us success in our undertakings, is the first thing we deny ourselves: sleep. Estimates are that losses in productivity from insufficient sleep reach into the billions. Next time you consider cutting into your sleep so you will have extra time to exercise, or when you reach for a nutritional supplement in the name of health, consider the following.

A study was conducted to determine the habits associated with good health. Americans were interviewed about their exercise, nutrition, smoking, sleep, and other health-related habits. The survey was repeated six years later. The investigators learned that of all the lifestyle factors investigated, a lack of regular sleep had the highest correlation with mortality. Sleep, this so often overlooked aspect of our lifestyle, was even more predictive of mortality than nutrition. Few things are more lifesaving than sleep; there are more automobile accidents and deaths caused each year from insufficient sleep than from drunk driving.

This is no surprise to Ayurveda. The *Charaka Samhita* states: "In the matter of keeping up the body, sleep is regarded to be productive of as much happiness as the taking of food." Happiness is the by-product of health, and from the perspective of the Vedic sages, sleep is on par with nutrition in offering health benefits.

Another study looked at the correlation between health and length and quality of sleep. The results were profound. Male poor sleepers were 6.5 times more likely than good sleepers to have health problems. Female poor sleepers were 3.5 times more likely than good sleepers to have health problems. It seems that modern science and ancient wisdom concur: high-quality sleep nourishes your health and your happiness.

Sunrise, Sunset, and Seasonal Change in Nature

Learning how to get a good night's sleep and understanding why it is important to do so can make you a better person overall. This is because it offers you an opportunity to get in sync with the rhythms of the natural world. Repaying your sleep debt to your physiology can liberate you from a life filled with offenses against wisdom. It can propel you into a life of balance.

Nature's cyclical patterns are evident. Since we are part of the natural world, we, too, experience cycles, except that our cycles are not always as evident, and they often suffer disruption because of our lifestyle. This exercise will help you to map out the current rhythms in your physiology. After you finish, invite a person close to you to help you confirm your impressions.

Principle 1: As Is the Macrocosm, So Is the Microcosm

- How do you feel physically in the summer, spring, fall, and winter?

- How is your mood affected by the changes in the seasons?

- How are your behaviors impacted by the changes in the seasons?

- How are your sleeping patterns impacted by the changes in the seasons?

- How are your dietary habits impacted by the changes in the seasons?

- What patterns do you see in terms of how the seasons of the year affect the cycles of your life?

Principle 2: Biorhythms Are Genetically Programmed into Our Physiology

Make use of an hourly appointment book to track the different cycles you experience in the day. During the course of each day, note the following:

- When do you have surges of physical energy?

- When do you have surges of mental energy?

- When do you get hungry?

- When do you feel clearheaded and creative?

- When do you experience bouts of emotional fatigue?

- When do you feel lethargic and slow-moving?

- When do you feel active and focused?

- When do you feel settled and comfortable?

As you continue to integrate the suggestions made in this chapter, notice if there are any changes in the daily natural rhythms of your physiology. Notice if the trend is toward becoming more in sync with the rising and setting of the sun.

14

Food: Nourishing Rites

> The belly rules the mind.
>
> —SPANISH PROVERB

Depression is not just in your head; its roots can be at the physical level of your being. The symptoms of depression might well mean that your body is depleted of energy. Like a perpetual hangover, these symptoms can signify that your system is gunked up with the remnants of unprocessed food. Undoing depression requires nourishing the body so that your spirit can have the physical support it needs to manifest itself.

Depression results from physiological imbalances that block the expression of our life force, which transports not only the natural intelligence that manages the universe but also the vibratory essence of our being. The flow of our life force is therefore the key to a properly functioning physiology, and we promote this through the manner in which we live our lives. In particular, how we eat and what we eat is very important. Consuming food is a nourishing rite that can help us to keep depression at bay.

The body, the mind, and the spirit form a seamless energetic system. If there is a snag in the fabric of any facet of one's physiology, it will affect the integrity of the totality. Similarly, health and wellness spread from one aspect of the mind-body to revitalize the rest of your being. Without a doubt, depression can make your body feel sick and tired, but can the reverse be true? Could emotional malaise and spiritual despair be a sign that your body is feeling blue? Nourishing rites that attend to the body offer a way into the seamless energetic system. We can infuse vitality into our entire being one morsel at a time.

When you are depressed, it becomes difficult to attend to your body. Those who are living with sadness are stuck in a vicious cycle. Like a tornado, depression threatens to draw the life force out of the physiology, but a tornado begins as a gentle shift that disturbs the balance of the elements of nature and then builds on itself.

So it is with us. Depression begins with an imbalance in our Vata, Pitta, or Kapha dosha. Left unattended, an imbalance in the mind-body can become a tumultuous event. The unbalanced physiology not only suffers symptoms of depression but also tilts the person in a direction of poor lifestyle habits. These habits, in turn, reinforce or introduce more imbalances and further increase disarray in all aspects of life. We find ourselves wondering how we encouraged the imbalances that threaten to topple us over into depression. How do we undo depression by nourishing our mind-body?

Diet: What's Eating You

Consider the things we do in the name of health. Disregarding Mother Nature, we adopt foolish lifestyles and take on the latest fad diet, thinking that it will make us look good and feel better. In general, our attention is focused on the superficial aspects of nutrition. We focus on what we put in our mouth because it impacts our body, forgetting that the highest purpose of eating is to nourish the spirit.

Food affects mood. All too often we discount the pivotal role that diet plays in mental health. For example, carbohydrates like breads, cookies, and cakes contain the biochemical building blocks that our body needs to make brain chemicals such as serotonin, so it is no surprise that such treats boost our mood and pacify negative emotions, at least short-term. On the other hand, the amino acids in proteins are used by the body to manufacture activating neurotransmitters such as dopamine, and unlike the mellow feeling we get from starch, foods like meats, eggs, and beans bolster our mental energy. Unconsciously, we use a variety of foods to fulfill our needs, but usually not with a long-term plan or deep awareness. Without thinking, we eat something for an immediate effect.

We often worry about what we eat and not about what's eating us. We may dive into food in a desire to fulfill an internal emptiness that has nothing to do with hunger, or we may restrict our food intake out of fear that it will increase our waistline, without realizing how this pattern of restriction impacts our emotional life.

Discerning how to care for the body is difficult when we are faced with an overload of nutritional information that points us in different directions. Almost daily, a new miracle food that will cure the ills of modern living is showcased. Faster than the speed of light, this natural product of the hour is artificially synthesized and packaged in a bottle. The list of books on diet and nutrition grows exponentially by the minute. Ironically, also growing is the incidence of chronic diseases in modern society. Perhaps Mark Twain put it best when he said, "I have never seen a man die of starvation, but I have seen many men die from eating." How can this madness be explained?

The madness behind the epidemic of sadness and other chronic illnesses is that we mess with what Mother Nature has given us. We have at our fingertips all we need in order to be healthy. Why add chemicals and preservatives to food? Why eat at the wrong times or in the wrong way? Why mess up natural metabolic processes by squelching our digestive fire? Why do we do this to ourselves? The Vedic sages would say that we all commit offenses against wisdom. With constricted awareness, we fail to intuit what is good for us. Love, nurturance, and comfort are the antidotes for depression—and from the Ayurvedic perspective, food serves as a medium to carry all of these qualities into our physiology.

The state of our general health is determined by the morsel of food at the end of our fork. Sadness is indicative that body, mind, and spirit are depleted of energy. The building blocks of our body come from the biochemicals in the food, but the liveliness that food imparts depends on its *prana*. If the food we eat lacks *prana*, we become energetically depleted and depressed. In this manner, food and mood are interlocking pieces of the holistic health puzzle. For this reason, we are going to focus not only on what to put in our body but also on how to feed our spirit.

Food: Courier of the Life Force

To create vitality and lightness of being, we must take a quantum leap from the mechanistic to the sublime. At the quantum level, the value of food is in its ability to transport the vibratory essence of the natural world into the body. Let's not talk about food in term of calories, protein, carbohydrates, fat, or even micronutrients like folic acid and vitamins. There's more to food than its biochemical building blocks. From now on, think of food as packets of information, couriers of universal intelligence and transporters of life-sustaining *prana*. (When consciousness meets food, life tastes good!)

We are familiar with Einstein's equation $E = mc^2$, but did you know that it applies to food? The theory of relativity echoes the ancient Vedic knowledge that all matter is energy and all energy becomes matter. The metabolic processes that take place in the body present a clear example of this principle in action. The conversion of matter into energy and of energy into matter is constantly going on in our physiology.

In light of this notion, what exactly is food? According to Ayurveda, it is matter that conveys energy to body, mind, and spirit. Ideally, food should carry with it good vibrations, or positive energetic imprints from the natural world. If what is consumed is correct for us, then these vibrations work synergistically to edify our physiology. What we eat carries energies and influences, imparting qualities and subtle effects to the mind-body. How different would our relationship to food be if, in addition to reading the label for calories and nutrients, we learned to experience the energetic message that food brings to us?

Good food becomes us. It's the life in our food that matters; the energy in the food becomes matter. We are what we eat, literally. Given this, how do we maximize the value of the food we consume? Ayurveda has suggestions.

Eat the freshest possible foods. In general, the fresher the food, the more *prana* it carries. The fresher the food, the more life you will extract from it. Food loses its value the longer it is stored. Even after only a few hours in the refrigerator, the vitality of food can be diminished. Stored food and leftovers bring little *prana* to our body. They fill us and give us some nutrients, but they do not give us liveliness.

In addition, highly processed foods are dead; they have had their natural intelligence wrung out of them. These make-believe foods have no real message or meaning to impart to our physiology. They do not bring the intelligence of the natural world into our bodies. When food neither nourishes the body nor feeds the spirit, we are left yearning for more.

Since the molecules of the food will be incorporated into our physical body, it is exceedingly important that the food's genetic makeup be compatible with ours. Food molecules must fit naturally in our body. We therefore recommend eating organically produced food. These foods come to us as Mother Nature intended. First, they are free of pesticides and other pollutants. Second, organically grown foods have not been genetically altered. The issue of genetically modified food has been politically controversial for the last several years. These foods have had their DNA altered. According to Ayurveda and many scientists in both the United States and Europe, we are best nourished by food that has *not* had its DNA altered.

Last but not least, take note of how your food is prepared. According to Ayurveda, the consciousness of the cook plays a huge role in the health-giving properties of the food. Cooks who care about their work infuse *prana* into the food they prepare. This can explain, in part, the healing properties of the traditional home-cooked meal: food made by the loving and attentive hands of a person who has a deep desire for the well-being of the recipients. The intention of the cook to prepare healing food that tastes good brings spiritual sustenance to the eater. Ideally, you should eat food that is prepared by a happy, settled cook.

The Process of Eating

Fresh and wholesome food brings wisdom and nourishment to us. Our body incorporates this wisdom and becomes infused with the liveliness of the food. Nourishing the body also calls for becoming cognizant of the many mechanisms at play when we eat. When we look at the causes of depression, we find that digestion is implicated. The roots of a depressed physiology can often be traced back to the following: suboptimal digestion, physiological imbalances, or an overload of toxins. Therefore, we must gain an increased awareness of not only what we eat but also how we eat, why we eat, when we eat, and how we feel after we eat. Regarding the nourishment of the physical body, ancient wisdom advises the following:

- **Optimize digestion**. From the Ayurvedic perspective, a primary concern is the ability to process what we put in our body, and this encompasses the four steps of ingestion, digestion, assimilation, and elimination.

- **Maintain doshic balance**. Once the digestive process is optimized, the next task is to utilize food in a manner that promotes physiological balance.

Let's investigate how to optimize digestion.

Ingestion: A Heady Experience

When we realize that we embody the food we ingest, we begin to understand why, for the Vedic sages, the process of eating is a beautiful and sacred ritual. According to Ayurveda, digestion begins in the eye of the beholder. There is no argument that the food itself feeds the cells in the body, but it is the full sensory experience of eating that enlivens the physiology.

Digestion begins when we look at our food. Indeed, the metabolic process begins even before food enters our mouth. Western scientific research estimates that 30 to 40 percent of the total digestive response to any meal is triggered by the brain. Haven't you observed noticeable changes in your saliva when you see a scrumptious meal sitting on the plate before you? You may have even witnessed a change in your digestive system just by thinking about food. Our perception of food prompts our digestive system to get to work. Salivating is a sign that your body is preparing to break down the food it's about to eat.

Eating is indeed a heady experience. Seeing, smelling, and tasting food begins a cascade of reactions in the physiology. Our sensory awareness of the food stimulates nerve receptors in the oral and nasal cavities that relay messages to the brain. In turn, the brain primes the digestive organs and mobilizes the intestines. The secretion of saliva, gastric acid, and digestive enzymes announces that the party has begun. A rush of blood floods the organs of digestion, and, as if dancing to a happy tune, the intestines do "the grumble": the rhythmic dance that ensures the proper movement of food through the digestive tract. Now we're cooking!

Awareness: The Flame of the Digestive Fire

Awareness is the spark that lights up your digestive fire. Without awareness, even the purest foods that carry the most vital messages can go unnoticed. The physiology assesses the messages that are brought in by the food; it prepares for the event. We need to eat and taste in order to heal.

When your mind does not digest the food, the digestive system is hurt. Eating puts us in a relationship with the food we consume. The mind must attend to the food that the body ingests if anything meaningful is going to be extracted from the interaction. What would happen if you were talking with a friend and he or she didn't pay any attention? At best, you'd walk away feeling unheard and unsatisfied; at worst, misunderstood and angry.

So it is with the process of digestion. Paying attention to the task at hand makes everything go better, whether the task is eating or talking with a friend. When we eat at high speed, or we make eating one of several tasks we perform simultaneously, we do not digest efficiently. Habitually engaging in inattentive eating, or attention-deficit eating, can mess up the workings of your gut by squelching your digestive fire.

Eating as a Sacred Ritual

Now that we have taken the steps to ignite our digestive fire, the next issue is to focus on maximizing the assimilation of the food we ingest. When we realize that the physical body is the vessel of the spirit, the mundane task of eating takes on a deeper meaning. Nourishing the body in order to nurture the spirit requires making the act of eating a sacred ritual. This means that how we eat (the process) is as important as what we eat (the food). A nice table setting can enhance the ritual of eating; gobbling food as we walk down the street or race somewhere in our car does not.

The Effect of Mood on Food

We have already discussed how food affects mood. Now let's discuss how mood affects food—that is, how our emotional state at the time we eat affects our ability to digest. Digestion is hard work for the body. It is even harder if it does not have the full support of the physiology, especially the brain and the nervous system.

The nervous system has a tremendous impact on the functioning of the digestive system. For optimal digestion and assimilation of food, the digestive system needs the nervous system to send messages to the pancreas asking for the production and release of digestive enzymes and hormones like insulin and glucagon. The nervous system also interacts with the circulatory system, enlisting it in the endeavor. As if sending troops on a mission, the circulatory system must divert blood and reroute it toward the trunk of our body in order to aid the intestines in the absorption of nutrients.

Stress makes a mess of digestion. We are evolutionarily programmed not to digest when we are under the influence of stress. Our primitive ancestors would not eat when a dangerous wild animal was prowling about, for this would threaten their survival. In modern times, however, the beast that's lurking about and causing stress comes in more subtle forms: as bits of information from TV, the newspaper, and thoughtless or argumentative conversation.

Relaxation ensures assimilation. We are wired to best assimilate food when we are in a calm environment. With its thorough and multidimensional understanding of the natural forces that underlie the functioning of our physiology, Ayurveda advises that food should be consumed in an environment that enhances relaxation. As much as possible, create an agreeable, quiet atmosphere. A pleasant dining experience will give you a good gut feeling. At the very least, do not argue, work, read, or watch TV while you eat; rather, focus on your food and the experience of eating. You will digest more efficiently if you pay attention to what you are doing. Pay attention to the taste and

Hero Pose

By focusing circulation on the abdominal region, Hero pose aids in digestion if it is done right after eating. this posture also dispels excess gas. Besides helping to break down food, this posture strengthens the knees, ankles, and legs as well as the pelvic region. It is also good for the back.

1. Kneel with your feet slightly apart. Drop down until you're sitting on your feet, buttocks on your ankles and heels. Place your hands on your thighs, thumbs and index fingers lightly touching. Hold your head high and your back straight.

2. Breathe comfortably and fully.

3. Lift up into a kneeling position, keeping your spine straight and your shoulders relaxed (not pulled up). Inhale as you rise, then exhale as you sit back down. Repeat once or twice, moving slowly each time.

Hero pose aids in digestion if it is done immediately after eating.

textures of the food. Eat food that is pleasant to both sight and palate. Eating should be a source of joy.

A settled mind means a receptive tummy. Try not to eat when you are upset or mentally distracted. Offer a smile to the food as a gesture of gratitude for the nourishment it will provide. (If this doesn't come naturally to you, we suggest that you pretend—fake it till you make it.) The nervous and digestive systems work well together only if they are given the opportunity to do so.

The Importance of Sitting While Eating

Always sit down to eat. This modicum of civility does more than you think. Sitting down to eat informs our mind that we are focused on the food we are about to consume, rather than on myriad other activities. Taking a few minutes to sit and look at your food induces a relaxation response in your physiology. This response triggers a release of biochemicals that aid in the digestive process. Additionally, the act of folding our hips directs our blood to the top half of the body, where it is needed for digestion, rather than to the legs, where it would otherwise go. In fact, this is the logic behind prescribing a yoga asana to aid digestion, such as Hero pose.

Finally, do not eat right before going to bed. If you eat late at night, the food will not be digested properly, and *ama* will be the result. During the night the body works hard to clean up the physiology. When the body is in shutdown mode, the digestive processes are far from efficient. A big meal in the belly often means a wakeful night.

Agni: Stoking the Digestive Fire

The Vedic sages used the term *agni* to describe the transformative power of digestion. *Agni* is our ability to change one substance into another while extracting energy from it. If your *agni* is low, your ability to absorb and digest is low. *Agni* exists in the mind as well as the body tissues, so it pertains to the ability to digest and assimilate thoughts as well as food. Physical *agni*, however, is the principal *agni*; the other forms of *agni* are related to it and can be determined to some extent by the state of the main source.

Low *agni* accounts for all toxic buildup in the physiology. This is very important when we are considering how to intervene in a case of depression. In general, a depressed mentality reflects a physiology with low *agni*. *Agni* burns up *ama* and confers vitality. If the body is not clogged with trash, digestion will be optimal. *Ama* can block any aspect of the digestive process and disrupt the full distribution of nutrients. You can eat the perfect food at the perfect time in the perfect setting, but if the digestive processes are not optimal, the food will not be metabolized. In these instances, large molecules of undigested food (*ama*) clog the digestive track and interfere with the free flow of natural intelligence in the body. When we diminish *ama*, the nutrients can be distributed throughout the body, and communication among the physical systems is unimpeded. The eventual result will be a healthy glow and a vibrant spirit.

Following are some tips for reducing the buildup of *ama*.

Eat when you are hungry. Hunger is Mother Nature's prompt that it is time to eat. Learn to recognize the natural signals, and eat only when you are hungry. The sages advise you not to engage in emotional eating. You probably already knew that, but did you know that if you eat when you are upset, nervous, or unhappy, the food is not digested efficiently?

Eat to only 75 percent full. How did you feel last Thanksgiving? After the meal, did you feel like the stuffed turkey? Nothing works efficiently on overload, including your digestive system. If you stop before you are full, you'll have room to breathe, and oxygen works wonders in the metabolic process.

Do not eat until the previous meal is digested. Digesting a meal can take anywhere from three to six hours. Digestion consists of a natural assembly line. If you throw something on the line while the previous items are still in process, you will create a jam. Give yourself time to thoroughly digest your food before eating again.

Avoid large amounts of liquid before, during, or after meals. Don't squelch your digestive fire. Sipping is fine during meals, but large amounts of liquid dampen the digestive process.

Make lunch the largest meal of the day. You are part of the natural world. When the sun is at its highest, your metabolic processes are at their strongest. Eat the largest meal at that time. At night the body is shutting down, preparing for rest. Eating large meals late turns your body into a tank of *ama*.

Avoid iced drinks and carbonated beverages. Your digestive enzymes and other vital factors were intended to operate at body temperature. Iced drinks hamper the digestive process. (Ice water is neither nice nor wise.) Enzymes also function best within a narrow pH range. Carbonated beverages are, in general, highly acidic. By altering the pH of the physiology, they impair the breakdown of food.

Chew your food well. Your teeth play an important role in the digestive process. By breaking food down into smaller pieces, chewing increases the surface area of the food particles. Enzymes and other biochemicals then have more area on which to work, and the food is broken down into nutrients more efficiently.

Avoid large quantities of raw foods. Raw foods do have a higher nutritional content than cooked foods, but they are difficult to digest. In order for our physiology to benefit from the extra nutritional value of raw foods, it must produce a more scorching digestive fire. Thus, we only succeed in taxing our digestive system if we eat raw foods in excess.

Drink and Be Merry!

When a physician trained in the healing arts of ancient India came to the United States, he was shocked by what he saw: obesity, uneven complexions, and puffiness; people who looked bloated and fatigued. "So much *ama!*" he exclaimed. His task was to come up with an intervention that was simple yet powerful, that could be easily interwoven into daily life.

His recommendation was to boil water every morning, pour it in a thermos, and sip it throughout the day.

Let's analyze why this works. Hot water balances all three doshas. Boiling water infuses it with lightness. The increased energy and lightness of the water lightens and stirs up Kapha dosha. The warmth of the water soothes Vata dosha. Water itself pacifies Pitta.

The act of sipping hot water clears *ama* and improves digestion. Hot water stimulates the digestive system to start digesting. If there is no food in the digestive tract, then *ama* is digested instead. Try it. We think you will be delighted by the effect.

Reducing *ama* in the physiology allows proper distribution of the nutrients in our digestive system. If we have blockages in our physiology and the nutrients have not been distributed, we receive false signals of hunger. In this way, hot water can even help with weight control. The cravings caused by *ama* are diminished, because the decrease in *ama* leaves one feeling energized and satisfied after eating. This is the sign of optimal digestion. Satisfied people are not as inclined to overeat or to have cravings.

Drinking spiced water is even wiser. Every substance we take into our body has an effect. For centuries, spices have been used for medicinal purposes. Each spice carries a unique effect. For instance, recent studies have shown turmeric to be an antioxidant and an anti-inflammatory agent. Other spices support the immune system, are natural pain relievers, and calm the nerves. Spices have power and can be used to enhance physiological balance. To spice up your life and reduce *ama*, try the following recipe.

¼ teaspoon cumin seeds (cumin helps to absorb and use nutrients)

¼ teaspoon coriander seeds (coriander helps to eliminate toxic chemicals and waste through your kidneys)

¼ teaspoon fennel seeds (fennel helps to normalize digestion, thereby reducing gas and bloating)

Add the spice seeds to 1½ quarts of plain, pure water, and boil for several minutes. After straining the spice seeds, pour the liquid into a thermal container that has a glass or stainless-steel (not plastic) lining. Sip the powerful concoction every hour or so throughout the day. Since this intervention may promote nighttime urination, stop drinking it by 6 p.m. so your sleep will not be disturbed.

Be careful not to chew and eat the seeds; this can aggravate your system. The wisdom of the spices becomes infused in the water, so imbibe the liquid and leave the rest. The subtle benefits of that wisdom will benefit your digestion over time.

We have never seen a case of a person being allergic to these particular spices, but anything is possible. If you are taking medications, there is always the chance of adverse effects when a new substance is added to the diet. Whenever you are introducing something new, it is a good idea to move cautiously.

Other Gut Feelings

Understanding your body's biological needs bolsters the desire to support those needs. After all, everyone wants to feel good. Knowledge precedes action. To know and understand your biological needs, listen to your body.

Your body is communicating with you constantly, attempting to engage you in the goal of nourishing every aspect of your being. Usually, there are three general messages being communicated: (1) Am I hungry? (2) Is my body prepared to digest the food? (3) What does my body need? Awareness will allow you to understand what your physiology is communicating.

The first and most apparent message, concerning hunger, we've come to recognize quite readily. The second message, concerning the body's capacity for digestion, requires a bit more awareness. The body may be saying, "Yes, you are truly hungry, but be sure you eat light foods, because you don't have the metabolic strength right now to process heavy foods." The third message, concerning the body's needs, requires even more discernment, for it is frequently relaying a message about emotional needs as well as biological needs.

If you discern your body's messages and follow through by consuming what it needs from food, you are bringing the gift of balance to your mind-body. This means clearing out disturbances that sustain mental, emotional, and physical unrest. Establishing nutritional habits in an effort to promote our well-being sometimes offers immediate results, but at other times it takes awhile for us to notice a difference. Always, however, what we feed ourselves will show over time. Bringing awareness to our eating habits is the key for good health, because our physiology is the product of our habits.

Being able to identify true hunger is a good first step in developing greater awareness of our body's needs. Many people are conditioned to eat a meal at a particular time each day and never stop to check to see if they are actually hungry. When we proceed to eat even though we are not hungry, we are probably lacking the digestive capability to assimilate the nutrients. Similarly, eating a second meal before the previous one has had sufficient time to digest can lead to disquieting gut feelings such as indigestion, bloating, gas, and burping—all symptoms that the physiology is wrestling with the food in an effort not to produce *ama*. Tuning in to your hunger and cultivating a good appetite is a general way to monitor the strength of your digestive fire. Eating when the fire is hot and strong will ensure that the nutrients are delivered throughout your system.

Cravings are gut feelings that can either assist or disrupt efforts to nourish our being. According to Ayurveda, cravings are the result of *ama*. They can represent either a biological need or a psychological desire. Both are messages from your mind-body that are asking you to address a pressing need.

To build the skill of learning how to differentiate between a biological need and a psychological desire, we offer the following general rule to guide you. A craving that is a biological need comes in the form of a desire for a particular taste that may be lacking in your diet; sweet and salty are the most common. A craving that is a psychological desire comes in the form of wanting a specific food, such as chocolate, pastry, potato chips, or ice cream. Consequently, the Ayurvedic answer to the question of cravings is twofold. First, it is important to discern the nature of the craving: Where is this need or desire coming from? Second, learn to decode the message the craving is trying to give you: What is it saying you need? In order to accomplish this goal, it is essential to learn to evaluate food for both its gross and its subtle properties.

When we can recognize a craving for an unhealthy food as psychological, there are a few options: (1) Satisfy the craving and suffer the consequence of the formation of toxins, (2) deny yourself the particular food and cause a mental deprivation that might impair appetite on the psychological level, or (3) choose a healthy substitute. Find a nutritious food that has similar taste and qualities to the item that is being craved. Finally, remember that drinking hot water throughout the day will help to dissipate cravings.

Ayurvedic Appetizer

How hungry are you?

If you are unclear whether you are hungry, consider doing either of the following before you begin to eat: (1) take a brisk walk, or (2) do some breathing exercises (see chapter 10).

Both of these exercises help to clear your palate, allowing you to better assess your hunger level.

If you are hungry, but you sense your digestive fire is weak, consider having an Ayurvedic appetizer (chutneys). Appetizers increase your appetite while stoking the digestive fire, thereby improving the digestive capacity. Especially if made fresh and with high-quality ingredients, a couple teaspoons of chutney can add a beneficial supply of antioxidants and zest to your meal. Additionally, it can bring elemental balance to your meal by introducing most, if not all, of the six tastes (sweet, salty, sour, bitter, pungent, and astringent) required. Not only will you find your cravings subsiding, but your meals will also be more satisfying.

Try nibbling on a thin slice of fresh ginger root with a spritz of lime juice and a sprinkle of rock salt to get your digestive juices flowing.

Alternatively, consider preparing the following dosha-specific chutneys:

Vata-Balancing Chutney

1½ teaspoons fennel seeds
1½ teaspoons cumin seeds
3 teaspoons ground coriander
2 tablespoons minced fresh ginger root
¼ teaspoon nutmeg
⅜ teaspoon salt
1 cup dates, pitted
⅜ cup or more of orange juice
1½ cups raisins

Combine all of the ingredients in a food processor and pulse to the desired texture.

Pitta-Balancing Chutney

2 ripe apples or pears
1 cup fresh cilantro
Juice of 1 or 2 lemons or limes
¼ teaspoon salt
2 teaspoons turbinado sugar (or to taste)

Peel and core the apples (or pears). Put them in a food processor along with the fresh cilantro. Add the lemon (or lime) juice, salt, and sugar and pulse to the desired texture.

This chutney pacifies Pitta dosha without diminishing your *agni*.

Kapha-Balancing Chutney

1 tablespoon lime juice
⅓ cup orange juice
¾ cup chopped peeled ginger root
½ cup raisins

Combine all of the ingredients in a food processor and pulse to the desired texture.

Reduce Stress to Increase Your Digestive Power

Ayurveda teaches that our bodies contain the wisdom to move toward balance. The digestive system relies on the parasympathetic nervous system to function properly. A smoothly functioning nervous system can aid in the efficient digestion of food. Making meditation, breathing exercises, and yoga postures part of your regular daily routine is exceedingly beneficial for the reduction of anxiety and stress in the body. Consequently, these interventions help to optimize digestion.

An additional intervention involves making a written or mental record of your energy level and emotional state before and after eating a meal. Healthy food choices will sustain your energy and impart a calm, pleasant mental state. Being able to reflect back on your food choices from day to day is a good way to discover which ones were nourishing to the body and which were the product of detrimental eating habits.

A Tasteful Way to Balance Emotions

Let's now take a look at our gut's lexicon. Our digestive system speaks to our doshas using a tasteful language. The point of the conversation is to assess the energetic qualities the food will bring to the physiology. The physiology recognizes six tastes: sweet, sour, salty, bitter, pungent, and astringent. Each taste has a particular effect on the doshas. Every aspect of nature, including taste, is composed of a unique elemental, or doshic, distribution. Just as each dosha is composed of two of the five elements of nature—earth, water, fire, air, and ether—so too is each taste (see the following table). According to Ayurveda, a meal must contain all six tastes in order to keep the physiology in perfect balance.

Ayurveda also evaluates food for qualities such as temperature (hot or cold), density (light or heavy), and texture (oily or dry) to assess the energetic impact on Vata, Pitta, and Kapha doshas.

The Six Tastes, Five Elements, and Three Doshas

Elemental Composition of Taste	Effect on Dosha	Benefits
Sweet = earth + water	Balances Vata and Pitta	Burning Depression
Salty = water + fire	Balances Vata	Airy Depression
Sour = earth + fire	Balances Vata	Airy Depression
Pungent = fire + air	Balances Kapha	Earthy Depression
Bitter = air + ether	Balances Kapha and Pitta	Earthy and Burning Depression
Astringent = earth + air	Balances Kapha and Pitta	Earthy and Burning Depression

According to Ayurveda, taste conveys and induces specific emotions. Sweet taste transmits nurturing emotions, which soothe an Airy Depression. Pungent taste stimulates the nerves, helping a person to break out of an Earthy Depression. Sour and salty tastes bring warmth to the physiology, which is why people with an Airy Depression often reach for foods with a preponderance of these tastes. Bitter and astringent tastes diffuse intensity and add lightness to the physiology; these two tastes, along with sweet taste, benefit individuals who suffer from a Burning Depression. All of us need all six tastes in various amounts to maintain a balanced physiology.

Herbs as Medicine

An Ayurvedic proverb states, "With proper diet and lifestyle, medicine is of no need. With improper diet and lifestyle, medicine is of no use." The importance of nutrition in bringing balance and health to the physiology cannot be overemphasized. By speaking the language of the doshas and serving as a carrier of *prana*, food imparts the healing properties of nature. Food is one of the main ways we keep the doshas in balance and maintain our physical integrity and optimal functioning. Hippocrates, the father of modern medicine, gave us the following words of wisdom: "Let food be thy medicine and medicine be thy food." Food provides the fuel that activates the healing potential in our physiology; it is the raw material from which the body will rebuild itself.

The body's natural inclination to heal remains active even in the face of disease. Herbs, a particular category of food, are of great help when the healing forces of the body are weakened. They strengthen and awaken the physician within, the dormant forces of healing. Herbs can be enlisted to help the physiology achieve its desired goal: wholeness. Herbs support the various systems of the physiology and assist the mind-body in moving toward balance. A favorable diet provides the foundation on which the herbs can work; without this foundation, the herbs will have only a limited impact.

Whether synthetic or natural, most medicines are inspired by nature. For instance, aspirin is derived from the white willow tree. Digitalis, a medication used to regulate the rhythm of the heart, comes from the foxglove plant, which is native to the Amazon. The shamans in that region have traditionally used the plant itself to help regulate the heart. The difference between the lab-synthesized digitalis and the substance used by the shamans is significant, because the traditional medicinal plant is administered holistically. Pharmaceutical companies, on the other hand, aim to identify, isolate, and use only the so-called active ingredient—the part of the plant that directly addresses the symptom. According to Ayurveda, this is problematic.

Plants have a natural state of balance. They are composed of active and inactive substances. Properly prepared herbs utilize the entire intelligence of the plant, whereas synthetically manufactured medicines recreate only the active substances. This explains why synthetic medicines work so quickly in diminishing symptoms. It also explains the toxicity that engenders negative side effects. Herbs work more slowly, but they correct underlying imbalances rather than remove symptoms.

Herbs, like pharmaceuticals, should be prescribed. All too often the media will pick up on the efficacy of a particular herb. Inevitably, of all the people who buy the product, some will benefit from it whereas others will not, and some will actually be harmed by it. Taking herbs haphazardly is dangerous. Just because something is natural doesn't mean that it cannot have deleterious effects. Poisonous plants are natural, too.

How an herb affects the physiology of an individual is intimately related to that individual's doshic imbalance. You should always speak with a health professional who is knowledgeable in the subject before you commit to an herbal regimen. The right herb, taken correctly, can be immensely powerful in helping your physiology to move in the desired direction.

Herbs are Mother Nature's primary medicine; Ayurveda understands the energetic qualities of herbs in depth. As medicine, herbs are used for fine-tuning our nutritional intake. Like food, they demonstrate their effect over time—usually in less time than food, of course. Unlike food, however, herbs are intended to be used for a limited period only.

There are mental and psychological correlates to physical health. When we are in a state of imbalance, we suffer from a lack of mental clarity and a degree of psychological unrest. Herbs have the ability to bring mental clarity, increased insight, and physical strength so that an individual can engage in undoing depression. Attaining physiological balance allows the unfolding of the finer aspects of our being: courage, insight, compassion, and happiness. These qualities fly in the face of depression.

Oxygen: Another Aid to Digestion

When it comes to consuming oxygen, the rule is this: the more breaths, the merrier. Consider the following facts about the role that oxygen plays in promoting metabolic efficiency:

- You could live for four months without food and four days without water, but only four minutes without air.
- Certain parts of the stomach lining consume more oxygen than other tissues in the body. The intestinal villi, the site where nutrients are absorbed in the gut, have organelles (mitochondria) that also require large quantities of oxygen in order to function properly. When the blood lacks oxygen, the absorption and assimilation of nutrients by the villi is hampered.
- The more you eat, the more the body needs to breathe. After you eat a meal, your parasympathetic nervous system reroutes circulation to the organs of digestion and causes your body to breathe

more deeply and fully in order to increase oxygen intake—unless you interrupt this process. So vital to the metabolic process is oxygen that your brain automatically increases air intake to accommodate the need for more oxygen. This is, in part, what causes you to yawn after eating a big meal.

- Oxygen is the power that drives your metabolic engine. Ninety-five percent of the energy generated by your body comes from the process of combustion: oxygen + food = energy. Calories are a measure of the energy that is derived from the combustion of food. It is oxygen that allows you to burn the calories in the food you've consumed. By increasing the amount of oxygen available to the body, you are therefore better able to burn the food you consume. Oxygen is indispensable in burning fat, the body's fuel reserve.

- Exercise is a way to help your body breathe better. The long-term benefit of a regular exercise regimen is twofold: (1) breathing helps your body to take in more oxygen, and (2) it teaches your body how to use the oxygen more efficiently.

- If your body is hungry for oxygen, go for a short walk before you eat. Besides relaxing your body and clearing your mind, this helps to ignite your digestive fire so you can be better prepared to ingest and break down the food. By treating yourself to a gentle walk after your meal, you give your body the opportunity to enhance assimilation and elimination. However, vigorous exercise—the kind that causes you to break a sweat—is not recommended either right before or immediately after a meal. This could induce a stress response.

Airy Depression: Is Grabbing Food on the Run Making You Light-headed?

For Arial, eating was yet another task on her endless to-do list. Eating was a chore to get over and be done with. It was best if she could take care of the eating nuisance while doing something important, such as checking e-mails or running errands. Arial joked that her desk and her car were her two favorite eating spots. The evidence of this was apparent: her car was littered with napkins from all the local fast-food joints. Arial often skipped dinner because she was busy folding laundry and preparing lunch for the next day. As she cleared off the table, she would graze on her children's leftovers. Later in the evening, after the children were tucked into bed, she would often eat popcorn or potato chips while watching TV.

There was no rhyme or reason to her eating pattern. Arial had gotten into the habit of grabbing a salad and a diet soda before a meeting and wolfing it down at top speed. On other days she would skip lunch altogether. This was easy for her to do because she rarely felt hungry. Sometimes it was not until she felt light-headed that she would remember to eat.

Settling a Nervous Tummy

Arial was leaning in the direction of her imbalances and creating a whirl-wind of problems in her digestive tract. A Vata imbalance makes a person feel ungrounded and anxious. Unfortunately, people with this imbalance select foods and engage in eating habits that perpetuate the imbalance. Arial ate in a hurried and mindless way. She sought out light foods like salads, popcorn, and rice cakes, then indulged in the effervescence of carbonated drinks. From the energetic perspective, these are all cold, dry, and light foods, which worsened the imbalance in Vata dosha.

Nervousness made Arial feel as if sitting down to a meal was a waste of time. She felt rushed and overwhelmed by all of the things that she *perceived* she needed to do. Arial was borrowing from her reservoir of physical strength to muster the energy to get through her day. This is, in part, why she felt so tired and why she sought the help of stimulants such as caffeine.

We never intend to cause ourselves deliberate harm. If we eat on the run occasionally, drink diet sodas every so often, and even skip an occasional meal, we will not cause irreparable damage to our doshas. One bad meal is not likely to harm us, either. Nevertheless, we need to realize that we are the sum of our habits. If our habits gain control over our intentions, we eventually bring disarray to the total system of body, mind, and spirit. The sum of Arial's habits was making her depressed and predisposing her to further ill health.

A fundamental step in undoing Airy Depression—gaining strength and settling anxiety—is to establish a daily routine. By habituating the mind-body to an established routine, we train the physiology to function optimally. If the physiology must constantly react to an unpredictable schedule and a lack of food at the necessary times of day, chaos inevitably ensues.

Arial needed to establish an external structure in her life in order to establish an internal rhythm for her body. As creatures of nature we possess an internal clock that mirrors the rhythms of the natural world. Following the trajectory of the sun maximizes our digestive fire; it favors eating the main meal at noon, when the sun (and our digestive system) is at its peak. The timing of our meals is thus critically important.

However, how we eat is as important as when we eat. Arial needed to relax, slow down, and smell the food! Eating while you are in a state of stress is damaging to the digestive system. Eating on the run, driving while gobbling fast foods, and chomping on bites of food while multitasking all served to accelerate Arial's nervous system. These behaviors are reactions to stress that simultaneously generate more stress. This is bad for our digestive system. We are evolutionarily programmed to eat when we are relaxed. This is when the body focuses its resources on the digestive processes.

To undo Airy Depression, it is essential to establish and maintain a daily routine. Eating regular meals at approximately the same time every day was vital if Arial's body was to regain internal order. Arial needed to learn to place nourishing food on a plate, sit down, look at the food, and eat slowly and with awareness and pleasure.

Fine-Tuning Nourishment

Arial was not hungry. From the Ayurvedic perspective, this symptom is of concern because it means that her digestive fire is low. Hunger is the message the brain receives when the body is telling it that it is primed for digesting food. It is no wonder that when Arial forced herself to eat a full meal, she became bloated and suffered symptoms of indigestion. She felt as if food was stuck in her gut. The culprit was cold beverages.

Habitually drinking cold sodas was creating problems for Arial. It was dousing her digestive fire, and the caffeine in the sodas was enhancing her stress response. In addition, these sodas were sometimes filling her up, and she was neglecting to eat because of it. In order to build her digestive fire, we suggested that Arial eat an Ayurvedic appetizer (see the sidebar "Ayurvedic Appetizer" on page 231). Sipping hot, weak ginger root tea before meals was also a gentle way of informing her body that food was on the way.

As Arial regained balance, she felt better and also regained her physical strength. She was ready to fine-tune her nutrition, so we recommended that she follow a Vata-pacifying nutritional path. Her food choices would ideally infuse the body with nutritious grounding and calming foods. We recommended that she choose warm, heavy foods prepared with good fats such as ghee (clarified butter) and oils rich in omega-3 and omega-6 fatty acids. Her nervous system needed good fats for nourishment.

Once Arial came to understand food from the Ayurvedic perspective, eating was no longer a nuisance. She learned to view food as packets of information that transport the elements of nature into her physiology. We advised her to favor sweet, sour, and salty tastes. By imparting the heavy and solid qualities of earth and water, sweet taste grounded her physiology by slowing down and consolidating her energy. The heavy and fiery qualities of sour and salty tastes balanced the scattered, light, and cold nature of Vata. Indeed, our physiology's ability to understand the message encoded in food goes well beyond what the taste buds perceive.

Initially, Arial thought that eating sweet, sour, and salty tastes could mean favoring salt-and-vinegar potato chips and chocolate chip cookies. Think again, Arial! Sweet comes to us from whole grains, such as rice or millet. It also comes from some vegetables, such as peas, carrots, and beets. We suggested that Arial get the six tastes through healthy food. An ideal dinner for her would be rice pilaf with chicken, peas, carrots, almonds, and raisins, seasoned with warming spices such as cinnamon, turmeric, ginger, pepper, and salt.

Herbs: Taking Nourishment Up a Notch

In Arial's case, we recommended Ayurvedic herbal formulas (see Resources for suppliers) to assist in the settling and rebuilding of her nervous system. The principal herbs in the formulas were ashwagandha

(*Withania somnifera*), shankapushpi (*Evolvulus alsinodes*), and tagarah (*Valeriana officinalis*).

Arial's nervous system was exhausted, so it needed something to rejuvenate it. Ironically, however, her exhaustion was manifesting with signs of hyperactivity, both mental and physical. Her symptoms were insomnia, anxiety, excessive thinking, and the need to be in constant motion. She required an herb that served both as a tonic (to revitalize) and a sedative (to calm), all in one—and this is what ashwagandha does. This herb is very useful in conditions that are caused by stress, because it regulates the impact of Vata dosha on the circulatory system and the functioning of the heart muscles. Ashwagandha therefore resolves emotional instability and suffuses the physiology with calmness.

Shankapushpi is an herb that has a strong affinity for nervous tissue. It effectively treats disorders like the anxiety, insomnia, and aches and pains that are brought on by an imbalance in Vata dosha. By inducing the flow of energy through the channels of the brain, it increases brain functioning and alleviates emotional instability. It is also beneficial when nervousness and anxiety are interfering with hunger and the ability to digest food properly.

For Arial's difficulties with sleep, tagarah was useful because it is a natural relaxant. By pacifying Vata, tagarah sedates the nervous system. Tagarah is a valuable botanical gift and should not be used chronically to treat unresolved emotional and physical imbalances that disturb sleep. Instead, it should be used as a temporary measure until the root of the problem is eradicated.

Tagarah is a heavy herb that contains the vibratory nature of the earth element; hence it is used to induce emotional stability and promote sleep. The heaviness that this herb passes on to the physiology grounds the agitation that is caused by the excessive tension, anxiety, and restlessness resulting from an imbalance in Vata dosha. It effectively treats insomnia and panic attacks. One of the possible mechanisms for tagarah's calming effect is its ability to increase the level of an inhibitory brain chemical called gamma-aminobutyric acid (GABA); tagarah thus performs a similar function as the synthetic tranquilizers Valium and Ativan do. Other important neurochemicals, including dopamine and serotonin, are also influenced by tagarah. This herb's effect on the mind may be more complex than the mere stimulation of calming receptors in the brain.

Tagarah is preferable to a synthetic sleeping pill because it has an established history of safety and efficacy. Studies around the world have demonstrated that taking this herb before bedtime improves the quality of rest a person receives. It is substantially more effective than a placebo in enhancing sleep without side effects. Brain-wave studies demonstrate an increase in the amount of time that people spend in the deeper stages of sleep after they have taken tagarah. The herb also reduces both the amount of time it takes to fall asleep and the number of times a person awakens during the night, and there is no side effect of drowsiness in the morning.

Burning Depression: Are Power Lunches Leaving You Hungry for More?

Barbara's appetite was sharp. She could set her watch by it. At midday, her stomach demanded her attention no matter what she was doing, and she was happy to oblige.

Barbara approached social dining with the same fervor she took to a power lunch. Lively and opinionated, she enjoyed intense conversation. After two glasses of wine everything became a debate. (This was taking quite a toll on her digestion!)

All of her digestive power was directed toward metabolizing the conversation rather than the food. Thus it is not surprising that even though Barbara ate good food, she derived no good feeling from it. In addition, she noticed that she was eating less yet gaining weight. Her palate was blunt, not registering subtle tastes; consequently, she favored tongue-burning, spicy foods, but even then she barely tasted what she ingested. For the most part, eating was a mechanical process. Barbara left the table with a certain degree of dissatisfaction. She was left hungering for more. At the physical level, she desired more food; at the emotional level, she wanted a greater sense of social connection; and at the spiritual level, she yearned for a little bit of fulfillment in her life.

Barbara has never considered herself a sickly person, but lately she has been visiting the doctor frequently. A gnawing burning sensation in her stomach was becoming severe. She had small, frequent bouts of diarrhea, especially after several nights of going out to dinner. Adult acne had reappeared. Migraine headaches were getting in the way of her work. She was worried that her body was having a breakdown.

Cultivating Awareness

Barbara's case serves as an example of what happens when your mind does not digest your food. Her awareness was not on the process of eating. If you do not pay attention to the food you ingest, an important phase of digestion is missing. This first, mental stage of the digestive process is of primary importance, because it sets the stage for optimal metabolism.

The priming of the digestive system occurs in the brain. When this doesn't happen, there is less preparation of the enzymes and inefficient movement in the intestines (peristalsis), so food is neither being broken down properly nor moved along the intestinal walls. In the long run, there's an increased vulnerability to digestive upset, bowel disorders, hypersensitivity, and fatigue—all of which Barbara was experiencing.

The way that Barbara was digesting food was similar to the way that she was processing her life experiences. Barbara does not pay attention to her internal world. All of her awareness is focused on what is going on in the external world. This is a recurring theme in her life. Recall that her depression was due, in large part, to the fact that she didn't pay attention to her inner life, her feelings. Emotions have a function. They are guideposts, giving important information about how we are navigating through life. Ignoring them is dangerous.

Unfortunately, merely asking Barbara to observe a protocol for priming her digestion would not address the ailments that already existed because of her history of disregarding gut feelings. At this point, it was important to balance her Pitta dosha. Eliminating spicy condiments and following a Pitta-pacifying diet contributed greatly to this goal. Barbara was asked to refrain from drinking alcohol until the majority of her physical distress was gone. These interventions brought almost immediate relief, motivating her to follow additional Ayurvedic suggestions.

Cultivating awareness for the taste, smell, and texture of food was a great lesson for Barbara. She aptly carried this skill of increased awareness over to her emotional life. In time, she learned to better monitor and appreciate her feelings. This heightened awareness of how she felt allowed her to make connections between perception and behavior. Understanding herself opened her heart to understanding others. Her relationships improved, which gave a lift to her spirit.

Barbara's Pitta-pacifying diet consisted of foods that are rich in sweet, bitter, and astringent tastes—especially sweet. These flavors correct the excess emotional and physical heat that radiates from a person with a Pitta imbalance. They induce a cooling and diffusing quality in the physiology that balances the heat and intensity that are so characteristic of a Burning Depression.

Milk, butter, and ghee were good for Barbara's physiology. Olive oil and lemon juice were ideal for salad dressing. Regular servings of white rice, barley, and oats decreased the acidity in her stomach. Barbara liked fruits and was delighted to learn that sweet fruits such as grapes, cherries, and mangoes would be great for her physiological needs. A variety of vegetables also suited her: asparagus, squash, carrots, sweet potato, okra, green leafy vegetables, broccoli, cauliflower, celery, sprouts, and zucchini. Spices such as fennel, cinnamon, turmeric, coriander, and cardamom gave her food the zing she loved without irritating her intestines. Occasionally, small amounts of fresh ginger, cumin, and black pepper were fine additives. Seafood and poultry were the animal proteins of choice.

Herbs: Feeding the Mind-Body

In Barbara's case, Ayurvedic herbal formulas (see Resources for suppliers) were recommended to assist in the settling and rebuilding of her nervous system. The principal herbs in the formulas were arjuna (*Arjuna terminalis*), brahmi (*Bacopa monniera*), and jatamansi (*Nardostachys jatamansi*).

Arjuna is a heart tonic that also clears excess Pitta dosha from the blood. We mention it as a key herb for depression because chronic sadness hurts the heart. Studies have shown that depression is one of the strongest contributors to heart disease. Arjuna heals the heart at the emotional and physical levels. At the emotional level, it reduces the inflammation (Pitta) of heated emotions and the congestion (Kapha) produced by emotional *ama*. At the physical level, it strengthens the muscles of the heart and tones the blood vessels so they remain flexible, thereby preventing high blood pressure.

Brahmi is used to aid in recovery from mental stress. It is bitter and sweet in taste, cooling in energy, and light in quality. This herb has an affinity for the brain and for nervous tissue. It relaxes the latter throughout the physiology, releasing muscular tension while improving memory, learning ability, and concentration.

Jatamansi is an herb that belongs to the same family as tagarah (Indian valerian), but it has a more cooling effect on the physiology than tagarah does, so it is helpful in relieving the mental pressure that triggers early-morning awakenings.

Earthy Depression: Are Comfort Foods Taking a Bite Out of You?

Food was one of the few things that still made Ed happy. A little sweet something could go a long way in helping him through the emotional trials of the day. At times his internal pain and heaviness was too much to bear; almost automatically, he would reach for the comfort of a pastry. Chocolate milk was also particularly soothing. A moment or two of immersion in the taste of these foods took him away from his incomprehensible sadness. Afterward he would beat himself up for falling into the rut once again. Feeling angry at himself and guilty made him feel alive, at least, so it was all well worth it.

In the past, Ed enjoyed cooking. He loved paging though cookbooks; the mere sight of beautiful food would stimulate his taste buds. During the past year, however, as his depression has taken hold of him, he hasn't had either the energy or the desire to prepare a meal. The responsibility of cooking had fallen squarely on his wife Janice.

Unlike Ed, Janice did not enjoy cooking. Their meals consisted mostly of canned and frozen foods. Prepared foods that could be quickly heated in the microwave frequently made up the menu of choice. Ed ate listlessly. Out of respect for his wife's efforts, he felt compelled to finish what was put in front of him. He couldn't remember the last time he had had a pang of hunger. With the exception of the sweet treats that helped to transport him, for a few minutes, away from his depression, Ed ate out of duty.

The Discomfort in Comfort Food

The notion of comfort food is well established in our culture. The dictionary defines it as "food that gives a sense of emotional well-being" or "any food or drink that one turns to for temporary relief, security, or reward." The type of food that is regarded as comfort food depends on the individual, but inevitably there are three standard ingredients: lots of simple carbohydrates and sugars, high levels of fat, and some element that transports us back to the nurturing days of childhood. In light of this, let's analyze Ed's cravings for sweets.

Thriving on predictability, Ed has a history of finding it difficult to make life transitions. It is always during times of major change that he is in danger of becoming unbalanced. Ed is a caretaker by nature. He intuits the emotions of others and responds well to them. When he is in a state of physiological balance, he is sweet, sentimental, and easy-going. When he begins to lose balance, he looks for comfort to regain his feeling of stability. Always the one who others lean on, Ed is not accustomed to asking for emotional support. He uses food to bring his sweet feelings back to him.

From the Western scientific perspective, studies have provided evidence that comfort foods, particularly those high in carbohydrates and fat, can influence a person's mood. Cholecystokinin (CCK) is a hormone that affects the brain, the gallbladder, and the pancreas. It is released shortly after a person begins to eat, particularly if fatty food is being ingested. Researchers have suggested that high levels of CCK in the blood induce a certain degree of sedation by activating the opioid pathways in the brain, as do drugs like opium (but to a lesser degree).

The sweetness of sugar does soothe the nerves. Food contains the building blocks with which the body creates biochemicals. In the case of white sugar, sucrose contains the basic molecules that are necessary to create the brain chemicals associated with sweet emotions. Sucrose contains tryptophan, an amino acid that the brain requires to make serotonin. On a short-term basis, fatty-sweet comfort foods leave a person feeling physically satiated and emotionally satisfied.

From the Ayurvedic perspective, taste transmits messages from the natural world. Sweet taste, which imparts the qualities of earth and water, relates to Kapha dosha. This grounding taste is therefore generally used to balance Vata dosha as well as Pitta dosha. In Ed's case, the taste of sweet was merely exacerbating his imbalance.

Ed would benefit from foods with bitter, pungent, and astringent tastes. Bitter foods such as olives, grapefruit, and leafy greens like kale, chard, and spinach would help him to feel lighter. Brussels sprouts and cabbage would also be good. Pungent spices like chili and black pepper, mustard seeds, ginger, cumin, and garlic were recommended, along with vegetables like radish and onions. Astringent legumes such as lentils and garbanzo beans and grains like barley helped him immensely. Honey is a healthful source of sweetness that also imparts the quality of astringency. Ed was advised to follow a Kapha-pacifying diet. However, at that point, as depressed as he was, he was not likely to have the energy to embrace a new way of eating.

The most pressing issue that Ed could readily address was lessening the level of *ama* in his body. The dead foods he was ingesting were gunking up his physiology. Dead foods lack *prana*. They grant no energy to the eater and impart no intelligence to the physiology. Think of processed foods as "virtual foods." They look like they are imparting a message of health, and they may even taste good, but there is no real energetic substance behind them. They only burden the body with the task of eliminating them from the system. Eventually, eliminating dead foods would decrease Ed's level of *ama* and contribute greatly to the relief of his cravings for comfort foods.

It helped Ed to understand the effects of food on his physiology. Once he understood where the cravings came from, he was open to *ama*-reducing interventions. Ed did lack motivation, but he was also desperate to end his depression. Nothing had worked so far. He was willing to try and could make changes as long as these did not overly tax him. The first step was to minimize eating dead foods as much as possible. An even easier, albeit powerful, intervention was to begin to drink hot water with spices throughout the day (see the "Drink and Be Merry!" sidebar on page 227). The hot water and the spices brought Ed the soothing warmth that he needed. This drink also activated his digestive system and initiated the breakdown of *ama*. Drinking hot spiced water throughout the day was something that Ed thought he could do. As his physiology was relieved of the *ama*, he began to feel lighter and more energetic. He could then begin to incorporate other changes in his eating patterns.

An *ama*-reducing diet for Ed consisted primarily of warm and light foods prepared with high-quality fresh products. Those who suffer from an Earthy Depression—with its hallmarks of mental dullness, emotional heaviness, physical congestion, and lack of motivation—profit from increasing bitter, pungent, and astringent tastes, as we noted above. Let's analyze why this is so.

Bitter taste is composed of air and ether, so it infuses the physiology with the properties of these elements. At a more subtle level, since these are the same elements that predominate in the mind, it is not surprising that bitter taste has the profound effect of creating mental space (opening the mind). Bitter tastes, according to Ayurveda, induce a sense of calmness, coolness, and detachment.

Pungent taste is composed of fire and air. It stimulates mental *agni*, promoting clarity, perception, and increased reasoning ability. Pungent foods are hot and spicy. They burn through us when we eat them. They lessen an Earthy Depression by increasing the flow of blood and nutrients, at the gross level, and of *prana*, at a subtle level. Pungent tastes infused Ed with heat and some get-up-and-go. This is just what one needs to clear *ama* and undo a Kapha imbalance.

Astringent taste is composed of earth and air. It causes your mouth to pucker. Therapeutically, it has a drying effect that especially balances Kapha.

Herbs: Lessening the Load

Earthy Depression is perpetuated at the level of the body. It is common for individuals who suffer from an Earthy Depression to have a strong craving for heavy and sweet comfort foods. Ed's excessive consumption of comfort food, especially sweets, was creating *ama*. In addition, the dead foods he was habitually ingesting were not bringing him vitality.

As we can see from Ed's case, an imbalance in Kapha dosha leaves people feeling as if they have been dipped in mud. Heaviness clings to them, and dirt clouds their vision. They feel as if they are pulling the weight of the world behind them. With zero motivation, they experience every task as drudgery. This is a by-product of an *ama*-filled physiology.

We prescribed some formulas with herbs that would further the goals of Ed's nutritional program: to reduce *ama* and balance Kapha dosha.

Punarnava (*Boerhaavia diffusa*) is an herb whose Sanskrit name means "new again." Punarnava renews the physiology by opening channels of transport. Its cleansing activity effectively allows nourishment to reach the tissues. It carries bitter, cooling, dry, and light qualities. Once it's digested, its bitter taste yields to a pungency that brings heat to the physiology. Punarnava kindles the digestive fire and is useful in a sluggish digestive system. It reduces Kapha in the lungs and the chest, allowing for more flow of *prana* by clearing the channels of obstructions. It nourishes the heart muscles and promotes a sense of vigor by lightening the physiology.

Vacha (*Acorus calamus*) is an herb with a stimulating effect, which makes it useful in treating depression that is marked by lack of motivation and mental sluggishness—the hallmarks of an Earthy Depression. Vacha's primary application is to open the mind, improve concentration, and increase mental clarity. It is heating, and it has a dry, light, and penetrating quality. Its combination of pungent, bitter, and astringent tastes balances Vata and Kapha doshas while also balancing Pitta dosha, thereby reducing stagnation from the subtle channels of the mind. By nourishing the mental and emotional *agni*, it strengthens the ability of the mind to digest life experiences. At a more fundamental level, it also awakens the digestive fire of metabolism so that *ama* in the digestive tract is eliminated.

Metabolizing Life: Are You Eating Your Heart Out?

Metabolism is not limited to the body. The metabolic reality is that everything we come in contact with undergoes some degree of ingestion, digestion, assimilation, and elimination. Scientific research is increasingly demonstrating that, as the Tibetan lama Tartang Tulku asserts: "when positive or joyous feelings and attitudes pass through each organ and circulate throughout our whole system, our physical and chemical energies are transformed and balanced."

There is a definite connection between what we think and feel and the chemistry created in the body—the cascade of biochemicals that floods the system. For instance, a stressful circumstance may trigger anger. This emotion, in turn, can induce the release of chemicals in the body such as adrenaline and cortisol, which impede the efficient working of the digestive and immune systems.

Developing awareness is an ongoing task throughout our lives. The purpose of this questionnaire is to help you get in tune with your dietary habits and how they pertain to your mental and emotional inner workings. The questions are meant for your reflection. If you feel stuck on some of them, ask a significant person in your life for his or her opinion. Sometimes a person who knows us well can be of great assistance in helping us to develop an increased awareness of how we function. After all, we are so used to being who we are that we often fail to take note of our habits. These questions are designed to make you take a closer look at yourself.

1. What happens to your nutritional habits when you are anxious?
   * Do you tend to eat more or eat less at those times?
   * Do you do one or the other depending on the situation?
   * Does a particular time of day trigger anxious eating?
   * What types of situations trigger anxious eating?
   * Do you eat more on certain days of the week?
   * If you are a woman, do you eat differently before or during your menstrual cycle?
   * Is anxious eating work-related or family-centered?
   * What happens to your nutritional habits when you are under stress?
2. How often do you eat under stress?
   * Do you tend to eat certain foods when you feel stressed?
   * If yes, list which ones; how do they make you feel an hour after eating them?

- Are there any common physical symptoms you've noticed during or after such times?
- How much time do you take to eat your meal during stressful times?
- Do you taste your food?
- Do you chew your food thoroughly, or do you shove it down?

3. Recall when a meal left you feeling physically and emotionally satisfied.
   - Where were you?
   - With whom were you eating?
   - Who was the cook?
   - What was the occasion?
   - What were the lingering sensations?

15

Now What?

You have learned about a consciousness-based paradigm that offers a deep understanding of depression. Now you know that depression is not just in your head and that it is about more than a broken brain.

By now, we hope, you are viewing yourself as a seamless energetic system, a pattern of vibrations floating in a sea of intelligence. You are more aware of the myriad ways in which you are in constant interaction with your environment. Increased depth and breadth have been added to your life by your current knowledge of how consciousness underlies all. With this life-enhancing knowledge in hand, you have begun to metabolize life's experiences in a different, more holistic way.

The message that we hope to have imparted is that happiness is a by-product of a physiology filled to the brim with vitality. According to Ayurveda, as beings of consciousness, we are essentially programmed for happiness—this is our birthright. However, in the course of life, especially if we don't assist our physiology in maintaining balance, we inevitably become gunked up with remnants of an unprocessed lifestyle. Physical, mental, emotional, and spiritual *ama* (toxins) create blockages in the flow of our life force. When this happens, our physiology eventually loses vitality and we become depressed. Let us underscore the notion that in the same way that depression is created, it can also be undone—one act at a time.

Revitalizing your being is a worthy undertaking. There are many agents of vitality at your disposal. In general, their goal is to infuse your physiology with vital energy, to undo blockages, to promote the free flow of your life force, and to integrate the many aspects of your being into a vital whole. Ayurvedic interventions are consciousness-based. It is at the level of consciousness that we draw the energy we need to make positive change and multifaceted growth a possibility. The systematic practice of self-referral, which is enhanced by meditation, can help us to develop the necessary strength for untangling the deep-seated roots of depression.

Indeed, by moving your body, posing for life, recharging your battery through sleep, engaging in nourishing eating rites, and breathing in *prana*, you *can* transcend darkness. Yet how do you know where to begin? Of all the interventions that are available, which one can help you get a jump-start on the process of healing depression the mind-body way?

Putting Knowledge into Action

Our advice is that you do as much or as little as you can—just do *something*! Take your healing into your own hands. Here are some questions to help you figure out where to start: Which idea in the book gave you cause to ponder? Highlight it, memorize it, or write it down on a piece of paper. Allow it to serve as an inspiration as you embark on your healing journey. Use it as a point at which to turn your life around. Which chapter spoke the most clearly to you? Read it again and use it to develop a plan of action for yourself. Which intervention intrigued you the most? Commit to instituting it right away.

Your healing journey can start with interventions that address *any* of the many aspects of your being. If you start with a few of the steps suggested in this book and incrementally add others as your momentum increases, you'll soon notice improvements. You'll feel healthier, and happiness will begin to shine through your physiology. We are sure of it.

It is a prime tenet of Ayurveda that we must minimize stress and strain. Life should be lived in accordance with the laws of nature, but living should be easy. With this thought in mind, we caution you not to take on too many changes at once. Decide what will be the most helpful for you and begin to make that part of your everyday life. Over time you can add more interventions, but *never* do too much at one time.

Where to Begin: To Thine Own Self Be True

By now you should have an understanding of the three different archetypes of depression. You may have a good sense or simply an inkling of where your experience of depression fits into these archetypes. Then again, perhaps you have not resonated with any one case in particular but rather have seen bits and pieces of yourself in all the archetypes—this is frequently the case. It is common for symptoms of depression to overlap, to run the gamut of imbalances.

Depression can change in its expression, especially if it is untreated and long lasting. It can morph from one archetype of depression to another. It is highly possible that you have experienced different symptoms at different times in your life.

Maybe depression has been a lifelong companion for you. For some individuals, sad feelings followed them from childhood into adulthood. It is not uncommon for depressed adults to recall a childhood punctuated by periods of sadness or to identify themselves as having been sad children. People are often so familiar with being depressed that they do not even realize that a different way of being is possible. They have come to understand depression as a personality trait rather than a condition. For them, identifying the type of depression they have is a challenge.

Having read this book and digested its contents, you are now better equipped to take a closer look at the tendencies and experiences that define your unique manifestation of depression. We urge you to deeply reflect and then answer all the questions in each of the three sections below. This exercise will help you to fine-tune your healing protocol.

The Mind-Body Questionnaire: Assessing Our Imbalances

The following questionnaire is designed to assess the habits and tendencies that contribute to your imbalances. It is divided into three sections. Our suggestion is that you read through all the questions first and cross out the ones that do not fit you at all. Then go back and reread the remaining questions, this time assigning a value to each question that indicates how well it describes your personal experience and tendencies. Given that you may have expressed different tendencies at different times in your life, we suggest that you answer these questions by keeping in mind your *present* state of mind. Use the following scale:

1: It applies to me infrequently.

3: It applies to me with some regularity.

5: It applies to me strongly.

At the end of each section, write down your total score.

Finally, consider asking someone who knows you well to answer the questionnaire on your behalf. Compare his or her responses to yours. Use any discrepancies to further fine-tune your assessment of yourself.

Section 1

1. People say that I respond to stress with fear.
2. I worry about people disliking me.
3. I become overly sensitive to criticism.
4. I have difficulty coping with uncertainty.
5. I feel that my needs are not met in any way.
6. I have difficulty trusting my own judgment.
7. My energy level waxes and wanes.
8. If I don't get sufficient downtime, I easily succumb to physical illnesses.
9. My thinking becomes scattered when I feel stressed.
10. My memory becomes irregular when I feel stressed.
11. I frequently have difficulty concentrating on tasks.
12. I often have trouble falling asleep.
13. I feel weak and nervous.
14. My enthusiasm and liveliness plummet, but I can still pick myself up easily.
15. I lose hope easily but can regain it quickly.
16. I can bounce back from disappointments relatively easily.

17. I become moody—I feel as if I am riding an emotional roller coaster.

18. I feel restless and fretful most of the time.

19. I can't organize and manage time well.

20. I have difficulty following through on tasks.

21. I feel as if I can't depend on myself (my body) to get things done.

22. I believe that the grass is always greener on the other side, so I get twinges of envy.

23. When depressed, I feel a void that nothing can fill.

24. I fear that people wouldn't like me if they really knew how I felt inside.

25. I grow impatient, wanting things to change.

26. I easily grow disenchanted with life.

27. I have only fleeting moments of satisfaction.

28. When depressed, I feel deprived and I worry about all the things I don't have.

29. I am inconsistent in my daily routine, or I lose control of my daily routine.

30. I become overly sensitive to other people's perceptions of me and responses to me.

31. Dealing with change becomes increasingly stressful.

32. My first symptom of depression is feeling insecure and anxious.

33. I worry excessively about the future.

34. I feel easily overwhelmed by change.

35. I crave stimulants such as coffee and cigarettes to keep up my energy.

36. I create fearful scenarios in my mind.

37. I am easily excitable.

38. When I am not stressed, I am enthusiastic and vivacious by nature.

39. I worry that bad things are going to happen.

40. I ruminate about the events of the day.

41. When I am depressed, my appetite shuts down and I don't feel hunger.

42. People say that my mind appears to be somewhere else.

43. I have difficulty making decisions, or I can't make up my mind about things.

44. My mind gets caught up in unproductive overactivity.

45. I feel that everything I do is not good enough.

46. I ruminate on potential problems.

47. I experience moments of despair.

48. When stressed, I feel my physical resources eroding.

49. I feel a lack of self-worth.

50. When I feel depressed, my greatest wish is to feel anchored and joyous once again.

Total score for Section 1: _____

Section 2

1. People say that I respond to stress with anger.

2. I feel easily frustrated.

3. Initially I have lots of energy, so I can handle stressful events fairly easily at first.

4. I believe that I put forth more effort than anyone else does, and without complaint.

5. Because I like to work hard, long, and fast, I often feel revved up, overly energized, and pressured.

6. I tend to overdo everything.

7. I worry that people are going to let me down, so I keep the world at a distance.

8. I feel betrayed when people let me down.

9. I am constantly comparing myself to others to see how I measure up.

10. When depressed, I fear that I am not good enough.

11. I experience a great deal of mental pressure.

12. My sleep is disrupted.

13. I set unrealistically high expectations of myself.

14. I set unrealistically high expectations of others.

15. I fail to appreciate my efforts.

16. I fail to appreciate the efforts of others.

17. People say that I push myself too hard.

18. When I am under stress, my thinking becomes rigid.

19. I feel as if I am not getting enough done.

20. People say that I become self-centered and block out everything around me, including other people.

21. People say that I become aggressive in my desire to accomplish things.

22. My body feels rigid and uptight.

23. I like things to go my way; when they don't, I become irritated.

24. When I am depressed, everything becomes very serious to me and I lose my sense of humor.

25. I tend to grow resentful of others' lack of participation and effort.

26. I respond to frustration by becoming irritable.

27. People say I become increasingly competitive with myself and others.

28. I become increasingly compulsive in my routine.

29. I always keep my goals in sight.

30. I don't lose motivation easily.

31. People say that I am often crabby.

32. Being regarded as competent is exceedingly important to me.

33. I become impatient very easily.

34. I value efficiency and attention to details.

35. When stressed, I know what I need to comfort myself.

36. I seek anything that will help me to get rid of tension in my body.

37. Although I am usually warm and engaging, when I am stressed I behave in an angry and demanding manner.

38. When depressed, I grow increasingly intolerant of people and things.

39. I feel the need to take control of things because people are not doing things "right."

40. My mind gets caught up in criticism and judgment.

41. Nothing seems just right; everything could be made better.

42. I tend to fly off the handle.

43. When stressed, I become more goal-oriented, but I grow impatient with my perceived lack of productivity.

44. When I am stressed, my appetite increases.

45. I disregard physical discomfort until it becomes unbearable.

46. I have difficulty identifying my emotions.

47. I have difficulty saying no, but then I feel resentment building up from the demands that are placed upon me.

48. I feel easily betrayed and can grow bitter.

49. My interest in matters of the spirit quickly wanes when I am faced with disillusionment.

50. When I am depressed, my greatest wish is to feel supported and understood.

Total score for Section 2: _____

Section 3

1. People say that I respond to stress with inertia.

2. I fear that people will abandon me if I express negative emotions such as anger and sorrow.

3. People say that I go into denial when I am stressed—I tend to let things get very bad before I deal with problems.

4. I worry that people will think I am a bad person.

5. I am unable to express my wants and needs because I am uncertain of what I feel.

6. My emotional steadiness becomes a sense of feeling stuck.

7. I don't confront people; instead I stifle my emotions.

8. I blame myself for everything.

9. I shut down emotionally when I am upset.

10. When depressed, I feel emotionally numb.

11. People say that the first sign they notice when I am becoming depressed is that I am hard to read.

12. When I am stressed, at first I respond with calmness, endurance, and stability.

13. I freeze under excessive pressure.

14. I stop taking care of myself when I am depressed.

15. I lose motivation when I am depressed.

16. Prolonged stress makes my mind sluggish and plodding.

17. The first sign of depression is that I feel lifeless.

18. Everything tends to slow down for me.

19. I have difficulty motivating myself to move.

20. I feel as if my brain won't function, so my thinking is dulled.

21. Although I am otherwise content, when I am depressed my life seems boring.

22. I feel as if I am carrying the world on my shoulders.

23. I can't get rid of my fatigue.

24. One of the first signs of depression is that I lose interest in physical activity.

25. When depressed, I withdraw emotionally from those around me.

26. Eating my favorite food comforts me.

27. When stressed, I feel physically sluggish.

28. When stressed, I feel emotionally listless.

29. When depressed, I tend to oversleep.

30. I feel drowsy after eating.

31. I grow increasingly set in my ways and unable to adapt to change.

32. I like to engage in activities that are relaxing.

33. When stressed, I grow increasingly attached to my possessions.

34. People say that I grow emotionally clingy when I am depressed.

35. I have trouble remaining focused and alert.

36. When stressed, I grow increasingly inefficient and more plodding in my performance.

37. I stuff away my emotions.

38. I feel alone and alienated.

39. Usually forgiving by nature, I hold on to hurt feelings when I am depressed.

40. I feel a sense of apathy.

41. I easily become overly sentimental.

42. When depressed, I find great comfort in familiar people, places, and things.

43. I long for the way things used to be.

44. When stressed, I tend to overeat and gain weight easily.

45. I feel hopeless and can't imagine a way out of things.

46. People say that I become increasingly passive—I can't do anything to change my attitude.

47. I feel stuck in a rut but feel powerless to change—I want someone to do it for me.

48. People's demands of me hurt my feelings.

49. I feel anxious and irritable at the thought of stimulating activity.

50. When I am depressed, my greatest wish is to feel alive and energetic.

Total score for Section 3: _____

Maximizing Your Plan of Action

Interpreting the results of this questionnaire can give you insight into how you express yourself and interact with the world. A three-step process is required. Please follow each step sequentially. First, define your unique expression of depression; second, identify the patterns, tendencies, and themes that emerge in your life; third, create a tailor-made program for yourself—one that offers long-term solutions and also addresses immediate needs. Let's begin!

Step 1: Define Your Unique Expression of Depression

What if you fit neatly into one category?

If this is the case with you, you likely resonated with the questions in a single section. If Section 1 best describes your experience, you have a predominance of symptoms that fit the archetype of Airy Depression. Your main doshic imbalance is Vata. If your experience is best described in Section 2, you are experiencing a predominance of symptoms that fit the archetype of Burning Depression. Your main doshic imbalance is Pitta. If your experience is best described in Section 3, you are experiencing a predominance of symptoms that fit the archetype of Earthy Depression. Your main doshic imbalance is Kapha.

Now proceed to step 2.

What if you did not fit neatly into one category?

A large number of people straddle two categories, and some even demonstrate characteristics of all three archetypes. If this is the case with you, add up the scores for each section. If your score is significantly higher in one section than in the others, this section corresponds to your archetype of depression.

What if all of your scores are similar? If they are too close in value to help you discriminate one section from the others, identify which section has the highest number of statements with a rating of 5. This section will best describe your predominant manifestation of depression.

Is what you have now determined really your predominant manifestation of depression? Check in with yourself. Does this make sense to you? You have read the cases and are familiar with the experiences that people have with Airy, Burning, or Earthy Depression. Where do *you* think you fit in best?

Step 2: Refine Your Assessment

Now we want to refine your assessment. The goal of this exercise is to help pinpoint the area of your mind-body that is most affected by the experience of depression. The value of this is that you can use this information to help you identify a starting point for your healing interventions.

Whether or not you distinctly fit into one of the three archetypes, review *all* your answers in each section. Highlight the questions to which you assigned a rating of 5. If you like, write them down on a piece of paper.

1. Put a *p* next to the questions that pertain to the physical aspect of your being.

2. Put an *m* next to the questions that pertain to the mental aspect of your being.

3. Put an *e* next to the questions that pertain to the emotional aspect of your being.

In order to aid you in this process, we have evaluated the questions ourselves (see the appendix). You may wish to compare your designations to ours. However, it is our recommendation that you label your questions *before* you check our designations, because we want you to reflect upon the questions and your responses to them. This is an important exercise in and of itself. It is by improving your awareness that you awaken the physician within, thereby accomplishing the primary goal of Ayurveda.

By assigning a value to the questions yourself, you are bringing awareness to the different aspects of your being. We encourage you to use this kind of thinking in your everyday life. Imbalances come and go. If your awareness is primed, you will easily be able to identify an imbalance when it occurs, as well as the area in which it is affecting you, and you'll know what to pull out of your Ayurvedic toolbox to help you to regain balance.

As you look over your answers in each section, which subcategory stands out the most? The answer to this question reveals the aspect of your being that is most affected by your doshic imbalance. Does it appear that depression is mostly affecting the physical, mental, or emotional aspect of your physiology? Are these results congruent with your experience of depression? Do these results offer you additional insight into your predicament?

Step 3: Identify a Starting Point for Your Journey

The ultimate goal in defining and refining your assessment of depression is to utilize this knowledge to create a tailor-made program that offers long-term solutions. Based on your answers for step 2, identify which aspect of your being is in the most immediate need of attention. This will be your starting point.

Although it is true that in the long run, every agent of vitality presented in this book will help the totality of your being, each has a distinct domain where it is most immediately efficacious. Finding an agent of vitality that directly addresses the aspect of your mind-body that is most currently affected will expedite the process of undoing depression.

What if most of your symptoms relate to your physical well-being? Consider which of the following interventions will best suit your needs:

- Regulating your sleep patterns (chapter 13)
- Evaluating how you are supporting your mind-body with nutrition (chapter 14)
- Starting an exercise program (chapter 11)

What if most of your symptoms relate to your ability to process thoughts? Consider which of the following interventions will best suit your needs:

- Joining a yoga class (chapter 12)
- Practicing breathing techniques (chapter 10)

What if most of your symptoms relate to your ability to process emotions? Consider which of the following interventions will best suit your needs:

- Becoming serious about meditation (chapter 9)
- Embracing a new paradigm of life (chapters 7 and 8)

What If One Size Does Not Fit Me?

Now you have reflected on your answers to the questionnaire, but you still can't find a niche for yourself or feel confident about choosing a starting point. Think about the evolution of your experience of depression. A possible scenario is that at this point you may be experiencing a mixed depression. This is commonly the case, especially when the roots of depression are not eradicated. Think back and trace the onset of your depression. You will realize that in the beginning your symptoms most likely fit into one category more than the others. With this in mind, reread the questionnaire and focus on which section best describes your initial experience of depression. Start there; address that imbalance first.

Our experience working with clients has revealed that most cases of depression begin with an imbalance in Vata dosha. This Airy Depression can subsequently morph into a Burning Depression or an Earthy Depression. As we explained in the case studies, an acute event, prolonged stress, or long-term physical exhaustion all have the same impact on the physiology—they cause an imbalance in Vata dosha. When Vata dosha is not balanced, the physiology can't obtain the support it requires to function properly.

With an imbalance in Vata dosha firmly set in place, the physical, mental, or emotional *ama* caused by grief, stress, or exhaustion creates blockages in the flow of the life force. Suffering from a lack of vital energy, the body will eventually collapse into an Earthy Depression. If a person keeps going and going, however, he or she may trigger a Pitta imbalance, leading to a Burning Depression. The general rule is that if you suffer from a mixed type of depression, balance your Vata dosha first.

At the physical level, we balance Vata with the following interventions:

- **Meditation**: Reread the section in chapter 9 on how meditation helps to support the nervous system by providing deep rest and purifying the physiology.
- **Sleep**: Reread the section in chapter 13 on how to address sleep disorders. Consider incorporating oil massage into your nightly routine.

- **Nutrition**: Reread the section in chapter 14 on balancing Vata dosha.

- **Yoga**: Reread the section in chapter 12 on how to approach yoga poses in order to soothe the nervous system.

- **Infusion of *prana***: If one of the issues you are contending with is low energy, then it's unlikely that exercising will be a means of infusing *prana* into your physiology. In fact, it might deplete you further. Consequently, we suggest that you focus on breathing exercises to clear the way for the flow of *prana*. Reread chapter 10 in order to learn, at the very least, the Three-Part Breathing technique. A full belly breath can blow the blues away—especially if you make it a habit.

Appendix

Authors' Evaluation of the Mind-Body Questionnaire: Assessing Our Imbalances

Here we list our categorical designations (whether physical, mental, or emotional in nature) for each statement from the Mind-Body Questionnaire in chapter 15. Compare them to the designations you came up with on your own.

Section 1

1. Emotional	13. Physical and Emotional	25. Mental
2. Mental	14. Mental and Emotional	26. Mental
3. Emotional	15. Emotional	27. Emotional
4. Emotional	16. Emotional	28. Mental
5. Emotional	17. Emotional	29. Physical
6. Mental	18. Emotional	30. Emotional
7. Physical	19. Mental	31. Mental
8. Physical	20. Mental	32. Emotional
9. Mental	21. Physical	33. Mental
10. Mental	22. Mental and Emotional	34. Emotional
11. Mental	23. Emotional	35. Physical
12. Physical	24. Emotional	36. Mental

37. Physical
38. Emotional
39. Mental
40. Mental
41. Physical

42. Mental and Emotional
43. Mental
44. Mental
45. Emotional

46. Mental
47. Emotional
48. Physical
49. Emotional
50. Emotional

Section 2

1. Emotional
2. Emotional
3. Physical
4. Mental
5. Physical and Mental
6. Mental and Physical
7. Emotional
8. Emotional
9. Mental
10. Emotional
11. Mental
12. Mental and Physical
13. Mental
14. Mental
15. Mental and Emotional
16. Mental and Emotional

17. Emotional
18. Mental
19. Mental and Emotional
20. Emotional
21. Mental
22. Physical
23. Emotional
24. Mental
25. Emotional
26. Emotional
27. Mental
28. Mental
29. Mental
30. Emotional
31. Emotional
32. Mental
33. Emotional

34. Mental
35. Emotional
36. Physical
37. Mental
38. Emotional
39. Mental
40. Mental
41. Mental
42. Physical
43. Mental
44. Physical
45. Physical
46. Mental
47. Emotional and Mental
48. Emotional
49. Emotional
50. Emotional

Section 3

1. Physical
2. Emotional
3. Mental and Emotional
4. Mental
5. Emotional
6. Emotional
7. Emotional
8. Mental
9. Emotional
10. Emotional
11. Emotional
12. Emotional
13. Emotional
14. Physical
15. Emotional
16. Mental

17. Emotional
18. Mental
19. Emotional
20. Mental
21. Emotional
22. Emotional
23. Physical
24. Physical
25. Emotional
26. Physical
27. Physical
28. Emotional
29. Physical
30. Physical
31. Mental and Emotional
32. Physical
33. Emotional

34. Emotional
35. Mental
36. Mental
37. Emotional
38. Emotional
39. Emotional
40. Emotional
41. Emotional
42. Emotional
43. Mental
44. Physical
45. Mental
46. Mental
47. Emotional
48. Emotional
49. Emotional
50. Physical

Resources

Ayurveda

Brooks, J. *Ayurvedic Secrets to Longevity and Total Health.* Upper Saddle River, NJ: Prentice Hall, 1996.

Clark, C., and H. Sharmi. *Contemporary Ayurveda.* Philadelphia: Churchill Livingstone, 1998.

Dugliss, P. *Ayurveda: The Power to Heal.* Ann Arbor: MCD Publishing, 2007.

Lad, V. *Ayurveda: The Science of Self-Healing.* Santa Fe, NM: Lotus Press, 1984.

Lonsdorf, N., V. Butler, and M. Brown. *A Woman's Best Medicine.* New York: Penguin Putnam, 1995.

Tiwari, M. *Ayurveda: A Life of Balance.* Rochester, NY: Healing Arts Press, 1995.

Mind-body medicine

Chopra, D. *Quantum Healing.* New York: Bantam Books, 1989.

Pert, C. *Molecules of Emotion.* New York: Simon & Schuster, 1997.

Sternberg, E. *The Balance Within.* New York: W. H. Freeman, 2001.

Complementary and alternative approaches to healing depression

Cousens, G. *Depression-Free for Life.* New York: HarperCollins, 2000.

Gordon, J. *Unstuck.* New York: Penguin Books, 2008.

Hyman, M. *The Ultramind Solution.* New York: Simon & Schuster, 2009.

Simon, D. *Vital Energy.* New York: John Wiley & Sons, 2000.

Controversies surrounding antidepressants

Glenmullen, J. *Prozac Backlash.* New York: Simon & Schuster, 2001.

Levanthal, A., and C. Martell. *The Myth of Depression as Disease.* New York: Praeger, 2006.

Breathing techniques

Instructional CD: *Breathe to Beat the Blues* by Amy Weintraub

Farhi, D. *The Breathing Book.* New York: Owl Books, 1996.

Lewis, D. *Free Your Breath, Free Your Life.* Boston: Shambala Press, 2004.

Yoga and meditation

Instructional DVD: *Lifeforce Yoga to Beat the Blues—Level 1 and Level 2* by Amy Weintraub

Begley, S. *Train Your Mind, Change Your Brain.* New York: Ballantine Books, 2007.

Deepak, C., and D. Simon. *The Seven Spiritual Laws of Yoga.* Hoboken, NJ: John Wiley & Sons, 2004.

Frawley, D., and S. Summerfield. *Yoga for Your Type: An Ayurvedic Approach to Your Asana Practice.* Twin Lakes, WI: Lotus Press, 2001.

Khalsa, D. S. *Meditation as Medicine.* New York: Atria, 2002. (www.drdharma.com)

McCall, T. *Yoga as Medicine.* New York: Bantam Books, 2007.

Weintraub, A. *Yoga for Depression.* New York: Broadway Books, 2004.

Nutrition

Douillard, J. *The 3-Season Diet.* New York: Three Rivers Press, 2000.

Kesten, D. *The Healing Secrets of Food.* Novato, CA: New World Library, 2001.

Khalsa, D. S. *Food as Medicine.* New York: Atria, 2004. (www.drdharma.com)

Morningstar, A. *The Ayurvedic Cookbook.* Santa Fe, NM: Lotus Press, 1990.

Yarema T., D. Rhoda, and J. Brannigan. *Eat, Taste, Heal.* Hawaii: Five Elements Press, 2008.

Exercise

Douillard, J. *Body, Mind and Sport.* New York: Harmony Press, 1992.

Sleep

Dement, W. *The Promise of Sleep.* New York: Random House, 1999.

Herbs

Lad, V., and D. Frawley. *The Yoga of Herbs.* Santa Fe, MN: Lotus Press, 1986.

Transcendental Meditation program

To get answers to your questions about Transcendental Meditation, visit TMeducation .org or call 1-800-LEARN TM.

Denniston, D. *The TM Book.* Fairfield, IA: Fairfield Press, 2001.

Ayurvedic herbal formulas providers

Ayurvedic Institute
505-291-9698
www.ayurveda.com

Kerala Ayurveda
831-662-2997
www.ayurvedaonline.com

Banyan Botanicals
800-953-6424
www.banyanbotanicals.com

Maharishi Ayur-Veda Products
800-255-8332
www.mapi.com

Index

CPSIA information can be obtained at www.ICGtesting.com
Printed in the USA
BVOW03n0220230416

445323BV00001B/1/P